THE THYMELE AT EPIDAUROS.
HEALING, SPACE, AND MUSICAL PERFORMANCE IN
LATE CLASSICAL GREECE

Theran Press

Theran Press is the academic publishing imprint of Silver Goat Media.

Theran is dedicated to authentic partnerships with our academic associates, to the quality design of scholarly books, and to elite standards of peer review.

Theran seeks to free intellectuals from the confines of traditional publishing.

Theran scholars are authorities and revolutionaries in their respective fields.

Theran encourages new models for generating and distributing knowledge.

For our creatives, for our communities, for our world.

WWW.THERANPRESS.ORG

THE THYMELE AT EPIDAUROS. HEALING, SPACE, AND MUSICAL PERFORMANCE IN LATE CLASSICAL GREECE. Copyright © 2017 by Peter Schultz, Bronwen L. Wickkiser, George Hinge, Chrysanthos Kanellopoulos, and John C. Franklin. All rights reserved.

Published by Silver Goat Media, LLC, Fargo, ND 58108. This publication is protected by copyright, and permission should be obtained from the publisher prior to any reproduction, storage in a retrieval system, or transmission in any form or by any means, electronic, mechanical, photocopying, recording, or likewise. SGM books are available at discounts, regardless of quantity, for K-12 schools, non-profits, or other educational institutions. To obtain permission(s) to use material from this work, or to order in bulk, please submit a written request to Theran Press, PO Box 2336 Fargo, ND 58108, or contact Theran directly at: info@theranpress.com.

This book was designed and produced by Silver Goat Media, LLC. Fargo, ND U.S.A.
www.silvergoatmedia.com
SGM, the SGM goat, Theran Press, and the Theran theta are trademarks of Silver Goat Media.

Cover photograph: John Goodinson
Cover design: Travis Klath and John Goodinson © 2017 SGM
This book was typeset in Palatino Linotype by Cady Ann Mittlestadt and Aurora McClain.

ISBN-10: 1-944296-04-2
ISBN-13: 978-1-944296-04-9

A portion of the annual proceeds from the sale of this book is donated to the Longspur Prairie Fund.
www.longspurprairie.org

Printed and bound in the United States of America.

THE THYMELE AT EPIDAUROS.
HEALING, SPACE, AND MUSICAL PERFORMANCE IN LATE CLASSICAL GREECE

Peter Schultz, Bronwen L. Wickkiser, George Hinge,
Chrysanthos Kanellopoulos, and John C. Franklin

With digital reconstructions by
John Goodinson, Modeler and John Svolos, Scientific Advisor
&
a technical appendix by Andrew Fermer,
Hann Tucker Associates Ltd

Theran Press

For our students.

Table of Contents

Contributors ix

Preface and Acknowledgments xi

List of Illustrations xvi

Note on Transliteration and Abbreviations xix

Introduction 21

Chapter One
    The Building 33

Chapter Two
    "Thymele" 45

Chapter Three
    Circularity, performance, and Acoustics 66

Chapter Four
    Paeans and Healing 86

Chapter Five
    Response: A Musical Maze for Asklepios?
    An Archaeoacoustic Assessment of the thymele
    at Epidauros 118

Conclusions and Beginnings 164

Appendix
    Acoustical Report on The thymele at Epidauros
    Andrew Fermer, Hann Tucker Associates Ltd 172

Illustrations 179

Bibliography 201

Index 233

Contributors

Peter Schultz is an archaeologist and conservationist. He is the former Olin J. Storvick Chair of Classical Studies at Concordia College and current Scholar in Residence at the North Dakota State University Department of Visual Arts. He took his Ph.D. in Classical Archaeology from the University of Athens in 2003 with his dissertation "Το εικονογραφικό πρόγραμμα του ναού της Αθηνάς Νίκης στην Ακρόπολη." He is co-editor of *Early Hellenistic Portraiture: Image, Style, Context* (Cambridge University Press, 2007), *Aspects of Ancient Greek Cult: Ritual, Context, Iconography* (Aarhus University Press, 2009), *Structure, Image, Ornament: Architectural Sculpture in the Greek World* (Oxbow Press, 2009), and *Artists and Artistic Production in Ancient Greece* (Cambridge University Press, 2017) — as well as the author of numerous articles on ancient Greek culture and art.

Bronwen L. Wickkiser is Theodore Bedrick Associate Professor of Classics at Wabash College. She specializes in ancient Greek history, religion, and medicine. Her first book, *Asklepios, Medicine, and the Politics of Healing in Fifth-Century Greece* (Johns Hopkins University Press, 2008), investigates the early development of the cult of Asklepios in relation to Hippocratic theories and practices. She is co-editor of *Aspects of Ancient Greek Cult: Ritual, Context, Iconography* (Aarhus University Press, 2009) and the author of many articles on topics that include the rituals of Athenian state burial, healing epigrams, and the role of medicine and magic in Ovid's *Metamorphoses*. Her most recent work examines the history and design of the Confederate Memorial at Arlington National Cemetery and its position within a highly contested landscape of memory.

George Hinge is a classical philologist and Associate Professor in the Department of History and Classical Studies at Aarhus University, Denmark. He took his Ph.D. in 2001 from Aarhus University with his dissertation *Die Sprache Alkmans: Textgeschichte und Sprachgeschichte* (Reichert Publishing, 2006). He is the co-editor of *Alexandria: A Cultural and Religious Meltingpot* (Aarhus University Press, 2009), *Aspects of Ancient Greek Cult: Ritual, Context, Iconography* (Aarhus University Press, 2009), and the author of numerous articles on ancient Greek language, philology, and literature. Dr. Hinge is the editor-in-chief of *Classica et Mediaevalia: The Danish Journal of Philology and History*.

Chrysanthos Kanellopoulos is an archaeologist specializing in classical architecture. He is Associate Professor in the Department of History and Archaeology at the National and Kapodistrian University of Athens and the historical architect at the American Center of Oriental Research in Amman, Jordan, where he has worked on the buildings of both Amman and Petra. His Ph.D. treated the Classical and Hellenistic phases of ancient Karthaia, Kea. He is the author of *Amman: The Great Temple* (American Center of Oriental Research, 1996) and *The Late Roman Temenos Wall at Epidauros* (Committee for the Restoration of the Epidauros Monuments, 1999), the co-author of *The Petra Church* (American Center of Oriental Research, 2001) and *The North Ridge in Petra* (American Center of Oriental Research, 2017), and author of many articles on ancient structures in Gytheion, Andros, Beidha, Keryneia, and Athens. Since 2012, Dr. Kanellopoulos's work has focused on the architecture of Hadrian's Library in Athens and the architecture at the Asklepieion of Lissos, Crete.

John C. Franklin is Associate Professor and Chair of Classics at The University of Vermont. He began life in composition and electronic music at the New England Conservatory (1988) before switching to Classics, taking a Ph.D. from University College London (2002). The cultural history of ancient music technology—both physical and conceptual—is central to his research, with a special interest in the interface between early Greece and the ancient Near East. He recently published *Kinyras: The Divine Lyre* (Harvard University Press, 2016). Dr. Franklin has held research fellowships at Warburg Institute (1999), the American Academy in Rome (2000–2002), the American School of Classical Studies at Athens (2002–2003), the Cyprus American Archaeological Research Institute (2003, 2012), the American Research Institute in Turkey (2003), the Center for Hellenic Studies (2005), the Institute for Advanced Study, Princeton (2011), and the W. F. Albright Institute of Archaeological Research, Jerusalem (2012).

Preface and Acknowledgements

The thymele at Epidauros is one of the most enigmatic buildings of the ancient Greek world. Thus, at the center of this book, there lies a mystery. It is a mystery that has intrigued scholars for almost two centuries. It is a mystery that revolves around unique marks, sacred geometries, perplexing architecture, hidden passages, uncertain timelines, and lost rituals. It is a mystery that we have not solved. Instead, in this book, we have compiled, synthesized, and speculated on a host of new (and old) clues that we think clarify the many puzzles that circle this remarkable structure. It is to these clues that we want to guide your attention—and your imagination. While the ancient ideas and intentions that motivated the construction of the thymele at Epidauros remain shrouded by time, the material evidence, the epigraphical record, and the literary testimonia (along with their many contexts) hold numerous potential answers. The range of ancient evidence that surrounds this building and the processes that we use to interpret it are our chief concern here. Through reexamination of this material, we hope to spark fresh debate regarding the form, the function, and the meaning of this most unusual and mysterious of ancient buildings.

Work on this project began in Athens during the winter of 2004 with a series of brainstorming sessions among Peter Schultz, Bronwen Wickkiser, and Chrys Kannellopoulos. At that time, we were interested in putting together a trans-disciplinary kind of project that would allow us to explore the thymele at Epidauros with a variety of scholarly tools, incorporating methodological approaches from the fields of archaeology, philology, cultural history, and religious studies. The goal at that time was not to produce yet another "solution" to one of Greek archaeology's most famous puzzles. Rather, we approached the project with an open spirit of adventure and curiosity: How could we explore this unique monument in a way that was both authentic and creative? How could we tell stories about this building that honored both the ancient material evidence and the ancient minds that produced it? How could we integrate our various disciplinary proclivities into a final form that was scholarly, rigorous, and accessible?

We realized quickly that in order to do the kind of work that we wanted to do—to tell the kind of stories that we wanted to tell—we needed to expand our team. Specifically, we needed authorities in the fields of linguistics, ancient Greek music and musical technology, contemporary acoustical engineering, and digital reconstruction. As a result, our team became more international and more interdisciplinary. Over the next several years, a linguist from Denmark (George Hinge), a digital modeler from England (John Goodinson), a restoration archaeologist from Greece (John Svolos), a music archaeologist from the United States (John Franklin), and an English acoustical engineer (Andrew Fermer) all joined the effort.

In the end, the book that you hold in your hands is the result of a kind of methodological experiment: a voyage into the archaeological imagination. During its composition, every team member brought different concerns, interests, and proficiencies to the project. Each of us saw—and continues to see—this strange building through a wide range of cultural, disciplinary, and personal frames. All of our various biases, ideas, and philosophies (delightfully!) influenced each other as our research and writing progressed. It is our hope that we have managed to capitalize on these diversities and from them craft something imaginative, coherent, and real—something that brings the ancient world to life.

For this reason, the hypotheses that we have generated and shared in this book are necessarily speculative. While rooted firmly in—and bound by—the ancient evidence, we see these ideas not as pillars of some kind of mighty intellectual edifice, but rather as living sparks set to kindle further discussion regarding this peculiar building and the embodied minds that shaped it. Just as importantly, we also see this book as a useful template for how the many tools within the fields of both classics and archaeology can effectively be used to imagine—and re-imagine—antiquity for ourselves, our students, our communities, and our world.

In that spirit, it is a pleasure to thank the following individuals for their kind support and their generous contributions to this project: Youli Anastasiadou, Bruce Baker, Karen Bassi, Getzel Cohen, Leo Coleman, Antonio Corso, Leslie Day, Sheila Dillon, William Engel, Kathryn Gutzwiller, Jeremy Hartnett, Carl Huffman, Craig Jendza, Nigel Kennell, Stefanie Kennell, Charalambos Kritzas, Carolyn Laferrière, Jill Lamberton, Astrid Lindenlauf, James McCredie, Tracy Miller, Steven Muir, Amy Muse, Naomi Norman, David Petrain, Betsey Robinson, David Scahill, Panagis Sklavounakis, Daniel Solomon, Brian Tucker, Heather Waddell, Steve Wernke, and Garth Whitcombe.

We are especially grateful to Angelos Chaniotis, Joseph Day, Gunnel Ekroth, Yannis Hamilakis, Jeffrey Hurwit, Jesper Tae Jensen, Mark Wilson Jones, Michaelis Lefantzis, Margie Miles, Jenifer Neils, Robin Osborne, Verity Platt, Olga Palagia, Spencer Pope, Rush Rehm, Ralph Rosen, Roger Schultz, Andrew Stewart, Olin Storvick, Petros Themelis, Barbara Tsakirgis, and Bonna Wescoat for their belief in our work, their comments on our numerous drafts, and their careful critique of the ideas that follow. This book would not exist in its present form without them.

Seven individuals deserve our special thanks. Armand D'Angour, Michael Barron, Mark Gealy, and Graeme Lawson provided extraordinary insight into the musical and acoustical issues surrounding the thymele and offered patient feedback on all matters harmonious and symphonic.

Andrew Fermer, the team member responsible for the production of both the acoustical appendix for this book and the digital reconstructions of the thymele's soundscape, helped us to better understand the thymele's acoustical properties; his work has been key to the nuance of the arguments that follow. The same can be said of team members John Goodinson and John Svolos. John Goodinson's digital reconstructions fundamentally transformed our discussion of the thymele's architecture, its design, and its place within the sacred landscape of the sanctuary at Epidauros. John Svolos's initial report on the thymele for the Committee for the Restoration of Ancient Monuments formed the basis of our work; his critical reading of the book you hold in your hands, his guidance of Goodinson's digital reconstruction of the monument, and his discussions with us on multiple issues (both great and small) have expanded and enhanced the depth, the tone, and the complexity of our arguments. We are grateful to these gentlemen for their limitless generosity, their unfailing grace, and—perhaps most importantly—their consistent good humor.

For financial support, we acknowledge Concordia College, Dartmouth College, the Great Lakes Colleges Association (New Directions Initiative Grant on "Hearing History," directed by Jeremy Hartnett), Gustavus Adolphus College, the Lake Ida Paradise Research Council, the National Endowment for the Humanities, the University of Cincinnati (Tytus Fellowship), Vanderbilt University, Wabash College, and the Institute for Advanced Study, Princeton (Elizabeth and J. Richardson Dilworth Fellowship). We are particularly grateful for the support of the American School of Classical Studies at Athens, whence this project was launched and which has long been an anchor and incubator for innovative work in classical archaeology in Greece. Any findings, conclusions, or recommendations expressed in this book do not necessarily reflect those of our sponsors.

This book was written at the Blegen Library at the American School of Classical Studies at Athens, at the John Miller Burnam Classical Library at the University of Cincinnati, at the Baker-Berry Library at Dartmouth College, at the Jean and Alexander Heard Library at Vanderbilt University, at the Lilly Library at Wabash College, at the Carl B. Ylvisaker Library at Concordia College, and at the Institute for Advanced Study, Princeton. We are happy to thank Karen Bohrer, Benjamin Millis, and Maria Tourna at the American School of Classical Studies; David Ball, Mike Braunlin, and Jacquelene Riley at the University of Cincinnati; Reinhart Sonnenburg at Dartmouth; Ramona Romero at Vanderbilt; Susan Albrecht, Diane Norton, Debbie Polley, and Laura Vogler at Wabash; and Amy Soma and Erika Johnson at Concordia for their generous and patient assistance during the course of its composition.

Preliminary versions of some of the ideas contained in this book were presented at the *107th Annual Meeting of the Archaeological Institute of America* (Montreal, Winter 2006), the *Sixth International Conference on Technology, Knowledge and Society* (The Free University of Berlin, Winter 2010), the *Twelfth Congress of the ICTM Study Group for Music Archaeology* (University of Valladolid, Fall 2011), *Aspects of Ancient Greek Cult II: Architecture, Context, Music* (University of Copenhagen, Spring 2012), the *Robert Penn Warren Center for the Humanities Seminar on Sacred Ecology* (Vanderbilt University, Spring 2012), the *Archaeological Institute of America 2011-12 Lecture Series* (Spring 2012), the *National Endowment for the Humanities Summer Institute on Mortality: Facing Death in Ancient Greece* (Athens, Greece, Summer 2014), and *Materiality, Representation, and Performance in Archaic and Classical Greek Poetry* (The University of Edinburgh, Summer 2017). Some early ideas were published by Schultz and Wickkiser in *The International Journal of Technology, Knowledge and Society* 6.6 (2010) 143-64.

List of Illustrations

Full color digital renderings are available at:
https://www.theranpress.org/the-thymele-at-epidauros.
All renderings are © John Goodinson. Please contact Theran Press for permissions and licensing.

Figure 1. Map of Greece, the sanctuary of Asklepios at Epidauros indicated. (© Theran Press.)

Figure 2. Plan of the Asklepieion at Epidauros, including theater, museum, and modern parking and paths. (© Theran Press.)

Figure 3. Plan of the central area of the Asklepieion at Epidauros, the thymele indicated. (© Theran Press.)

Figure 4. Cutaway plan of the thymele at Epidauros, from the southeast. (© C. Kanellopoulos.)

Figure 5. Restored cutaway elevation of the façade and foundations of the thymele at Epidauros, from the south. (© J. Goodinson; J. Svolos, scientific advisor.)

Figure 6. Top: The Parthenon's façade elevation (right) superimposed on the krepis and elevation of the thymele (left), with scaled stylobate width. Bottom: Ground plan of the thymele with section AB of the circumference marked on the first step of the krepis and with section CD marked on stylobate level. (© C. Kanellopoulos.)

Figure 7. Restored elevation of the thymele and temple of Asklepios at Epidauros, from the southeast, over the "altar court." (© J. Goodinson; J. Svolos, scientific advisor.)

Figure 8. Restored elevation of the thymele and temple of Asklepios at Epidauros, from the east along the axis of the "altar court." (© J. Goodinson; J. Svolos, scientific advisor.)

Figure 9. Plan of the central area of the Asklepieion at Epidauros in the third century BCE. The thymele and its "altar court." (© P. Schultz, after P. Kavvadias.)

Figure 10. A Corinthian capital from the thymele at Epidauros. (© Bryn Mawr College Library Lantern Slide Collection.)

Figure 11. Detail of a Corinthian capital from the thymele at Epidauros. (© Greek Ministry of Culture; photograph, P. Schultz.)

Figure 12. Drawing of the central capstone of the thymele's floor, inv. no. 12292. Point A marks the most well-preserved edge of the capstone's outer circumference; the restored diameter of the stone (ca. 1.236 m) was taken from this point. Point B marks the most well-preserved interior edge of the capstone's central hole; the restored diameter of the hole (ca. 0.38 m) was taken from this point. (© J. Svolos.)

Figure 13. Excavation photograph of the thymele at Epidauros showing the building's hollow foundation, and the size, scale, and position of the "labyrinth" corridors. ("Fundamente der Tholos zur Zeit der Ausgrabungen mit W.Dörpfeld." © D-DAI-ATH-Epidauros 7.)

Figure 14. Detail of the thymele's harlequin floor. (© J. Goodinson; J. Svolos, scientific advisor.)

Figure 15. Oblique, detailed view of the thymele's central elements and restored bronze grille. (© J. Goodinson; J. Svolos, scientific advisor.)

Figure 16. Phiale. The Painter of London D12. Attic. Ca. 450-440 BCE. (Museum of Fine Arts, Boston. Edwin E. Jack Fund. Photograph © Museum of Fine Arts, Boston.)

Figure 17. Digital reconstruction of the interior of the thymele with dancers and musician, as seen from the interior door lintel, door open. (© J. Goodinson; J. Svolos, scientific advisor.)

Figure 18. Digital reconstruction of the interior of the thymele with dancers and musician, as seen from the interior door lintel, door shut and lamps lit. (© J. Goodinson; J. Svolos, scientific advisor.)

Figure 19. Right: Distribution of signs within the labyrinth, following figures in Svolos 1988 (with minor corrections to his composite sign-charts by reference to his actual plans of the rings). Left: Composite chart to establish alphanumeric equivalents for each sign (for ease of reference in the main text). (© J. Franklin.)

Figure 20. Drawing of the marks in the substructure of the thymele. (© J. Svolos.)

Figure 21. Photograph of an inscription recording the text and musical notations of a paean by Limenios, ca. 128 BCE, inscribed on the Athenian treasury at Delphi. Musical notations are highlighted. (Delphi Museum, Inv. Nos. 489, 1461, 1591, 209, 212, 226, 225, 224, 215, 214; © Greek Ministry of Culture.)

Figure 22. Labyrinth signs compared with instrumental notation symbols. Those which are unmarked in left-hand chart find matches in the notation, as indicated by circles on the right-hand chart (taken from Hagel 2000). Those with "X" have no matches. Those with "?" could match if one permits alternative rotations. (© J. Franklin.)

Figure 23. Labyrinth signs compared with vocal notation symbols, following conventions of Figure 22. (© J. Franklin.)

Note on Transliteration and Abbreviations

In transliterating Greek words and names, we have tried to remain close to the Greek spelling (e.g., Asklepios, rather than Asclepius), except where the Latin spelling of words or names has become so popular in English that adherence to Greek transliteration would be distracting (e.g., acropolis, as opposed to akropolis).

Unless otherwise noted, all journal abbreviations follow those given by the *American Journal of Archaeology* at http://www.ajaonline.org/submissions/abbreviations.

Ancient literary and epigraphic sources have been abbreviated according to *The Oxford Classical Dictionary*.

INTRODUCTION

Music is the mediator between the spiritual and the sensual.
Ludwig van Beethoven

Sometime around 380 BCE, the citizens of the small Peloponnesian city of Epidauros launched a massive building program at the nearby healing sanctuary of Asklepios, son of Apollo (Figs. 1-3).[1] In terms of scale, expense, and design, nothing like the Epidaurian building program had been attempted since Pericles's grand imperial project in fifth-century Athens. In addition to many smaller buildings and improvements, the sanctuary was expanded to include a lavish temple designed and built by the architect Theodotos (*IG* 4² 1, 102.7-9), an expensive new chryselephantine cult statue created by the Parian sculptor Thrasymedes (Paus. 2.27.1-2; *SEG* 15.208; see also *IG* 4² 198), and an innovative theater attributed to Polykleitos the Younger (Paus. 2.27.5).[2] One of the most interesting pieces of architecture constructed during this time was an elaborate tholos, a round building that, like the sanctuary's famous theater, was said to have been the work of the younger Polykleitos (Paus. 2.27.5). The fourth-century building accounts (*IG* 4² 1, 103.125) call this building the *thymele* (Figs. 4-5).[3]

---

[1] Architectural development of the sanctuary, with bibliography: Burford 1969; Svolos 1988a, 225-26, with focus on the thymele; Gruben 2001, 143-53; Riethmüller 2005, 1: 279-324; Melfi 2007, 17-209. For a new edition, commentary, and German translation of the epigraphical evidence, see Prignitz 2014. Svolos (1988a) provides comprehensive discussion of the thymele's construction, excavation, and publication.

[2] It is assumed that Polykleitos "the Younger" is meant here on account of the sculptor-architect's middle fourth-century date and his association with the Asklepieion's famous theater. See: Pollitt 1990, 79, 106, and 195; and below, n. 18. Theodotos and the temple: Burford 1969, 141-44. Thrasymedes and the cult image: Mitsos 1967; Burford 1969, 59-61, 154-55; Krause 1972; Ridgway 1997, 36; Lapatin 2001, 109-11 (with comprehensive bibliography); and Muller-Dufeu 2002, 537.

[3] Polykleitos, the thymele, and the theater: Burford 1969, 141-45; and Seiler 1986,

In terms of labor, expense, complexity, and ingenuity, the Epidaurian thymele eclipsed the structures that surrounded it. From the physical remains preserved on site, it is clear that the variety, the quality, and the workmanship of the materials used in the thymele's construction were unmatched in the Epidaurian Asklepieion and, indeed, unmatched in most other Greek sanctuaries. This sumptuous building was central, both physically and ritually, to the panhellenic sanctuary it adorned. This is confirmed both by its position next to the temple of Asklepios and by its place directly across from the old altar of Apollo and Asklepios (Figs. 7-9). For its size, there was no more costly or more ornate building in the Peloponnese. The thymele was also innovative in terms of structure and design. Not only were tholoi rare in mainland Greek sanctuaries generally, but this particular tholos was built over a circular, labyrinthine foundation that was unique in the history of Greek architecture (Figs. 4-5; 13-14).[4] It is with good reason that Alison Burford described the thymele at Epidauros as "the most beautiful building in the sanctuary, surely intended by the planners to be a wonder to all beholders."[5]

Since its initial excavation by Panayiotis Kavvadias in 1881, scholars have proposed a wide range of interpretations for this enigmatic structure, all prompted by its prominent position in Asklepios's sanctuary and by its curious design.[6] John Svolos noted that the thymele must have "played a special role in the functioning of the Asklepieion and the cult of the god" and that the thymele "was just as important as the temple, as shown by

---

72, with n. 281.

[4] Rarity of tholoi: Lawrence 1957, 239-46; Seiler 1986, 72-89; Tomlinson 1988, 350.

[5] Burford (1969, 63) notes: "The thymele's proportions, nearly nine meters high and twenty-three meters across, must have made it dominate its surroundings."

[6] History of the thymele's excavation and reconstruction: Svolos 1988a, with bibliography.

its size, its site on an artificial terrace near the Abaton, [by] the cost of [its] construction, and [by] its sculptural decoration."[7] Indeed, the thymele cost roughly twice as much as Asklepios's temple to build.

But what "special role" did the thymele play in Asklepios's sanctuary? Here, many answers have been given.

The thymele has been considered to be either Asklepios's tomb (perhaps connected to chthonic aspects of his cult) or an architectural frame for an altar to the hero-god.[8] These readings seem logical, given the building's central position in the sanctuary and its name; the term thymele is often associated with altars or other places of sacrifice. Perhaps less well known, the thymele has been interpreted also as a prytaneion, a fountain, a sacred hearth, a dining hall, an astronomical tool, a library, a space for therapeutic incubation, a space to prepare patients for incubation, a storehouse for medicinal herbs, and most infamously, a residence for sacred snakes, or even a house for one enormous, revered python.[9] The curious hole at the

---

[7] Svolos 1988a, 225.

[8] Tomb of Asklepios: e.g., Roux 1961, 187-200; Burford 1969, 66-68; Svolos 1988a, 228; and Riethmüller 2005, 1: 318-21, all with a range of interpretive options. Connection between the thymele and chthonic ritual: Robert 1939, 423; Roux 1961, 187-88; Seiler 1986, 85-86; and Svolos 1988a, 225. Altar, particularly for rites of holokautesis: Robert 1939, 338-64 and below, pp. 49-51. During recent excavations at Epidauros, Vassilis Lambrinoudakis uncovered a ca. 3 x 5 m area of ash and burnt soil located near the ramp of the thymele and contemporary with construction of the thymele. Lambrinoudakis interprets this as an altar and believes there to be a ritual connection between it and a small pit found in the very center of the thymele's labyrinthine foundations. The latter pit he believes to be the core of an early altar, based in part on associations between the term "thymele" and sacrifice, and on the fact that the ground level of these two "altars" is the same. In his interpretation, then, the thymele is a monumentalization of this early altar, and the area of ash by the ramp is a temporary altar that was used while the thymele was being constructed (Lambrinoudakis and Katakis 2017).

[9] Prytaneion: Kavvadias 1900, 74-75 and Charbonneaux 1925. Fountain house: Defrasse and Lechat 1895, 100-5, 124-28. Well house: Burford 1969, 63. Sacred

center of the thymele's floor that opens into the labyrinthine infrastructure below has been interpreted as a well, as an offering pit (ἐναγιστήριον) for libations poured into it from the cella above, or as an entrance to a maze through which worshippers wandered like initiates in a mystery cult.[10]

While some of these interpretations have captured the popular imagination and appear now regularly in handbooks, guides, and introductions to Greek architecture and religion, all are problematic and all leave many questions unasked.[11] Indeed, the most popular among these interpretations—that the thymele served as a tomb or heröon for Asklepios, or that the building served as an altar or hearth—are implausible. The name *thymele*, which is sometimes used to indicate a hearth or altar, might indeed suggest a major rite of holokautesis, or ritual burning.[12] However, the notion that the Epidaurian thymele housed an altar or hearth is inconsistent with the restoration of a fully enclosed roof for the building; an altar or hearth would have required a building open to the sky, and no evidence of burning of any sort was ever discovered inside the building.[13] As for the hypothesis

---

hearth: Charbonneaux 1925, 158 n. 1, with earlier bibliography. Dining room: Kavvadias 1900, 48-71 and Cooper and Morris 1990. Library: Caton 1899, 11-12. Place for incubation: Elderkin 1911. Place of preparation for incubation: Askitopoulou et al. 2002; for incubation generally, see Renberg 2017. Storage area for medicinal herbs: Richards-Madzoulinou 1981. Snakes' house: Holwerda 1904 and Kerényi 1959, 102-5, et al. Giant python: Svornos 1901, 34 (cited in Burford 1969, 67 n. 7).

[10] Robert (1939, 340) suggested that the building was used as both a hearth and ἐναγιστήριον. Offerings, especially of eggs, are discussed by Riethmüller 1996 and 2005, 1:318-24. Kavvadias (1900, 75) suggested that the building's substructure was used by initiates.

[11] E.g., Burford 1969, 63; Reithmüller 2005, 1:318-21.

[12] See below, Chapter Two.

[13] Robert 1939, 340. We might also ask why yet another altar was desirable or necessary *inside* this building. Not only were altars rare within buildings of this period (Hollinshead 1999, 197-98), but the thymele itself already communicated with the sanctuary's early (ca. late sixth-century) altar ca. 40 m due east of the

that the thymele might be understood as a kind of hero shrine, it should be remembered that the vast majority of monumentalized heroa from the Geometric period and later are polygonal, not circular.[14] More importantly, early excavations discovered no traces of pottery in the center of the thymele's maze-like foundations, a curious absence if individuals were pouring libations regularly into the hole and consequently, on some occasions, dropping their vessels. Evidence for systematic libation, burning, or any other type of sacrifice, is therefore lacking. While it is certainly possible—and perhaps

---

thymele, as well as with the long, rectangular altar of the fourth century just east of Asklepios's temple. We should consider the possibility that the thymele, given its proximity to and alignment with the early altar, was built intentionally to communicate with it. As to rites of holokautesis, Ekroth (2002, 226) argues there is no clear evidence for holokautesis in any cult of Asklepios.

[14] Heroa can be any shape (*contra* Robert 1939, 423). Likewise, there seems to be nothing necessarily "heroic" about circular architectural form. See, for example, the rectangular temple/heröon of Herakles at Dodona (Dakaris 1993, 19-20), the trapezoidal heröon of Pelops at Olympia (Kaltsas 1997, fig. 14; Whitley 2001, 155); the rectangular heröon of Helen and Menelaus at Therapne near Sparta (Antonaccio 1995, 155-66); the triangular heröon at the west gate of Eretria (Bérard 1970); the rectangular heröon of Phrontis(?) at Sounion (Antonaccio 1995, 166-69) and the pentagonal shrine of Archemoros at Nemea (Antonaccio 1995, 176-77). Nevertheless, it cannot be denied that Bronze Age tholos tombs functioned as the locus for hero and/or ancestor cult from at least the eighth century (Alcock 1991 and Huguenot 2003, with comprehensive bibliography; Larson 2007, 196-207) nor is there any question that this practice continued well into the Roman period. The possibility that a connection existed between fourth-century tholoi and those of the Greek Bronze Age might repay systematic investigation. For instance, might the circular design of the thymele recall Mycenaean tholos tombs and hint thereby at the heroic past? Or might the tholos tombs themselves have served an acoustic function appropriate for the songs of heroes? It is an interesting coincidence that the Hellenistic theater at Orchomenos has roughly the same diameter (ca. 16 m) as the Mycenaean tholos tomb ("Tomb of Minyas") nearby (ca. 14 m) and that the latter was certainly reused for ritual/performance in the Hellenistic period. Equally interesting, in the context of this book, is the fact that both structures were not far from the city's Hellenistic Asklepieion.

even likely—that the thymele served, on some level, as a *symbolic* tomb or *symbolic* hearth or *symbolic* altar, it seems equally important to recognize, at the outset, that no archaeological evidence supports the interpretation of the building as an actual tomb or functional space for burning and/or sacrifice.

The meanings and purposes of this building remain poorly understood. Since this is so, perhaps there is room for yet another hypothesis? In this book, we will argue that, in addition to its many other possible functions, the thymele at Epidauros served as a space for sacred, musical performance. We will also suggest that the form and design of the thymele, particularly its circularity and its elaborate substructure, served important symbolic and acoustical functions that would have affected both the building's perceived role within Asklepios's temenos and the lived experience of music performed within and around the building's cella. Expanding on this hypothesis, we will also argue that the music performed inside the thymele can be connected to ritualized healing, the primary function of Asklepios's sanctuary at Epidauros. Finally, coming full circle, we will do our best to complicate and problematize the preceding arguments, thereby paving the way for further discussion that is both rigorous and creative.

Although we were unaware of it at the beginning of our research, two preliminary arguments along similar lines had already been made early on in the study of the thymele's meaning and function. In 1898, Samuel Herrlich suggested that the thymele served as a venue for musical performance; he was followed by Hermann Thiersch in 1909.[15] Both scholars have been ignored almost entirely since 1925, when Jean Charbonneaux criticized Thiersch's architectural comparanda during the course of his own interpretation of ancient Greek tholoi.[16] Although the general line of argu-

---

[15] Herrlich 1898, 22-23; Thiersch 1909.

[16] Herrlich (1898) focused his work primarily on linguistic evidence and, from

ment for the thymele's musical functions is clearly an older one, it seems equally clear that new approaches developed during the last century have transformed the ways we now view ancient evidence and that new discoveries have complicated and nuanced the ways in which this ancient puzzle might be assembled. These new data and methodologies form a tantalizing basis for renewed consideration of the possible musical functions of the thymele.

Our argument that the thymele was a locus of musical performance

---

that, suggested that the thymele was used for musical competitions. Given that "thymele" was often used to designate an area within the orchestra of a theater, and that "thymelic" musical competitions had become very popular by the third century BCE, Herrlich argued that the thymele at Epidauros was designed as a performance space. (As we shall see in Chapter Two, there is much evidence in support of this reasoning.) Thiersch (1909), on the other hand, focused on the design of the building, specifically the connection between circular space and performance. He argued that the thymele was a music pavilion, a kind of odeion, and that paeans to Asklepios were performed within it. He also argued that the labyrinth was a resonance chamber that transformed the structure into an acoustical engine. Thiersch's argument was questioned by Charbonneaux (1925, 169-71), who wanted to problematize the relationship between ancient Greek tholoi and civic council houses and who found (perhaps rightly) Thiersch's comparanda a bit too simplistic for his tastes. Charbonneaux's critique of Thiersch was accepted by Roux (1961, 189 n. 3; see also below, Chapter Three) and so the connection between music and the thymele was, for the most part, forgotten. The conclusion of Charbonneaux's article (1925, 177-78) is worth quoting in this context: "Je n'ai pas la prétention, pour conclure cette rapide étude, de rassembler en un corps de doctrine les observations qui l'ont motivée, ni de remplacer un système par un autre. J'ai simplement voulu montrer qu'une théorie préconçue peut difficilement rendre compte, à travers les étapes d'une civilisation complexe, des différentes apparitions d'un type d'édifice, fut-il aussi simple que la Tholos. Aussi bien, les monuments d'aspect nouveau, qui sortent presque chaque année du sol antique, témoignent-ils à quel point sont dangereuses, dans l'histoire de l'architecture, les excessives simplifications." We are in agreement with this final sentiment. Indeed, it is our hope to offer here an interpretation of the thymele that complements and enriches other interpretive possibilities and that does its best to avoid convenient simplifications.

draws strength from a growing body of scholarship that treats specifically the acoustics of ancient structures. This field of scholarship is known as archaeoacoustics. Archaeoacoustical studies encompass a wide range of ancient edifices, including prehistoric structures like Stonehenge or the sanctuary of Chavín de Huántar in Peru, classical theaters throughout the Mediterranean, medieval churches across Europe, and much more.[17] The sanctuary of Asklepios at Epidauros has itself long been at the center of archaeoacoustical research due to its well-preserved theater and its renowned acoustics, but no attention has been paid to the thymele in this regard, a rather strange trend considering that the ancient tradition attributes both the theater and the thymele to the same designer, Polykleitos the Younger (Paus. 2.27.5).[18] Here,

---

[17] For an introduction to the range of approaches and structures encompassed by the field of archaeoacoustics, see: Schafer 1977; Scarre and Lawson 2006; Garfinkle and Waller 2012; Eneix and Zubrow 2014; Mills 2014; Blake and Cross 2015; Eneix 2016; below, Chapter Five; and below, Conclusions and Beginnings. Gurd (2016) now treats auditory aesthetics in the ancient Greek world.

[18] Acoustics of the theater at Epidauros: Declercq and Dekeyser 2007, with bibliography; G. Kampourakis 77-99 in Gogos 2011. The dangers of relying on Pausanias for details such as the names of craftsmen are widely known and accepted; see, e.g., Schultz 2007a, 221 ns. 113-6, with bibliography. However, the fact that parts of the thymele were built by a predominantly Argive workshop (IG 4^2 I, 103.15 et al.) and made use of black Argive limestone lends some credence to Pausanias's claim that it was designed by Polykleitos the Younger, himself an Argive. Svolos (1988b, 245) points out that: "The unbridled, programmed use of this [Argive stone] in the tholos in all probability attests the presence not only of an Argive architect, but also compatriot artisans experienced in its quarrying and working." On this point, see also Burford 1969, 199-202. It is also important to remember that Athenian sculptors, too, played a major role in the construction of the thymele (Burford 1969, 199-202) and in Epidauros more generally. Athenian sculptors and Epidauros: Burford 1969, 155 and 202 (Table 10); Yalouris 1992; Smith 1993; Lattimore 1997, 257; Ridgway 1997, 41 and 366; Feyel 1998; Rolley 1999, 203-8; and Leventi 2003, 101-2. Of course, whether Pausanias is correct in ascribing the Epidaurian theater and the Epidaurian thymele to the Argive Polykleitos is hardly crucial to our argument. The tradition alone—that the same individual designed both structures—indicates

we hope to argue that the thymele at Epidauros belongs to a growing list of structures in which song, dance, and other forms of musical performance played important roles in ancient design, function, thought, and experience.

Given the paucity of material and literary evidence, all hypotheses regarding the many possible functions and meanings of the thymele—including our own—must remain tentative. That said, it seems equally clear that any thesis concerning the function of the thymele should take into account the four primary characteristics of the building that are not open to debate: first, the near obsession with expense and innovation evidenced by the thymele's sumptuous materials and decoration; second, the significance of the term "thymele"; third, the unusual form of the building, specifically its circularity and its unique foundations; and fourth, the prominent position of the building at the center of Asklepios's most famous healing sanctuary.

To address these interconnected topics and to explore our hypothesis, we have divided this book into five chapters. In Chapter One, "The Building," we sketch the physical remains of the thymele, with a particular focus on the builders' sustained interest in expensive architectural innovations and novelties; something *new* is going on with this building. Chapter Two, "*Thymele*," discusses the possible meanings of the building's unusual name and how this particular label might have been understood in late Classical and early Hellenistic Greece. As will be shown, the linguistic evidence points strongly at a performative function for the thymele. In Chapter Three, "Circularity, Performance, and Acoustics," we examine aspects of the building's design in more detail, especially the thymele's circularity and its unique basement. When considering the connection between ancient forms

---

that they were closely associated in the minds of those who visited the sanctuary in antiquity. Perhaps this was due to similarities not only in the design but also in the function of the two structures.

and ancient functions, the building would have offered much to those using its circular space for the performance of song and dance. Chapter Four, "Paeans and Healing," explores the close connection between music and healing in Greek antiquity, with a focus upon a particular type of song-dance that was sacred to Asklepios and his father Apollo in the sanctuary at Epidauros: the paean. Here, we suggest that paeans, as well as other types of music, were performed within the thymele not only as forms of supplication and thanksgiving to the gods but also as an important aspect of sacred therapy. In Chapter Five, "Response: A Musical Maze for Asklepios? An Archaeoacoustic Assessment of the Thymele at Epidauros," John Franklin takes stock of the hypotheses offered in Chapters 1-4 and complicates, nuances, and energizes the arguments. Finally, much as an epode follows strophe and antistrophe in ancient song, we round out our analysis with some conclusions, reflections, and prospects for further exploration.

◘ ◘ ◘

Of course, we are engaged in a particular kind of cultural study here, and it is not unproblematic. For us, archaeology—broadly conceived—is not only the study of "material culture in context," but also the study of the embodied, sensual, lived experiences that this material culture generated, reflected, and integrated across the ever-shifting social matrices of ancient communities. We believe that it is necessary to assume the full-blooded mindfulness of the ancient makers who were invested in the conscious (and self-conscious) creation of these experiences. Following the recent work of Yannis Hamilakis, which likewise considers ancient experience as a lived, holistic sphere that incorporated all senses and modes of cognition, we agree that, "A sensorial archaeology is not a representation of the past but an *evocation of its presence, its palpable, living materiality, its flesh."*[19] Indeed, as we will suggest below, the spiritual sounds, rhythms, and experiences that revolved around the thymele were deeply intertwined with the building's physical appearance, form, and function.[20] Likewise, ancient priests, worshippers, musicians, dancers, audiences, and communities engaged the thymele not just with their eyes and their minds, but with their whole beings. One productive way to examine the thymele and its contexts, then, is as a "sensorial assemblage"—a scintillating, heterogeneous arrangement of materials, beliefs, impressions, and memories—as a *living* place and artifact.[21]

Since this is our goal, our work adopts a holistic, trans-disciplinary approach that seeks to paint a vivid picture of ancient Greek experience as it may have been lived. Working with ideas most famously laid down by R.G. Collingwood, we see ancient material culture as a vehicle through which we can ask provocative and productive questions about a living past, a past that was—in its moment—every bit as complex, vibrant, and energized as our own present moment.[22] For this reason, the archaeology we practice here encompasses a wide array of methodological tools that we have used to

---

[19] Hamilakis 2002; 2013, 199 (our emphasis). Recent anthologies edited by Shane Butler and Alex Purves (2014), Jerry Toner (2014), Michael Squire (2016), Kelli Rudolph (forthcoming), and Alex Purves (forthcoming) are also essential reading.

[20] If this is correct, then it will also be important to consider what kinds of "presence effects" were produced in and around the thymele. Hans Gumbrecht (2004) has argued that being physically present at a musical or theatrical performance produces two different kinds of effects: "presence effects" and "meaning effects." These "presence effects" rise from performances and extend, enhance, and surpass questions of simple content. Also influential for our study is the work of Christopher Small (1998), who takes readers on an experiential tour of a concert hall to demonstrate that "music" has no meaning apart from the spaces and rituals that frame and create it.

[21] Hamilakis 2017.

[22] Collingwood 1946. See also: Morris 2000, 3-36; Hodder and Hutson 2003, 145-205; Hamilakis 2002; 2013; 2017.

craft dynamic answers to animated questions—answers that are coherent, answers that correspond to the current state of the material evidence, and answers that speak to our sense of a shared, human history. Our objective here is not to "set the record straight" with regards to this mysterious building, but rather to spark a dialogue based on the ancient evidence, the literary and archaeological imagination, and our own humanity. If we want to enrich our understanding of this unique structure and its makers, then we believe this to be an exciting, productive, and fulfilling path.

Chapter One
The Building

*Whenever we witness art in a building,
we are aware of an energy contained by it.*
Arthur Charles Erickson

Soon after the builders at Epidauros completed the new temple of Asklepios in ca. 375-365 BCE, they embarked upon a much larger, much more costly and much more time consuming project: construction of the thymele.

Georges Roux and Alison Burford, followed by Florian Seiler and John Svolos, place the beginning of the thymele's construction at ca. 365-360 BCE.[1] There is little reason to doubt this chronology, although it should be admitted that these dates are based solely on the style of the building's architectural details, the letter forms of the building's inscribed construction accounts, and rough estimates of construction logistics. For our purposes, 365-360 BCE is a safe range for the structure's foundation date.

Whenever work began specifically, it is clear from the thymele's building accounts (*IG* 4^2 1, 103 A-B) that construction on this building lasted at least twenty-seven years.[2] It is unknown how long the builders took to complete the thymele, since the accounts for the final years of construction are missing. Both Seiler and Svolos suggest that the work lasted around four decades (365/0-325/0 BCE), a hypothesis based on masonry style, tooling, and other construction details.[3] Even if we adopt a shorter estimate for the thymele's construction—and say that it was completed in about thirty years (365/0-335/0 BCE)—the thymele at Epidauros still took longer to assemble

---

[1] Roux 1961, 175-84; Burford 1969, 208 (VI); Seiler 1986, 80; Svolos 1988a, 225. So, too, Kavvadias 1900, 49.
[2] Burford 1969, 220-22. On the thymele building accounts, see now Prignitz 2014.
[3] Seiler 1986, 80; Svolos 1988a, 225.

and finish than any other monumental building of fifth- or fourth-century Greece. The nearby temple of Asklepios in the sanctuary of Epidauros provides a useful comparison: it was finished in four years and eight months (*IG* 4^2 1, 102 A-B). The precise reasons for the thymele's long construction period are unknown, but political factors are sometimes given as a possible, albeit problematic, explanation.[4]

When it was finished finally in ca. 335-320 BCE, the thymele at Epidauros was, and would remain, the largest and most ornate peripteral, round building of Greek antiquity—a unique structure. The thymele was adorned with 52 finely carved, twelve-petal rosettes on each of its 52 metopes and an elaborate raking cornice that was carved with a winding, horizontal anthemion interposed with palmettes and lion-headed water spouts. The

---

[4] Seiler (1986, 80; followed by Svolos 1988a, 225) suggested that the "unstable" political climate of fourth-century Greece might account for the thymele's long construction period. But Seiler gives no specifics, nor does he explain why Asklepios's temple and other major projects at the Epidaurian Asklepieion were finished promptly, whereas work on the thymele continued for decades. Seiler also leaves unexplained the epigraphical evidence for massive fines levied on contractors who failed to complete their work on the thymele on time. These fines sometimes amounted to almost 2/3 the amount of the contractor's original contracts; there can be little doubt that the contractors responsible for the thymele had ample incentive to stay on task and to complete their work in a timely manner (Burford 1969, 106). It is also unclear if the political environment of fourth-century Greece had any effect on other Peloponnesian construction sites. Indeed, after the Battle of Leuktra (371 BCE)—whose date might mark the beginning of construction on the temple of Asklepios itself (Burford 1969, 55)—we have evidence for several major building projects in the Peloponnese that were both launched and completed over the course of the fourth century. These include substantial undertakings in Argos, Corinth, Megalopolis, Messene, Nemea, Olympia, and Perachora, among many others. Downey (2003) provides an analysis both of the projects and of the fourth- and third-century political environment; Scahill (2012, 318-25) gives an essential discussion of the boom in Peloponnesian building projects in the second half of the fourth century BCE. It seems unlikely that "politics" alone can provide an adequate explanation for the thymele's long construction period.

rosettes may have been gilded.⁵ The thymele was topped with an elaborate akroterion, almost certainly of the floral/anthemion type.⁶ While larger round buildings are known from the Aegean (such as the tholos at Athens, or the rotunda of Arsinoe II at Samothrace, among others), the thymele was the largest tholos with a full colonnade in the Greek world. Likewise, while there are more heavily adorned sacred buildings on the Greek mainland, all are rectangular, not circular. Within the class of fourth-century *Rundbauten*, only the earlier tholos in the sanctuary of Athena Pronaia at Delphi comes close to the thymele's complexity and monumental impact, and the tholos at Delphi is only two-thirds the size of the Epidaurian thymele.⁷

In terms of its technical geometry, the thymele was equally sophisticated. The design of a large, round building presents a number of complications within the rules of the Doric system. If the architects had chosen simply to copy the column proportions of the tholos at Delphi, for example, the final design would have appeared proportionally squat because of the thymele's larger diameter (Delphi: ca. 13.5 m at the stylobate, 20 columns; Epidauros: 20.15 m at the stylobate, 26 columns). This would not do. As a solution to this design challenge, the height of the thymele's columns was increased and the columns were given excessively slender proportions (height:lower

---

[5] Roux (1961, 140) identifies phialai in the form of the rosettes. The possibility that the rosettes were gilded is suggested by the gilding of the rosettes of the Erechtheion (*IG* 1³ 476), a building to which the thymele owes a major debt for its adornment; e.g. Gruben 2001, 360-61; Svolos 1988a, 225. For gilding of marble architectural elements generally: Paton 1927, 227-31 and Schultz 2001, 2-5, with bibliography.

[6] Central floral akroterion: Kavvadias 1900, fig. 11. Floral akroteria in ancient Greece: Danner 1989. Not only is the amount and level of detail in all of the floral decoration of the thymele astounding, but some of it may have been designed specifically to represent healing plants; on the latter point, see Richards-Madzoulinou 1981.

[7] The diameter of the stylobate of the tholos at Delphi: ca. 13.5 m; diameter of the stylobate of the thymele at Epidauros: ca. 20.15 m.

diameter proportion = 6.93:1) — a ratio unprecedented for the Doric order in the fourth century BCE.[8] The resulting elevation is quite different from the familiar appearance of a typical Doric, hexastyle elevation. Instead, the proportional elevation of the thymele is almost identical to the octastyle, densely spaced, façade of the Parthenon.[9] The twenty-six columns of the thymele's circular peristasis represent two canonical wings of a peripteral Doric temple (thirteen columns long) that have been positioned opposite to each other and "wrapped" around a conceptual cylinder. The portion of the circumference of the first step of the krepis (corresponding to the thirteen columns and twelve intercolumnar slabs) is 100 "feet" of 0.3275 m each, thus introducing — for the first and last time — the famous and revered hekatompedos temple schema into a round building (Fig. 6, AB).[10]

A number of other innovations first introduced in the thymele became widespread thereafter. For example, the Corinthian colonnade of the thymele's interior freed the Corinthian order from Ionic theory: hereafter,

---

[8] This same issue was confronted thirty years later during the construction of the Philippeion. In that case, however, the Ionic order was used, which is "naturally" slender (Roux 1988, 296).

[9] In the Parthenon, the stylobate width:(column height + entablature height) ratio = 2.956:1. In the thymele, the stylobate diameter:(column height + entablature height) ratio = 2.937:1. The difference is negligible. We are grateful to Youli Anastasiadou and Panagis Sklavounakis for their assistance with these calculations. Athenian craftsmen at Epidauros: Burford 1969, 155 and 202 (Table 10); Yalouris 1992; Smith 1993; Lattimore 1997, 257; Ridgway 1997, 41 and 366; Feyel 1998; Rolley 1999, 203-8; and Leventi 2003, 101-2.

[10] Specifically, the diameter of the first step is ca. 21.68 m. The circumference is ca. 68.11 m. The 25:52 parts of the latter (circumference AB in Fig. 6) equal ca. 32.74 m. For the Doric pous, see: Pakkanen 2013, 2 and Pakkanen 2008. The section of the stylobate circumference that corresponds to 13 columns (13 column slabs + 12 intercolumnar slabs or 25:52) is calculated as ca. 30.37 m (circumference CD in Fig. 6) This length could be equal to 100 Epidaurian podes with a length of ca. 0.30 m. The length of the sprint in the Epidaurian stadium would thus be ca. 180 m = 600 x ca. 0.30 m each.

Corinthian columns could now reach ceiling height with extraordinarily slender proportions (in the thymele, the overall height:lower diameter = ca. 10:26) without the need for an upper, "stacked story" of columns.[11] The frieze of the inner colonnade was also designed as a large cyma recta frieze and was thereafter implemented in all of the Ionic monuments at Epidauros as well as the Propylaea on Samothrace; this "Corinthian frieze" would enjoy great popularity through the Roman period.[12] Finally, instead of a common Doric (or Ionic) doorframe, the doorway of the thymele was composed from two doorjambs bridged with a lintel in the form of an Ionic entablature.[13] Recent discoveries reveal that this type of doorway was only a few years later employed in the lateral doorway of the temple of Athena Alea at Tegea.[14] Though this type of doorway was rarely used again in Greece, it became highly popular in the baroque schemes of Alexandrian architecture.[15] The

---

[11] The Corinthian capital is "naturally" taller than the Ionic when placed on a shaft of identical diameter, further increasing the column's proportions and its overall height.

[12] Roux 1961, 157; Kanellopoulos and Zavvou 2014, 368-69.

[13] Roux (1961, 149-50 and pl. 44.3) comments that such a doorway is unattested in any Greek temple. Justifiably so, as the thymele was not a temple.

[14] Pakkanen 2014, 369, fig. 22. Interestingly, the temple of Athena Alea at Tegea was also intimately connected to the Philippeion, which was the next tholos to have been constructed in Greece; Schultz 2007a, 210-11 and ns. 29-33.

[15] Doorways with jambs that carry entablatures appear in Macedonian tombs in Rhodope (Tomb of the Symbols, end of the fourth century BCE) and in Stavroupoli in Xanthi (first half of the second century BCE), as well as in the shops of the Hellenistic stoa at the stadium in Messene. The same type of doorway appears in the Tomb of Mustafa Pasha I at Alexandria, the villas at Ptolemais, the tombs of Petra, and the early frescoes from Pompeii (Villa of P. Fannius Synistor at Boscoreale), all executed by Alexandrian workshops (Rekowska 2012, 169, pl. 5; Laidlaw 1985, pl. 45). At least four such Hellenistic/Roman doorways on Crete are due to Cyrenaean/Alexandrian influence. One is in the temple of Asklepios at Lissos and another, published example comes from Aptera (Niniou-Kindeli and Chatzidakis 2016, 142, fig. 10.26).

thymele's innovations must have been widely studied in antiquity; certainly they were imitated.

In addition to its refined superstructure, its elaborate exterior adornment, and its imposing size, the thymele's position within the space of the Epidaurian Asklepieion added to its overall impact and novelty (Figs. 7-9). The thymele was situated on a broad, artificial terrace, at the head of a long (ca. 30 m) "altar court" at the center of the sanctuary (Fig. 9). The terrace itself was a major expense and was conceived as an integral part of the thymele's design from the beginning of its construction.[16] With the exception of the western half of the Asklepieion's large fourth-century stoa, which formed part of the terrace's northern retaining wall, no other monumental building made use of the terrace's space. This is significant in its own right because the terrace allowed the thymele to be distinguished spatially—to stand slightly apart—from the other monuments of Asklepios's crowded temenos.[17] The altar court in front of the thymele was a space bounded on its eastern side by an altar and on its western side by the thymele itself. Its northern and southern edges were framed by dedications and exedrae. This altar court not only distinguished the thymele spatially, but also provided an ideal, open venue for a wide range of ritual and performative acts, or even just gathering. These activities would have drawn further attention to

---

[16] Svolos 1988b, 248. Svolos (1988b, 256 n. 1) suggests that this terracing might take as its inspiration the grand terraces of the fifth-century Athenian Acropolis, and this would certainly make sense when we remember that Athenian craftsmen were employed in the thymele's construction (Burford 1969, 202). Another parallel is provided by the famous terracing at the Argive Heraion (Antonaccio 1995, with bibliography), which would certainly have been known to the Argive workers on the thymele and, perhaps, to its Argive architect, Polykleitos, if Pausanias is correct in his identification of the building's architect; see above, p. 21 n. 3.

[17] The ground level just west of the Temple of Asklepios slopes downward. Here, the addition of the wide platform symbolically elevated the thymele so that it stood on the same plane as the rest of the Askelpieion's monumental topography.

the thymele. In this panhellenic temenos, where space was at a premium and where dedicatory competition transformed sacred land into symbolic battle grounds contended over by poleis and elites alike, the demarcation of a large, open space reserved as an unoccupied "showcase" for a specific building is testament to the building's importance.[18] This reading of the area is at least partially confirmed when we take note of the relationship between the temple of Asklepios and its surrounding structures and dedications; there are no other clearly defined open spaces like the thymele's altar court anywhere else in the Asklepieion—other than the altar court in front of Asklepios's temple itself. Further confirmation for the significance of the thymele's altar court comes from the presence of at least five expensive exedrae—monumental viewing benches—that both border and frame the space (Fig. 9), again in a manner quite similar to that seen in the open area in front of Asklepios's temple. The prominent position of the thymele, as well as its imposing façade, would have made a dramatic impact on any visitor to the sanctuary.

The interior of the thymele was equally lavish. The building's details have been treated at length elsewhere, but three of the most novel and expensive features of the thymele's design deserve brief comment here: the first freestanding interior colonnade of the Corinthian order, the first triple-ringed "harlequin" floor mosaic, and the first hollow foundation. While the original design of the ceiling and roof is lost to us, there can be little doubt that it, too, would have provided a striking, suitable counterpoint to the other carefully designed elements of the interior.

The interior Corinthian colonnade was composed of fourteen columns. A Corinthian capital, intentionally buried on the site (Figs. 10-11), gives us the

---

[18] Landscapes of power: Veronese 2007, Ch. 2. See also Scott (2010, 5-28, with bibliography) and Ma (2013, 67-154, esp. 108).

best impression of the appearance of the design of the interior colonnade's order. This capital has been interpreted as either a flawed or damaged piece or, perhaps more likely, a paradigm on which the team of sculptors based their finished pieces.[19] Regardless, the complexity of the design, the innovative use of the new Corinthian order, and the technical skill with which the piece was finished (Fig. 11) all point to a level of unprecedented expense and novelty.

Svolos describes the black-and-white harlequin design of the floor of the thymele as "masterly," "impressive," and "audacious" (Figs. 12; 14-15).[20] In particular, the floor's dark Argive stone, when polished, would have become a lustrous, luxurious black—almost like ebony.[21] A central ring of black Argive stone rested prominently at the center of this swirling circle of geometry. The ring of black stone was originally ca. 5 m in diameter and was comprised of seven arced blocks, each 0.255 m thick; about fifty percent of the material belonging to this ring is preserved. This central, black ring was the heaviest decorative element of the floor and also served as the "hub" of the floor's harlequin decoration, anchoring and focusing the visual energy of the floor's decoration on the very center of the thymele's cella. A typical fragment from this block shows evidence of perfect

---

[19] Corinthian capital as model: Burford 1969. The use of paradeigmata by sculptors is sometimes considered problematic (see, e.g.: Scranton 1969, 33-34, followed by Ridgway 1969, 117). The Erechtheion accounts provide relevant evidence, since the formal (and we may presume practical) connection between the Erechtheion and the thymele is clear (see above, p. 35 n. 5). These accounts indicate that the model-maker for the Erechtheion's rosettes (a sculptor named Neseus) was paid 8 drachmas for his design (*IG* I³ 476, ll. 258-66). There is little reason to doubt Burford's assertion that the "model capital" was in fact a paradeigma, at least on practical or logistical grounds.

[20] Svolos 1988b, 280.

[21] Svolos 1988b, 245.

anathyrosis on three exterior sides, while its fourth (interior) side is left smooth. This interior side is beveled at a 3.6 degree angle to allow for the reception of the central capstone of the floor.

This central capstone (no. 12292) is massive (Fig. 12). It is a single slab of Pentelic marble with a restored diameter of ca. 1.236 m.[22] The slab was ca. 0.231 m thick at its outer edge, but tapers in thickness to 0.227 m near its center. As only about twelve percent of the total volume of the stone is preserved, the evidence is extremely fragmentary. Even so, it is clear that the capstone's exterior circumference (Fig. 12, A) was perfectly beveled to sit within the "socket" created by the beveled edge of the central ring of black Argive stone.

Most significantly, the interior surface of this capstone (Fig. 12, B) shows the arced contour of a large hole ca. 0.38 m in diameter that penetrated the center of the capstone.[23] Roughly the size of a modern manhole opening, this hole would likely have been covered in antiquity to prevent accident or injury since it leads directly to the building's hollow foundations. Svolos speculates that the hole's cover may have been made of another piece of Pentelic stone that could have been removed as needed for maintenance or other purposes (Figs. 12 and 14).[24] Another possibility—one to which we subscribe and to which Svolos has lent his support—is that the cover was made of wood or bronze, perhaps even an elaborate bronze grille (Fig. 15),

---

[22] Svolos 1988b, 281. Svolos writes: "The central slab was of Pentelic marble and had a *diameter* of 61.88 cm" (emphasis added). But his drawing of no. 12292 also notes "R = 61.88." This is confirmed by Svolos's drawing of the ring of black Argive stone (plan 24, bottom right) in which Svolos again gives the *radius* for the central stone as 0.6188 m when he writes "R = 61.88 (κεντρικός λίθος)." In his text, "diameter" is an error; the text should read "radius." Svolos, personal communication.

[23] The existence of this hole was confirmed by Svolos, in personal correspondence and conversation, and by autopsy; see also Svolos 1988b, 281.

[24] Svolos, personal communication.

the design of which would have corresponded to the elaborate design of the thymele proper. A decorative, open pattern for this hypothetical grille would have reduced the cover's weight, facilitated removal of the cover and access to the thymele's foundations, and allowed the volumes of the two spaces to communicate.[25]

This hole provided the sole access point to the thymele's hollow foundations: the so-called "labyrinth" (Figs. 13-14). "Labyrinth" remains in quotation marks here since there is little evidence that individuals, whether worshippers, priests, or any others, entered and moved around the interior of the thymele's foundations at all. This "labyrinth" is itself a unique space in Greek architecture: three concentric rings of limestone walls, pierced by doorways and bisected by a single cross wall, produce a series of corridors roughly 2 m tall and 0.65 m wide that could be navigated only in a fixed route. Anyone or anything entering through the hole in the cella's floor would have been forced by the cross wall and doorways to move in a single pattern. The narrow width of the corridors, moreover, suggests that any human traffic in the infrastructure would have been limited to occasional service personnel as opposed to streams of worshippers.[26] Quite unlike the cella, this was not a fancy space in terms of decoration: the floors were of trampled earth and the walls were unplastered.

Even so, considerable time and money were spent on this aspect of the building's construction. Svolos notes that the construction of a circular building like the thymele presents several challenges in execution:

[The building's circularity] placed far greater demands on the ancient architect and builders, both in time and effort, consequently increasing the

---

[25] Svolos, personal communication. See below, pp. 75-76.
[26] While it is possible that worshippers wandered in the subterranean maze in rituals akin to those of mystery cults, as proposed by Kavvadias (1900, 75), no physical evidence supports this hypothesis.

cost of construction and prolonging the time required for its completion. It should not be forgotten that it took well over 30 years—perhaps as many as 50—to finish [the thymele]. It is obvious that, apart from some incidental delays not connected with the work force, a major part of this not inconsiderable period of time was due to the specific construction demands that this building posed.[27]

This exceptional decision—to create a hollow, circular foundation—prompts a series of interconnected questions. Why did the thymele's designers not just create a traditional foundation with easy-to-cut, rectangular stone? Why the necessity for spatial circularity throughout the entire volume of the thymele's building envelope, extending even into its basement? Why spend perhaps three times as much treasure on a unique foundation system that would have been seen only rarely? Regardless of how we choose to answer these questions, there can be little doubt that this unique substructure was a fundamental element of the thymele's overall design. To this day, the space remains one of the most enigmatic of the ancient Greek world.

This brief summary of the extraordinary aspects of the building's design points to three interconnected characteristics. First: meticulous craftsmanship. The architect, designers, model-makers, sculptors, masons, painters, and gilders responsible for the thymele's final effects were obsessed with quality. Every decision within the building was carefully thought out to maximize the thymele's visual and aesthetic impact. Second: lavish expense. None was spared. Round buildings are already more costly than their rectangular counterparts, but at Epidauros it is almost as if the designers went out of their way to discover new, extravagant ways to elaborate and expand on previous models and paradigms.[28] Third and finally: innovation. In a recent

---

[27] Svolos 1988b, 245 and above, ns. 23-25.
[28] Svolos 1988b, 245.

monograph on Greek novelty and the "new," Armand d'Angour argues for complex, embodied definitions of "newness" in the ancient world.[29] These definitions, he suggests, can be used to subvert the traditional view that the ancient Greeks were "held in the grip of the past," an entrenched notion most famously articulated by Bernard van Groningen in 1953.[30] "Novelty and innovation," D'Angour writes, "were no less real phenomena for the Greeks than for us."[31] On every level, the design of the thymele speaks to this reality: the designers of the building were deeply concerned with the new.

Any argument for the thymele's possible function should take these three interconnected factors regarding the building's design and construction into account: meticulous craftsmanship, lavish expense, and—perhaps above all—innovation. The building's details throughout point directly to a concern with artistic and aesthetic "modernization." Whatever activities went on inside or around the thymele, these experiences were deliberately framed and richly enhanced in a way that was both new and unique to the ancient Mediterranean world.

---

[29] D'Angour 2011.
[30] See Tate 1955.
[31] D'Angour 2011, 62.

Chapter Two
"Thymele"

The gold-beaten thymelai were opened wide, and all over the city of Argos altar fires shone.
The pipe, the servant of the Muses, played its beautiful sound.
Euripides, Elektra 713-17

In addition to the tholos's extraordinary design, the name of the building—*thymele* (Θυμέλη)—also offers important clues as to its functions. It is from this most basic point—the building's name—that our argument begins to take shape.

Θυμέλη is the term used for the building in a series of inscriptions, now fragmentary, that documented its construction year-by-year. In these inscriptions, we find the term *thymele* in two instances: during year seventeen and during year twenty-six.[1] In year seventeen, thymele seems to refer to the interior of the Corinthian colonnade (τὸν σακὸν τᾶς θυμέλας, IG 4² 1, 103.125). In year twenty-six, by contrast, the term seems to apply to the peristasis pavers (τᾶς θυμέλας τὸ στρῶμα τὸ ἐν τᾶι περιστάσι, IG 4² 1, 103.162) and thus to an area larger than that defined by the colonnade.[2]

How would this word have been understood?

The discussion that follows is a philological analysis of the usage and etymology of the word thymele. As we shall see, one of the primary

---

[1] In the same inscription we also find the derivations θυμελοποίαις (ll. 119, 134, 137, 139) and θυμελοποιοῖς (l. 142).

[2] It is worth considering the possibility, strongly suggested by these accounts, that at first only the floor was identified as a "thymele" due to its function as a locus of song and dance, much like an orchestra floor, but that the entire building became synonymous to the term soon after it was completed. The same phenomenon is apparent in the case of the Parthenon, where the term describing the opisthodomos chamber of the temple came to be applied, over time, to the entire structure: Hurwit 2004, 106-10.

semantic fields of thymele is a place for musical performance, which leads to our hypothesis about the function of the Epidaurian thymele.

Since antiquity, θυμέλη has been associated with the verb θύω, "to offer by burning, to sacrifice," and most ancient grammarians considered the primary denotation of the word to be a βωμός, or "altar."³ This definition is the basis of much modern work as well. Wilhelm Dörpfeld ascribed a central role to a hypothetical altar of Dionysos, or θυμέλη, in the ancient Greek theater.⁴ And A.S.F. Gow, in his diligent study of the term θυμέλη, concludes that although the "etymology of θυμέλη does not seem open to very much doubt," its proper meaning is "hearth" rather than "altar."⁵

These conclusions are mirrored in our lexica. The three authoritative etymological dictionaries—Frisk, Chantraine, and Beekes—include the word under various derivations of θύω and thereby define its meaning as "Herd, Altar," "autel où l'on brûle les victims, autel," and "hearth, altar."⁶ Liddell and Scott (LSJ) also derive θυμέλη from θύω and define its primary meaning as "prop. *place of burning, hearth*."⁷ But we find a more specialized meaning farther into the LSJ entry: "II. esp. of the *altar* of Dionysus which stood in the orchestra of the theatre…hence in later writers, b. the *orchestra* …hence of the chorus, opp. actors,…c. the *stage*…(hence generally *platform, stage*)." This extended LSJ entry suggests that the semantic field of θυμέλη in many of our extant sources is a place for musical performance.

---

³ Hsch. s.v. θυμέλαι, θυμέλη, *Suda* s.v. θυμέλη, σκηνή, *Etym.Magn.* 743; the etymology also in Phrynichos *Eclogae* 135; Porph. *Abst.* 2.59; the same definition, but without this etymology in Poll. *Onom.* 4.123; Phot. s.v. θύμελον; *Etym.Gud.* 266.
⁴ Dörpfeld 1902.
⁵ Gow 1912; essentially followed by Robert 1939. See also Seiler 1986, 86; Prignitz 2014, 267.
⁶ Frisk 1960-72, I 699; Chantraine 2009, 431-32; Beekes 2010, 568 (the latter with the reservation "unclear").
⁷ Liddell and Scott 1996, s.v. θύω (A).

This is confirmed, moreover, by the ancient grammarians. Phrynichos, a second-century CE Atticist, also believed that θυμέλη originally meant "sacrificial place," but he clarifies that the contemporary (i.e. second-century CE) meaning is "the place in the theater where aulos-players and cithara-players and others compete."[8] In accordance with his linguistic purism, he discards the contemporary usage of θυμέλη and prescribes that the word ὀρχήστρα be used for this performance space instead. Similarly, Timaios, another grammarian of the Roman period, states that the ὀκρίβας (mentioned in Plato as the location of the προαγών) was "a stage put up in the theater where the public speakers stood; for there was no θυμέλη yet."[9]

Moreover, in a discussion of the terminology of the Greek theater, the second-century CE lexicographer Julius Pollux specifies, "The σκηνή belongs to the actors, and the ὀρχήστρα to the chorus. The latter was also the place of the θυμέλη, either a speaking platform or an altar, whereas on the σκηνή there was the street altar too before the doors and a table with pastries, which was called θεωρίς or θυωρίς."[10] He thus offers two different translations of θυμέλη: βῆμα "speaking platform" or βωμός "altar." It is hardly a coincidence that he uses two Greek words that both belong to the root of βαίνω "to step up" (also causal); he may have believed that θυμέλη

---

[8] Phrynichos *Eclogae* 135: οἱ δὲ νῦν ἐπὶ τοῦ τόπου ἐν τῷ θεάτρῳ, ἐφ' οὗ αὐληταὶ καὶ κιθαρῳδοὶ καὶ ἄλλοι τινὲς ἀγωνίζονται. σὺ μέντοι, ἔνθα μὲν τραγῳδοὶ καὶ κωμῳδοὶ ἀγωνίζονται, λογεῖον ἐρεῖς, ἔνθα δὲ οἱ αὐληταὶ καὶ οἱ χοροί, ὀρχήστραν (in *Praeparatio Sophistica* 74, the word is simply translated as τὴν τοῦ θεάτρου σκηνήν).

[9] Timaios *Lexikon* 997a: ὀκρίβας· πῆγμα τὸ ἐν τῷ θεάτρῳ τιθέμενον, ἐφ' οὗ ἵστανται οἱ τὰ δημόσια λέγοντες· θυμέλη γὰρ οὐδέπω ἦν.

[10] Poll. *Onom.* 4.123: καὶ σκηνὴ μὲν ὑποκριτῶν ἴδιον, ἡ δ' ὀρχήστρα τοῦ χοροῦ, ἐν ᾗ καὶ ἡ θυμέλη, εἴτε βῆμά τι οὖσα εἴτε βωμός. ἐπὶ δὲ τῆς σκηνῆς καὶ ἀγυιεὺς ἔκειτο βωμὸς ὁ πρὸ τῶν θυρῶν, καὶ τράπεζα πέμματα ἔχουσα, ἡ θεωρὶς ὠνομάζετο ἢ θυωρίς.

was derived from τίθημι "to put," an etymology that is also recorded in a Byzantine lexicon.[11] So, a θυμέλη can be something erected, but it can also denote a space where one places oneself.

At any rate, it is evident that Pollux was not sure what the θυμέλη actually was, other than some feature of the ὀρχήστρα.[12] He seems to imply that, just as the σκηνή of the actors had its own altar, the ὀρχήστρα of the chorus should have had some sort of altar too. It is significant that Pollux articulates his description in the preterit (ἔκειτο, ὠνομάζετο, etc.); he is not describing contemporary practice of the Roman period, but the classical theater, which was known to him and his peers only from scattered references in Attic dramatic texts of the Classical period. The grammarians of the Second Sophistic read these references through the lens of etymology, interpreting the classical evidence in terms of sacrifice (θύω) or dedication (τίθημι).

As we shall see below, both the ancient and modern etymologies are problematic from a linguistic point of view. The phonetic structure of θυμέλη precludes a derivation from the verb θύω, with the meaning "to sacrifice." Instead, the semantics of θυμέλη should be established on the basis of an analysis of how the word is used in the extant texts. The following discussion takes into account all occurrences of θυμέλη and its derivations in Greek literary and epigraphic texts until ca. 600 CE.

---

[11] *Etym.Gud.* 266: θύμελαι, τράπεζαι, ὀρχήσεις· Αἰσχύλος τοὺς βωμοὺς λέγει, ἀπὸ τοῦ θέσθαι ἢ ἀπὸ τοῦ τίθεσθαι.

[12] Sandin 2005, 17 n. 51: "Thus he is not, pace Arnott (1962, 43-44), certain about what the thymele actually is, but apparently makes two conjectures with the aid of the literary sources available to him. If Pollux could not with any certainty identify the thymele as an altar, he probably did not have access to more crucial evidence than we, or the *Suda*."

ΘΥΜΕΛΗ = "OBJECT OF WORSHIP, ALTAR"

The clearest instance of the meaning "altar" in literature occurs in Euripides's *Suppliants* (64), where the chorus says that it has come δεξιπύρους θεῶν θυμέλας, "to the fire-receiving θυμέλαι of the gods." The altars of the gods are the conventional places for suppliants to go, and the epithet makes this interpretation all but self-evident. However, it is possible that the poet has attached the unequivocal epithet "burning" in order that θυμέλαι can be understood as metaphors for altars in particular. So this verse proves only that θυμέλη might refer to an altar, not that this meaning is inherent to the word.

In a hymn to Hestia, composed by Aristonoos and inscribed on the Athenian treasury at Delphi, the chorus ends with the wish: ἀεὶ λιπαρόθρονον / ἀμφὶ σὰν θυμέλαν χορεύειν, "to dance forever around your greasy-throned θυμέλη."[13] An altar or a sacrificial hearth could easily be called the greasy seat of the god, and the epithet λιπαρόθρονος is probably borrowed from Aeschylus, where it is used with ἐσχάραι (*Eum.* 806).[14] Furthermore, λιπαρός is not only "greasy," but also "shining" or "rich." The hymn has described how the goddess "personally lights the honorable altars of the gods" (μούνα πυ[ρὶ φλ]έ[γ]ουσα / βωμοὺς ἀθανάτων ἐριτίμους). On the other hand, we also hear that she "dances throughout the high-gated temple of Apollo" (ναὸν ἀν' ὑ[ψίπυλ]ον Φοίβου χορεύεις), as a role model for a chorus. In the Homeric hymn to Hestia, we hear that the goddess attends to the temple of Apollo, and "oil is always dripping from your hair" (αἰεὶ σῶν πλοκάμων ἀπολείβεται ὑγρὸν ἔλαιον). This piece of information points to the holy stone of Delphi (swallowed by Kronos instead of Zeus), which was anointed

---

[13] This hymn is discussed also below, in Chapter Four.
[14] Gow 1912, 238; Furley and Bremer 2001, 2:45.

with oil every day.¹⁵ In other words, what is called θυμέλη in our hymn is perhaps not the eternal fire of the temple, but the Omphalos, which, being the center of the world, could be considered the seat of Hestia.¹⁶ However, even if θυμέλη does refer to a sacrificial hearth here, the connotation "fire" need not stem from the word itself but from the particular connection with Hestia.

A Hellenistic sacred law from Pergamon prescribes that "three nine-knobbed cakes should be offered at noon, two on the θυμέλη outside to Tyche and Mnemosyne, and the third one in the dormitory to Themis."¹⁷ The preposition ἐπί that governs θυμέλη suggests that we are in fact dealing with an altar of some sort here. A few inscriptions present the θυμέλη as a dedication to female deities. The only Hellenistic example is dedicated to Ennodia by a priestess (EKM 1. Beroia 23.5, 275-250 BCE). A longer verse inscription from Antioch in Pisidia starts with the words Μ[ηνὶ] θεῷ Πατρίῳ θυμέλην [ταύτην] | ἀν[έθη]καν, "This θυμέλη was dedicated to the national goddess Men…" (CMRDM 4 127.1, imp.), but it is not clear whether the θυμέλη is the stone block itself or something else. A rock inscription from the same sanctuary refers to θυμέλαι given *ex voto*, but it does not specify the nature of these votive gifts.¹⁸

A dedication to Meter Zizimene found in Ikonion (*RPh* 1912:73,46.1-2, imp.) includes the words πάπου θυ|μέλη written as a sort of headline at

---

¹⁵ Furley and Bremer 2001, 1:117-18 (quoting Paus. 10.24.5).
¹⁶ Roussel 1911.
¹⁷ *IvP* 3 161A.10: [εἰς δὲ τὴ]νέσπέραν ἐπιβαλλέ[σ]θω πόπανα τρία ἐννεόμφαλα, | [τούτων μὲ]ν δύο ἐπὶ τὴν ἔξω θυμέλην Τύχηι καὶ Μνημοσύνηι, | [τὸ δὲ τρίτ]ον ἐν τῶι ἐγκοιμητηρίωι Θέμιδι.
¹⁸ CMRDM 1 252.3: [Οὐ]είβιος Φίρμος Καπίτων μετὰ | [γυ]ναικὸς καὶ τέκνων τεκ[μ]ορεύσας | [θυ]μέλας Μηνὶ Ἀσκαηνῷ εὐχήν (Ramsay's supplement in CMRDM 4 20). We have ca. one hundred inscriptions from Pisidia with the formula τεκμορεύσας Μηνὶ (Ἀσκαηνῷ) εὐχήν, but this is the only one with an extra object before the dative.

the top. The editor describes the object as "un petit βωμός," but adds that "[l]es deux premiers mots annoncent la destination de l'autel."[19] Another inscription from Ikonion has more or less the same headline: θυ[μ](έλη) πάπω[ν] (ca. 160-170 CE), and the word πάπος, attached to θυμέλη in both texts, is interpreted as incense.[20] However, the latter inscription is funerary and θυμέλη is described in the text of the inscription as a στήλη, not an altar. It remains unclear to what these headlines refer.

The word θυμέλη occurs also in several Delian accounts and inventories from the Classical and Hellenistic periods, but the context rarely allows us to make any inferences as to the precise nature of the object.[21] In two cases, however, the θυμέλη is described as part of an altar: *IG* 11² 161.A95: τὴν θυμέλην τοῦ βωμοῦ τοῦ ἐν τῆι Νήσωι | κονιάσαντι Φιλοκράτει and *IG* 11² 164.A76: θυμιατή]ριον ἀνεπίγραφον [χαλ]|κῆν [ἔχο]ν θυμέλην (this phrase has also been supplemented in *ID* 104(16).8 and 104(17).3+4). Obviously, the word cannot be translated "altar" *tout court*. Carl Robert, associating θυμέλη with the root of τίθημι, believes that it is the substructure ("Unterbau") of the altar,[22] while A.S.F. Gow identifies it with "the top surface or depression on which the fire burns" (also called βώμιος ἐσχάρα).[23]

ΘΥΜΕΛΗ = "RITUAL SPACE, SHRINE"

One of the earliest occurrences of θυμέλη is in Aeschylus's *Suppliants*: καὶ γεραροῖσι πρεσβυτοδόκοι γεμόντων θυμέλαι φλεγόντων (667-69).

---

[19] Calder 1912, 73.
[20] Ramsay 1941, 166-67. See also: Liddell and Scott 1996, supp., 238. This meaning is supported by *Alt.v.Hierapolis* 227, ἀποκαυσμὸν τῶν πάπων.
[21] *IG* 11² 144.A109; *IG* 11² 199.B90; *ID* 316.125; *SEG* 36 731.27.
[22] Robert 1897, 441. This meaning is given as an alternative in Hsch. s.v. θυμέλη ('...ἢ ἱερὸν ἔδαφος').
[23] Gow 1912, 230.

Unfortunately, the transmitted text does not make much sense grammatically and is therefore difficult to translate. We cannot have two uncoordinated imperatives in the same sentence, and as it stands, the dative γεραροῖσι would readily be understood as an instrumental dative to φλεγόντων, with the unfortunate consequence that the elders themselves are the burnt offerings.[24] One popular conjecture is γέμουσαι instead of γεμόντων (Kruse), but it solves only the first problem (and leaves the corruption unexplained). A more promising conjecture is προβούλοις θυμέλαι φλεόντων (Hermann), i.e. "let the θυμέλαι that receive the elders thrive with counselors." Accordingly γεμόντων has intruded into the text as a gloss on φλεόντων (cf. Hsch. φλεῖ· γέμει). Holger Friis Johansen and Edward W. Whittle argue that "as θυμέλαι denotes hearths, not buildings, Hermann's text uncomfortably situates the counselors *on the hearths*."[25] However, if we accept that θυμέλη may be a ritual space of some sort, the conjecture makes perfect sense.

Θυμέλη occurs four times in Euripides's *Ion* (at 46, 114, 161, and 228), all with reference to Apollo's temple in Delphi.[26] Nothing indicates that we should think of an altar or hearth. On the contrary, the protagonist says, εἰ μὲν ἐθύσατε πελανὸν πρὸ δόμων / καί τι πυθέσθαι χρῄζετε Φοίβου, / πάριτ᾽ ἐς θυμέλας· ἐπὶ δ᾽ ἀσφάκτοις / μήλοισι δόμων μὴ πάριτ᾽ ἐς μυχόν (line 228), "If you have offered a πελανός at the entrance and are going to ask Phoebus something, please proceed into/onto the θυμέλη. If the sheep are not slaughtered, you cannot proceed into the innermost part

---

[24] Johansen and Whittle 1980, III 34-36.

[25] Johansen and Whittle 1980, III 34-36. They declare that the etymology of θυμέλη "is clear: it is a derivative of θύειν 'smoke', and its basic meaning must be 'place of smoke' i.e. 'hearth'" (referring to Gow 1912).

[26] Each instance is discussed by Gow 1912, 225-29; Winnington-Ingram 1976, 491-500.

of the house."²⁷ Some commentators do in fact understand θυμέλη as a second altar, so that the text describes two successive sacrifices.²⁸ However, if it were an altar, one would expect the preposition πρός instead of εἰς (cf. Aesch. *Ag.* 1298, Eur. *Hec.* 144, *IA* 1555 πρὸς βωμόν, Hdt. 2.39, 4.87 πρὸς τὸν βωμόν), unless the suppliant is placing himself on the altar. So, it is more likely that these two sentences describe two alternatives: either you make a sacrifice or you stay out (though with a different kind of sacrifice in the negative sentence). It may be important to our argument that this θυμέλη is also the location of the protagonist's long monodic performance (vv. 82-183; see also Chapter Four).

Euripides seems to have used the word with an even more general meaning. In *Iphigenia in Aulis*, Agamemnon refers to Mycenae as Κυκλώπων... θυμέλας, "the θυμέλαι of the Cyclopes" (152), and in the *Rhesos*, the chorus calls Troy θυμέλας οἴκων πατρὸς Ἰλιάδας, "the Trojan θυμέλαι of the paternal house" (235). In both instances, the word means little more than "dwelling" or "home." This is compatible with the hypothesis that the original meaning is "hearth." Greek literature is full of examples of ἑστία used with the meaning "house" (which is never the case with βωμός).²⁹ However, ἑστία is not the word for an actual physical hearth, but is rather the "hearth" as an idea, the center of a household or community. The place of fire over which people cooked their food was called ἐσχάρα, which is not used in the metaphorical sense "home." At any rate, there is nothing in Euripides's text to suggest that we are dealing with a metaphorical "hearth" instead of "sacred space" (cities are frequently called "holy" in the poetic tradition).

---

[27] On procedures for consulting the Delphic oracle, see Dillon 1997, 82-86.
[28] Lee 1997, 184-85: θυμέλαι "is used here...in the narrow sense of altar or area of altar and refers to the altar inside the temple itself..."
[29] Gow 1912, 219-20.

In Euripides's *Elektra*, it is evident that θυμέλη can be some kind of building: θυμέλαι δ' ἐπίτναντο χρυσήλατοι, / σελαγεῖτο δ' ἀν' ἄστυ / πῦρ ἐπιβώμιον Ἀργείων, "The gold-beaten θυμέλαι were opened wide, and the altar fire shone all over the city of Argos" (713). Gow believes that the chorus sings about portable hearths that "were set out."[30] However, πίτνημι / πετάννυμι may mean "to spread out" (light, clouds or water), but hardly "to distribute" (individual objects). It also covers the meaning "to open wide" (of doors in *Il.* 21.531, πεπταμένας ἐν χερσὶ πύλας ἔχετ'). Fernand Robert imagines a golden perfume-burner (the shape of which he compares to the thymele of Epidauros), and he renders the sentence "la fumée s'envolait des brûle-parfums ornés d'or."[31] He seems to associate the verb with πέτομαι "to fly," but this verb has nothing to do with πετάννυμι, at least in the historical phase of the Greek language.[32] J.D. Denniston, who is convinced by Gow's reconstruction of the semantics of θυμέλη, admits that if θυμέλαι "could mean (as has been maintained) 'halls' or 'chambers,' the verb would be natural enough, 'opened wide'...."[33] In the most recent Loeb translation, the verse is rendered: "The temples of wrought gold were opened."[34]

In later literature, θυμέλη occurs only in connection with musical performances (see below), except in Lucian's tragic parody *Podagra*. The chorus describes how the personified Gout walks with her stick πρὸς θυμέλας, "to the θυμέλαι." It is possible that the author believes that the word means "altar," but "temple" would fit the context just as well (cf. Eur. *IA* 1431, πρὸς

---

[30] Gow 1912, 224-25.
[31] Robert 1939, 268-71.
[32] Rix (2001, 478-79) conjectures that these two verbs are cognates in Proto-Indo-European ("die Flügel ausbreiten" > "fliegen"), but cf. Hackstein 2002, 140-43.
[33] Denniston 1939, ad v. 713.
[34] Kovacs 1998.

ναὸν θεᾶς; 1555, πρὸς βωμὸν θεᾶς). At the same time, we can be sure that the contemporary meaning of the word (that is, a place for song and dance), would have added to the comic effect of the limping personification.³⁵

It is possible that the word also denotes a ritual space, such as a temple, in a Hellenistic verse inscription dedicated to Aphrodite (*SEG* 8.496, Terenuthis, Egypt). The giver states that he has made the dedication τιμαλφῶν τὰν σὰν εὐλίβανον θυμέλαν, "worshipping your incense-rich θυμέλη." The same epithet εὐλίβανος qualifies a temple in Aristonoos's paean to Apollo (εὐλιβάνους ἕδρας, 23), though of course an altar could just as well be associated with incense and would be the natural focus of worship.³⁶

ΘΥΜΕΛΗ = "STAGE, THEATER"

The most widely attested meaning of θυμέλη in all of Greek literature is "stage or theater" (or a meaning related to dramatic and/or musical performance). It may occur already in an elegiac couplet ascribed to Alcibiades, which is allegedly directed against the comic poet Eupolis (fr. 1 W.): βάπτε<ς> μ' ἐν θυμέλῃσιν, ἐγὼ δέ σε κύμασι πόντου / βαπτίζων ὀλέσω νάμασι πικροτάτοις, "You may wash me on the stage (?), but I shall wash you in the sea and kill you in the grim water."³⁷ An even earlier occurrence is possibly Pratinas (fr. 708 P., quoted in Ath. 14, 617c-d): τίς ὁ θόρυβος ὅδε; τί τάδε

---

³⁵ If the Epidaurian thymele was indeed a place for musical therapy, as we are arguing, and if this function were still known in the second century CE, then this passage in Lucian—wherein Gout, a personification of an ailment known to have been cured by Asklepios, walks towards *thymelai*—may contain yet another level of humor.

³⁶ It is an epithet of the region of worship in the Orphic hymn to Aphrodite (*Hymn. Orph.* 55.17, εὐλιβάνου Συρίης ἕδος).

³⁷ Quoted in *Sch. Aristid.* 3.444 and Tzetz. *Prol. de com.* 1. The first source has βάπτε με ἐν θυμέλῃσιν, the latter βάπτε με σὺ θυμέλῃσιν; both are unmetrical. We follow the emendation of Meineke.

τὰ χορεύματα; / τίς ὕβρις ἔμολεν ἐπὶ Διονυσιάδα πολυπάταγα θυμέλαν; "What noise is that? What dance is that? What insolence has entered the tumultuous θυμέλη of Dionysos?" One could, of course, read the meaning "altar" or "hearth" into the text, but the verses themselves speak only about a ritual space filled with choruses. Furthermore, the epithet πολύπαταξ "full of noise" goes much better with "stage" than with "altar."[38]

In our texts from the Hellenistic period onwards, the word θυμέλη is used almost exclusively in connection with musical or dramatic performances. Sometimes we hear about a θυμέλη being constructed, suggesting that the word designates a building of some kind.[39] The word is occasionally juxtaposed with σκηνή, indicating a close synonymy between the words, e.g. Simias *AP* 7.21, πολλάκις ὂν θυμέλῃσι καὶ ἐν σκηνῇσι τεθηλώς.[40] More often a performance or a performer is described as being ἐπὶ θυμέλῃ, "on stage" (or similar expressions, generally without the article), indicating not so much a topographical location but rather the nature of the performance, viz. a musical or dramatic show other than tragedy and comedy, e.g. *SEG* 33 973, line 9 (Colophon, 2nd cent. BCE) τὸν ἀγῶνά τε ἔθηκαν [γυμνικόν τε] καὶ μ[ου]σικὸν ἐπὶ θυμέλας.[41] The word may also designate simply the

---

[38] Sandin 2005, 17 n. 51.

[39] *IK Knidos* I.301.7; Plut. *Sull.* 19.6.

[40] Also Poseidonios fr. 370 (in Strabo 10.3.9); Plut. *Quaest. conv.* 621B; Just. *Nov.* 502; Epiph. *Adv. haer* 3.414. In juxtaposition with θέατρον in Plut. *De cup. div.* 527F. In Lucian *Salt.* 76 a dancer is asked to φεῖσαι τῆς θυμέλης, "spare the stage."

[41] Also Hedylos ap. Ath. 4, 176c; Antip.Sid. *AP* 16.290; Oinomaos in Euseb. *Praep. evang.* 5.32; Plut. *Demetr.* 12.9, *De Pyth. or.* 405D, *Quaest. conv.* 711B, *Prae. ger. reip.* 822F; Artem., *Onir.* 2.3, 2.69, 3.4; Hdn. *Ab exc.* 1.9.2 (suppl.); Origen *Hom. in Job* 17.101; Porph. *Adv.Chr.* 23; Them. *Or.* 331a; Nonnos *Dion.* 12.150; [Manetho] *Apotel.* 4.186, 6.510; Procop. *Anec.* 1.11, 10.12; Just. *Nov.* 502; Theodoretos *Hist. eccl.* 159; Sozom. *Hist. eccl.* 4.25.4; Christodoros *AP* 2.1.35; Malalas *Chron.* 315.3; Picard, *Éphèse et Claros* 143 middle; *IG* 2^2 3117, 12664.2; *IG* 10^2 1 436.2; *IG* 14 2124, 2342.7; Miletos 453.6.

musical or dramatic show itself, cf. Plut. *Galb.* 14.2, ἢ ποίαν αἰδουμένους θυμέλην ἢ τραγῳδίαν τοῦ αὐτοκράτορος; most examples are found in poetry, which suggests that we are dealing with metaphorical usage.[42]

In an epigram transmitted in the *Palatine Anthology* (*AP* 10.103), Philodemos employs θυμέλη in a way that has frustrated philologists:

τὴν πρότερον θυμέλην μήτ' ἔμβλεπε μήτε παρέλθῃς· / νῦν ἄπαγε δραχμῆς εἰς καλὰ χορδόκολα.[43] / καὶ σῦκον δραχμῆς ἓν γίνεται· ἢν δ' ἀναμείνῃς, / χίλια. τοῖς πτωχοῖς ὁ χρόνος ἐστὶ θεός.[44]

Do not peep into the former θυμέλη first nor pass by it. Now go away to the good one-drachma sausages. You can have one fig for a drachma, but if you wait, a thousand. Time is the god of beggars.

The most recent commentator, David Sider, proposes a completely new meaning for θυμέλη here, namely "butcher's shop."[45] He derives the word from θύω "to sacrifice, slay" or, occasionally, "to slaughter" (LSJ s.v. I2b), assuming that this meaning, "although now unattested, was in common parlance." By contrast, earlier commentators assumed that these verses had an erotic content; their understanding of θυμέλη seems more

---

[42] Poseidippos fr. 118.4; Antip.Sid. *AP* 6.46.4; Archias *AP* 6.195.3; anon. *AP* 9.505d.2; Agathias *AP* 5.218.1; SEG 55 723.6; *IG* 2² 9145.7; *IG* 5¹ 734.4; EKM 1. Beroia 396.6, 399.6-7; Marek, *Kat. Pompeiopolis* 28 11-12. In prose only Hdn. *Part.* 61; Alkiphron 4.18.16; [Manetho] *Apotel.* 5.141.

[43] Sider's (1997, 177) emendation of the transmitted "κολοκορδόκολα."

[44] The beginning has now been confirmed by P.Oxy. 3724 col. iv.16 (τηνπροτερονθυμε). The papyrus is a catalogue of *incipits*, many of them transmitted under the name of Philodemos elsewhere. Cf. Sider 1997, 203-25.

[45] Sider 1997, 176-77. Similarly already van Lennep 1822, 233: "Hinc notare etiam potuit popinam, ubi sacrificiorum reliquiae venum exponebantur, atque inde quemvis cupediariorum apparatum."

convincing.⁴⁶ σῦκον is known as slang for the female genitalia (Ar. *Pax* 1350), and χορδόκολα, a compound of χορδή "guts" and κόλον "intestine," leaves plenty of room for obscene associations. Giuseppe Giangrande translates θυμέλη as "eine Speise...die mit Mehl, Wein und Öl zubereitet wurde," seeing a contrast between expensive and cheap delicacies (read: prostitutes).⁴⁷ However, this special meaning, which is only ascribed to the comic poet Pherekrates without any context, is not reliable.⁴⁸ At any rate, since sexual misconduct was regularly ascribed to musical and dramatic performers since the Classical period, and even more so in Rome, it would hardly be surprising if θυμέλη, as a theater, was readily associated with prostitution. So, the joke is basically about competing sources for sexual satisfaction: theater or brothels.

Plutarch uses the word for a transportable platform on which Alexander and his men celebrated their return to western Persia (*Alex.* 67.2): μετὰ τῶν ἑταίρων ὑπὲρ θυμέλης ἐν ὑψηλῷ καὶ περιφανεῖ πλαισίῳ πεπηγυίας εὐωχούμενον συνεχῶς ἡμέρας καὶ νυκτός, "feasting constantly day and night with his friends on a θυμέλη built on a high and conspicuous frame." The choice of word presents the revelers as some kind of theater production or focus of a religious festival. The procession surrounding the platform is described in words reminiscent of such a festival. It is full of drinking, music, song, and the Bacchic frenzy of women: "there followed also the play of Bacchic insolence, as if the god himself were present and escorted the parade" (παρείπετο καὶ παιδιὰ βακχικῆς ὕβρεως, ὡς τοῦ θεοῦ παρόντος

---

⁴⁶ Giangrande 1963, 255-57.
⁴⁷ Giangrande 1963, 256. Gow and Page (1968, vol. 2, 395) are skeptical.
⁴⁸ Pherekrates fr. 247 Kassel and Austin in Phrynichos *Praeparatio Sophistica* 74: Φερεκράτης δὲ τὰ θυλήματα, ἃ πέρ ἐστιν ἄλφιτα οἴνῳ καὶ ἐλαίῳ μεμαγμένα, ὡσαύτως καλεῖ θυμέλην (sim. Hsch. θυμέλαι· οἱ βωμοί. καὶ τὰ ἄλφιτα τὰ ἐπιθυόμενα).

αὐτοῦ καὶ συμπαραπέμποντος τὸν κῶμον). The climax of the chapter is the famous scene, at the end of the processional route, where Alexander kisses his favorite, the victorious dancer Bagoas, in the theater.

Here we should mention also the frequent adjective θυμελικός, which is used exclusively of musical or theatrical performances, especially with the nouns ἀγών[49] and σύνοδος,[50] but it is also common as a noun, meaning "actor" or "actress."[51] Thymelic competitions are attested beginning in the fourth century BCE (*Syll.*³ 457, 1), but may well have existed earlier.[52]

As we have seen, most modern scholarship has worked with the hypothesis that the primary meaning of θυμέλη is "altar" or "sacrificial hearth." It is assumed that the classical theater had a θυμέλη (altar or hearth) in the orchestra and subsequently the word was transferred to designate the orchestra as such and later any stage for choruses. The present discussion,

---

[49] ἀγών: Polemon fr. 45 (in Ath. 15, 699a); Memnon fr. 3 (in Phot. *Bibl.* 224.223b); Charicles *FHG* IV 360 (in Ath. 8, 350b-c); Diod.Sic. 4.5.4, 17.110.7; Origen *C. Cels.* 5.42; IThesp 156.1, 157.3; Paton-Hicks 8; *IG* 4² 41; *CID* 4 117.17; *IG* 2² 1134.24-25; *FD* 3(2) 69.17, 49.24, 48.29; *IvP* 2 268 fr. AB. col. I.6 + col II.6-7; *IG* 12² 58.10.7; *EKM* 1 / Beroia 117.14, 118.4; *IG* 12⁷ 53.33-34, 54.24-25, 397.22, 405.37-38; Keramos 13-4; Panamara 227.11, 228.11; Aphrodisias 328.16; Priene 1270.2; *TAM* V(2) 983.14, 998.8-9; Side Kitabeleri 148.1, .2, .3; *BCH* 1886: 219,3.22; *BCH* 1900:338,1.15.

[50] σύνοδος: *IK* Side 1 31.3, 32.2; *IG* 14 2496.1, 2500.3; Bosch, *Quellen Ankara* 155,128.8, 166,130.A1-2+B14; Erythrai 94.2; Petzl/Schwertheim 8/16.5, .58, .86; *IG* 2² 1350.3; *TAM* 5(2) 1033.1-2; Smyrna 95.29-30; *IG* 14 2495.5; *IScM* 2 70.9; *IK* Heraclea Pont. 2.A21; I.Napoli 1 47.4; *IG* 12¹ 83.6; *OGIS* 713.2, .9; *TAM* 2 496.9, 910.12; *PdP* 5 (1950) 76,1.1; *IK* Prusias ad Hypium 49.25. Other nouns: *Lyr. adesp.* 113 P.; *IG* 7 4138.15, 4139.9, 4142; Panamara 200.29; Cornutus *Nat.deor.* 62; Plut. *Fab.* 4.6; *BCH* 1900:343,7.6, 344,10.7, 345,11.7; Cyril. *De exitu animi* 77.1084.

[51] Panamara 176.23-24; Joseph. *AJ* 15.270; Plut. *Sull.* 36.1, *Cat.Mi.* 46.4; Pausanias Dam. fr. 5 (in Malalas *Chron.* 225, 248, 249, *Chronicon paschale* 364); Artem. *Onir.* 2.3, .30, .37; Ptol. *Tetr.* 4.4.6; *Vita Aesopi (W)* 81; Heph.Astr. *Apotel.* 169; Jul. *Ep.* 89b; Cyril. *De exitu animi* 77.1076. Also in the neuter: Plut. *Comp. Ar. et Men.* 853B; *IG* 7 2712.75; *IMT* Skam/NebTaeler 170.28; IThesp 175, 161.

[52] See *RE* VI A 1:704 s.v. Θυμελικοὶ ἀγῶνες; Frei 1900; also below, Chapter Five.

however, has identified a common denominator among all the different usages of the word. They all relate to ritual practices of some kind by which worshippers seek to satisfy a divinity, and most examples associate these practices with a particular space. One such space is, of course, an altar, which is the proper understanding of some of the examples we have studied, but other examples seem to suggest a sacred building or a sanctuary in general. The dancing place is also a ritual space, since Greek choral lyric is, in most cases, an integral part of a particular cultic context and is a form of communication between gods and men. In all these instances, contact with the divinity is important. The prosaic definition of θυμέλη could be "a performative meeting point between man and god."

Towards an Etymology of ΘΥΜΕΛΗ

Etymology plays an essential role in establishing the core meaning of the word, but things are not as plain as the handbooks and lexica would have us believe. First, the phonological structure of the word makes a derivation from the verb θύω—"to sacrifice"—problematic. The first syllable in θυμέλη is always treated as short in poetry, e.g. Eur. *Ion* 46, ὑπέρ τε θυμέλας διορίσαι πρόθυμος ἦν (iambic trimeter) or *SEG* 8.496, τιμαλφῶν τὰν σὰν εὐλίβανον θυμέλαν (dactylic pentameter). Yet, the other μ-derivations from θύω consistently have a long ῡ: θῦμα "sacrifice" (e.g. Eur. *Med.* 1054),[53] θῡμός "spirit" (*Il.* 1.24 etc.), θῡμιάζω "to burn so as to produce smoke" (e.g. Soph. *OT* 4). We have a short ῠ in θύμον "thyme," but it is probably unrelated and pre-Greek (like many other names of indigenous plants); as the most recent etymological dictionary says, "a variant of θῡμός

---

[53] The only exception is the pentameter line Γα[μα]λίου πραπίδων, τοῦτο φέρω τὸ θύμα (*IGUR* I.127, fourth century CE).

with short *u seems impossible in IE terms."⁵⁴ As a matter of fact, θυμός has a clear cognate in several Indo-European languages: Sanskrit *dhūmá*, Latin *fūmus*, Lithuanian *dūmai*, Old Church Slavonic *dymŭ*, all with the meaning "smoke" and consistently with a vocalism that points to a long *ū.⁵⁵

Greek has a short ῠ in certain forms of θύω, like the perfect τέθυμαι or the passive ἐτύθην, and in certain verbal nouns, like θυσία "sacrifice" or θυτήρ "sacrificer." Here, the short vowel is probably regular,⁵⁶ but whatever the historical reason may be, this kind of "secondary ablaut" is typical in the verbal paradigm of Greek.⁵⁷ At any rate, the derivations in -μος/-μα/-μων from roots ending in -υ- and -ι- generally have a long vowel,⁵⁸ and there are only a few exceptions, all of which are either isolated or young.⁵⁹ So the overall rule is that the derivations with -μ- have a long vowel before the suffix. This means that if θυμέλη is derived from θύω or θυμός, the short vowel would be extraordinary in terms of the Greek language itself.

If θυμέλη belongs to the root of θύω, it should formally be an expansion of the verbal noun θυμός with the suffix *-lo-*. This suffix was

---

⁵⁴ Beekes 2010, 564.

⁵⁵ Most scholars agree that this ū derives from an older *uH (i.e. with a laryngeal).

⁵⁶ The short vowel can be explained as a regular omission of the laryngeal in *uH in the second part of compounds and in the reduplicated perfect, cf. Beekes 1969, 242-45.

⁵⁷ Due to analogy, a paradigmatic contrast between long and short vowels is introduced into roots that originally had a long vowel throughout the paradigm or a contrast between a diphthong and a monophthong: ἔφῦν : ἔφυμεν (< *ephūn : *ephūmen), ὄρνῡμι : ὄρνυμεν (< *orneumi : *ornumen). Cf. Schwyzer 1939, 364.

⁵⁸ E.g. ἀ-μύμων, δρῡμός / δρῦμα, ἔν-δῡμα, ἔλυμα, ζύμη / ἄ-ζῡμος, κνῦμα, κρῡμός, ἄ-κῡμος/ κῦμα, λύμη / λῦμα, ῥῡμός / ῥύμη / ῥῦμα, στῦμα, τρύμη, φῦμα, χῡμός, τῡμός / θῦμα; βρῖμός, βρίμη, βρῑμάομαι; κλίμαξ; κρῖμα (later κρίμα); λῑμός; πῑμελή; σῑμός; τῑμή, τῑμάω, ἄ-τῑμος; φῖμός.

⁵⁹ δί-, ἀμφί-δυμος, ἔρυμα, ἔτυμος / ἐτήτυμος, πλύμα, ῥύμα (older ῥεῦμα), χύμα (older χεῦμα); ὄβριμος; κλίμα.

no longer productive of new word formations by the historical phase of the Greek language, which means that the derivation must have occurred in an earlier phase of the language. There are a few words showing the combination *-me- + *-lo- in Greek: θεμέλιος "foundation-stone" (τίθημι "to put") and πῑμελή "soft fat, lard" (πίων "fat").⁶⁰ Since θεμέλιος has a cognate in Latin *familia* "household" (orig. "basis"?), this derivational type is in all likelihood Proto-Indo-European.⁶¹ However, a *-lo- derivation from θυμός should have a long vowel. This is the case in Sanskrit *dhūmrá-* "grey, purple"⁶² and Latvian *dūmals* "smoke-colored."

In the historical phase of the Greek language, the noun θυμός means "spirit, mind, desire, temper, etc.," which is hardly consistent with the semantics of θυμέλη. There are, however, other μ-derivations from θύω that are closer to the assumed core meaning of this word, like θῦμα "victim, sacrifice" or θυμιάζω "to burn incense, to fumigate." None of these are attested in the early literature: θῦμα does not occur before Aeschylus, and since the μα suffix is extremely productive in the Classical period, it is in all likelihood not an inherited form but derived directly from θύω in the contemporary meaning. The first known occurrence of θυμιάζω is in Hipponax (fr. 175 W.), but the formation is exceptional, and it has in fact retained the

---

⁶⁰ Frisk 1943, 50-55.

⁶¹ *Famulus* "slave" is perhaps a back-formation from *familia*, cf. de Vaan 2008, 201. Latin *cumulus* "heap" may be related to Greek κυέω "to be pregnant," κῦμα "wave," in the same way that θεμέλιος is related to τίθημι, θέμα. The short vowel is explained either as some shortening of long vowels before resonants or on analogy with *tumulus*, cf. de Vaan 2008, 153. For the regular shortening of pretonic long vowels in Latin, see Schrijver 1991, 334-43.

⁶² Mayrhofer 1986-2001, I 796: "Die Form (statt *dhūma-rá-) erklärt sich durch Anlehnung an *tāmrá-*." The form *dhūmala-*, often quoted in the handbooks, is attested only in lexica.

original meaning, namely "smoke."[63] Another archaic derivation from θύω, namely θύος (attested in Mycenaean), designates "a substance producing a fragrant smell when burnt, incense, or sim."[64] Though associated with sacrifice and burning, it clearly points to the original meaning of the root.

So, if θυμέλη were indeed a Proto-Indo-European derivation, one should not ascribe to it without further ado the historical semantics of θύω. It would not be, properly, a "sacrificial place" or "hearth," but rather a "smoking place." Though it may be true that there is no smoke without fire, the cognates in the other Indo-European languages strongly suggest that this word has to do with smoke and air and not some kind of religiously motivated ignition.

Some scholars, both ancient and modern, have proposed that θυμέλη derives instead from the verb τίθημι, "to put, to place"; Carl Robert thereby proposed that the term means "foundation" (cf. θεμέλιον) and thus could designate any type of built structure, including, for example, houses and temples in addition to altars.[65] This etymology is, however, improbable because of the irregular root vocalism (-υ- instead of -ε-).

A more satisfying alternative, phonologically speaking, would be a derivation from the root of θέω "to run, hurry," as suggested by Wolfgang Aly, who translates θυμέλη as "Tummelplatz."[66] The cognate θόασμα is attested

---

[63] Meier-Brügger 1989.

[64] LSJ 1996, suppl., 153. Related forms are θύον "sandarac tree; incense," θυόω "to fill with sweet smells," and θυήεις "smoking incense, fragrant," which occur in Homer. It is more doubtful whether θεῖον (epic θέειον or θήϊον) "sulphur" derives from θύος. Meier-Brügger (1989, 245 n. 51) postulates a PIE *dhueh$_2$-es-io-, which would yield *thwāhion > θήϊον. However, the more common epic form θέειον and Lesbian θή[ϊο]ν (Alc. fr. 45.8 V.) point to *thewehion (*dheu(H)-es-io-) rather than *thwāhion.

[65] Robert 1897, 438-45.

[66] Aly 1914, 60-63.

with the meaning "dancing place" (*Hymn. Orph.* 49.6), but "dancing" is not part of the semantics in the words from which this noun has been derived (θοάζω "to hurry" < θόος "swift"). Furthermore, θέω has yielded no other μ-nouns in Greek. θυμέλη would be a completely isolated form with aberrant semantics.

One possibility that has not been suggested before is a derivation from the root of θέα "sight, spectacle," θεάομαι "to watch," and θαῦμα "wonder." If the root is indeed Indo-European,[67] it is at least conceivable that a derivation with *-*me-lo*- from such root could result in θυμέλη.[68] This word would mean something like "show" or "wonderwork."

◘ ◘ ◘

Of course, we must accept that often it is not possible to find a suitable etymology for a Greek word, as is clear to anyone who browses one of the etymological dictionaries. In most cases, an obscure Greek word is a borrowing from either pre-Greek (whatever that was) or one of the many extinct languages in Asia Minor and the Middle East. Regarding θυμέλη, a negative result is just as beneficial as a positive one, since it liberates us from the burden of the traditional etymology. False association has, since antiquity, distorted our understanding of the classical texts that employ this word, forcing us to read smoke, fire, or slaughter into contexts that do not

---

[67] Beekes (2010, 535-36) categorizes the Greek words as pre-Greek due to the vacillation between Att. θαῦμα and Ion. θῶ(υ)μα, which "cannot be explained in IE terms." However, the variation is also found in τραῦμα ~ τρῶμα "wound" (with a similar distribution between Attic and Ionic). τραῦμα is derived from τιτρώσκω "to wound," which certainly looks like a good Greek word (with a PIE origin, cf. Skt. *turá* 'ill').

[68] *dhh₂u-me-leh₂ > **dhu-me-lā-* > θυμέλη; for the development of *Hu in Greek, see Schrijver 1991, 512-25.

suggest these concepts in the first place.[69] And this, in turn, has caused confusion for classical archaeologists, who have tried to uncover in the ground what classical philologists believe they have discovered in lexica.

When we let the texts speak for themselves, the different semantic fields that can be reconstructed for θυμέλη connect much more neatly and coherently. The basic meaning of the word, which fits virtually all examples in our literary and epigraphic sources, without adding anything extraneous, seems to be: "a ritual space in which worshippers communicated with the gods through performance of sacrifice, prayer, and/or song and dance."

---

[69] In the Classical and post-Classical periods, the Greeks were no longer aware of the linguistic origin of the word and may have created their own folk-etymologies. We have already seen that later grammarians derived the word θυμέλη from θύω "to sacrifice," which in classical Greek was the general word for cult practices. It is conceivable that some speakers would also recognize the word μέλος "song" in it, even though this possibility has left no explicit traces in our sources (the words θύω and μέλος are juxtaposed in Aesch., Eum. 328-29 = 341-42 and Dio Chrys., Or. 32.57, but without reference to a θυμέλη, though it is striking that the latter passage talks about music as a form of therapy for the soul; a portion of this latter passage appears on p. 86 below as the epigraph to Chapter Four). Although a popular etymology may not be correct linguistically speaking, it still had a reality in the minds of ancient speakers and influenced the semantic development of the word.

Chapter Three
Circularity, Performance, And Acoustics

It is the pervading law of all things organic and inorganic, of all things physical and metaphysical, of all things human and all things super-human, of all true manifestations of the head, of the heart, of the soul, that the life is recognizable in its expression:
that form ever follows function. This is the law.
Louis Sullivan

The discussion in Chapter Two demonstrated that the word *thymele* could have communicated the idea of "sacred performance" or "sacred performance space" to an ancient Greek audience. In this chapter, we turn to other features of the thymele at Epidauros that further suggest that the building may have been used for some kind of ritualized dance, song, or both. These features include the circular form of the building, its unique, labyrinthine foundations, and a key element of the cella's interior decoration: a painting of Eros holding a lyre by the fourth-century virtuoso Pausias.

Circular space and performance

A famous—and sometimes problematic—conceptual tool employed by architectural historians is the idea that architectural form, function, and meaning are interdependent. While this idea was most carefully articulated by modernists such as Adolf Loos and his "followers"—Le Corbusier, Walter Gropius, Alvar Aalto, Mies van der Rohe, and Gerrit Rietveld—it has been rather common, for at least the last hundred years, to think of ancient architecture in similar terms.[1] The work of ancient Greek architects could be quite sophisticated intellectually.[2] Indeed, the

---

[1] Goodyear 1912; Robert 1939 (but see the criticism in Holland 1948); Jones 2003; Townsend 2003; Schultz 2007a, 221-25; Wescoat 2012.

[2] Townsend 2003; Wescoat 2012; Jones 2013.

formal analysis of ancient architecture is capable of sustaining a broad range of interpretative hypotheses that consistently link form, function, and meaning in bold and plausible ways. With regard to ancient Greek architecture specifically, Bonna Wescoat has recently noted that "Architectural form is not the mere handmaiden of function but has also semantic value and the capacity to transform the experience of those who engage it spatially, metaphysically, psychologically, emotionally, and associatively."[3] In sum, the form of an ancient Greek building—the combined physical composition of structural and decorative elements of which the building was made—*means* something. Since this is so, it seems appropriate to consider the connections between the function of the thymele at Epidauros and its most elementary formal characteristic: its circularity.

A long and well-known scholarly tradition connects performance to circular space in the ancient Greek world.[4] While the old notion that the circular orchestra of the Greek theater had its origins in the circular choros (dancing floor) or circular halos (threshing floor) has been recently problematized, it seems equally clear that circular spaces and performance were firmly joined in some ancient Greek minds.[5] When a group of dancers or singers clasps hands and steps backward, pulling their arms taut, the shape they make is never a square or a trapezoid—it is always a circle. There is something basic, and perhaps even primal, that connects circular form to

---

[3] Wescoat 2012, 66.

[4] See, for example: Kolb 1981; Polacco 1998; Rehm 2002; Rehm 2006; Schultz 2007a; and Wescoat 2012, all with bibliographies.

[5] Circular orchestra and agrarian cycles in ancient Greece: Ure 1955. Fourth-century date for the circular orchestra in ancient Greece: Ashby 1999, 25-26; van den Eijnde 2000, 11-12, 103-8; Rehm 2002, 37-41 (esp. 39 n. 17, with bibliography); Csapo 2014 (esp. with his Appendix, written by H.R. Goette). See also: D'Angour 1997, Schultz 2007a, 221-25, with bibliography, and Ceccarelli 2013.

group performance, specifically to group dance and song. This idea was not lost on Greek architects and it seems to have informed—consciously or not—many of the well-known circular performance spaces of the ancient Greek world, such as the halos on the Sacred Way at Delphi, the circular area in the Sanctuary of the Great Gods at Samothrace, or the theater of Dionysos in Athens.[6] Of course, this is not to claim the existence of some reductive equation (e.g., circle = performance) within the ancient Greek world. Rather, it is to suggest that, in addition to other possible formal and/or functional meanings, circular architectural form could, and often did, signify the idea of performance in some ancient Greek minds.

To begin, altars were often placed, and sacred performances often occurred, within circular or semicircular spaces. The archaic altar in the sanctuary of Demeter at Arkouda on Thasos, for example, was placed on a circular pavement that seems to have been designed to facilitate the viewing of rituals, such as the performance of hymns.[7] In the sanctuary of Amphiaraos at Oropos, worshippers convened in a semicircular, stepped theatron to one side of the altar, and the theatron was inscribed "the viewing area next to the altar" (τὸ θεάτρον τὸ κατὰ τὸν βωμόν, *IG* 7 4255.29-30).[8] Altars and the performances that rotated around them could also be

---

[6] The famous dancing model from the large tholos at Kamilari, Crete—in which four nude men hold hands and dance in a circle—springs to mind here. Similar models were found at Late Minoan Palaikastro, Olympia in the Geometric period, and from Hellenistic Corinth (see, for example, Branigan [1993, 130, fig. 7.6]). Lawler (1947) still provides good treatments of circular song and dance in ancient Greece. See also Fitton 1973, 258-59.

[7] Grandjean and Salviat 2000, 129, 217, no. 72; Ohnesorg 2005, 110-13, fig. 51; see also Wescoat 2012. Also Hölscher 2002, 336, on the large, open area east of the altar of Zeus at Olympia serving as a theater-like space for sacrifices, especially before construction of the Echo Stoa.

[8] Petrakos 1968, 67-69, 98-99. On steps as shaping participation in rituals, especially sacrifices, see Hollinshead 2012; Hollinshead 2015.

enclosed within monumental circular spaces bordered by walls, fences, or other visible boundaries. The altar area at the sanctuary of Zeus Agoraios on Thasos and the archaic altar of the temple of Apollo at Didyma are the two best known examples of such altar courts surrounded by stone parapets.[9] That altars themselves could be, and often were, round is also worth noting.[10]

Vase painting helps to confirm that this connection between sacred song and dance, altars, and circularity was well known and well established in antiquity. A famous white-ground phiale in Boston, attributed to the Painter of London D12 (Fig. 16), shows a group of women dancing around a flaming altar.[11] These women hold hands, wear sacred costume (red himatia over white chitons), and are pictured dancing to the music of an aulos player as they circle the interior of the vessel. Guy Hedreen has shown that images like these can be understood as spatial metaphors and that the women can be interpreted as dancing in a circle, in this case around a sacred altar.[12] Their clasped hands, the steady visual tempo created by their feet, and the cadence of the folds of their chitons (which slant ahead to show rhythmic motion, replicate the linear design of the phiale's central "hub," and point to the center of the vessel like spokes on a wheel) all confirm this hypothesis.[13] This impression is enhanced by the dancers' chiastic glances, by their

---

[9] Thasos: Grandjean and Salviat 2000, 76, figs. 31-32, no. 35. Didyma: Ohnesorg 1991, 122, pl. XXVIb; Ohnesorg 2005, 48-50, pl. 19; but see Fehr 1971-2, 29-34 and Cooper and Morris 1990, 69-71. James McCredie (1968, 219) has suggested that a round, molded block found on the Eastern Hill in Samothrace was an altar originally placed in the center of the Theatral Circle.

[10] Circular altars: Berges, Patsiada, and Nollé 1996, with comprehensive bibliography.

[11] Boston Museum of Fine Arts 65.908.

[12] Hedreen 2013.

[13] Ines Jucker (1963, 58-61) and Penelope Truitt (1969, 86-91) have also emphasized

gait—they seem to move both forward and backward as they step in time—and by the painter's emphasis on the ground line on which they dance, a line that emphatically stresses the cup's circular form, and by extension, the circular shape of the dance.

Also important in the context of performance and circularity are ancient Greek choroi. While some scholars have disassociated choroi from the "origins" of the well-known circular orchestras of Greek theaters built in the fifth century and later, these circular performance spaces are nevertheless significant; there can be little doubt that these circular spaces provided venues for sacred song and dance.[14] The word *choros* itself has several meanings in ancient Greek: it can signify the *act* of dancing, or a *troop* of dancers, or a special *place* for dancing—a dancing floor.[15] The fact that the performance space, the performance act, and the performers themselves are so closely associated philologically seems significant, especially when we consider the argument made above in Chapter Two.

The physical remains of ancient choroi are widely known across the Greek world.[16] There is evidence for circular dancing floors on Crete, including the sanctuary of Asklepios at Lebena, the city of Eltynia, ancient Vari, and ancient Istron, among many others.[17] Charalambos Kritzas,

---

that these *Reigentanz* scenes were especially suited and adapted to circular zones on pots and that painters often exploited a vessel's form to express circularity of performance. Additionally, Sheramy Bundrick (2005, 181-82) has suggested that a scene of girls holding hands and dancing around the shoulder of a well-known lekythos in the Metropolitan Museum of Fine Arts (56.11.1) might also have been associated with the physical arrangement of public performances of maiden choruses.

[14] Ceccarelli 2013.

[15] Kritzas 2006; also Burkert 1985, 102. But see also Polacco (1998, 105-16) who argues that the term most frequently applies to the act of dance rather than the space.

[16] Wescoat (2012) provides the fundamental discussion of this material; we follow her arguments and conclusions closely.

[17] Kritzas (1998 and 2006) provide the comprehensive lists.

building on Peter Warren's interpretation that the circular platforms outside Knossos are Bronze Age choroi, has discussed possible links between these round spaces and Homeric descriptions of the ornate dancing floors of the nymphs (*Od.* 12.315-318) and the dancing floor of Ariadne (*Il.* 18.590-592).[18] The early fourth-century choros at Argos is particularly important here, given its proximity to Epidauros.[19] This circular space was clearly meant to frame dances and other sacred performances: the area is surrounded by a limestone shelf wide enough to seat an audience. The same might be said of the large circular structure excavated below the acropolis of Sparta; Pausanias seems to refer to this area and calls it a "choros" (3.11.9), while both Herodotus (6.67.3) and Lucian (*Anach.* 38), if they refer to the same site, call it a "theatron."[20] For these later authors, connections between circularity and performance seem natural.

Also associated with the choros is the circular halos, or threshing floor. Most early scholars believed that the round orchestra of the Greek theater was derived from the halos, where the harvest both of grain and grapes was accompanied by celebration in song and dance.[21] This account seems logical given how closely the dithyramb and Dionysos were linked with agriculture. Although this hypothesis has since been called into question, there is little doubt that these circles served some performative function.[22] Indeed, these threshing floors number among the most prominent public

---

[18] Kritzas 1998 and 2006; Warren 1984, cited in Wescoat 2012.

[19] Marchetti and Rizakis 1995, 455-56; Nielsen 2002, 103; Wescoat 2012.

[20] Kourinou 2000, 114-27, 280-81; Nielsen 2002, 91-93; Wescoat 2012, all with bibliography.

[21] See above, p. 67 n. 5.

[22] Dionysos, dancing festivals, agriculture, and theater: Otto 1995; Kerényi 1976, 178, 185; Seaford 2006, 15-25; 87-104.

areas and most common circular spaces in the ancient Greek world.[23] The prominence of the halos is evident in many Greek sanctuaries. For instance, the Eleusinian accounts of 329/8 BCE (*IG* 2² 1672.233) mention a sacred threshing floor, and Eugene Vanderpool has suggested that this floor should be found on the raised terrace in front of the Telesterion.[24] The famous halos in the panhellenic sanctuary of Apollo at Delphi is also important.[25] Here, we see an explicit connection between circular space and performance: every nine years in this space (which was framed by five exedrae that provided benches for viewing and listening) a sacred play, the Stepterion, was performed to please both god and worshippers.[26]

Charalambos Kritzas has suggested that the word halos can indicate a choros and that the two terms are thus interchangeable to a certain extent. Steven Lonsdale has supported this notion, emphasizing the fluidity of purpose inherent in the circular dance floor, which he describes as "a locus with the magnetic power to attract a divinity or lover, to experience union, to dismember, to reconstitute, in short a theatron for recreating and manipulating the natural and supernatural worlds."[27] That every theater

---

[23] *Halos:* Young 1956, 122-24; Langdon and Watrous 1977, 173-75; Goette 2000, 83.

[24] Vanderpool 1982. Wescoat (2012) points out that there is a semicircular foundation from the Geometric period beneath the Telesterion that may be too large to belong to an apsidal temple, as it is often identified; it might be a performance space.

[25] *GDI* 2101, 2642; Plut. *Quaest. Graec.* 203c; *De def. or.* 418A (for the Doloneia); [*De mus*] 1136; Ael. *VH* 3.1.

[26] While the particulars of this ritual are uncertain, most scholars believe that it included a reenactment of the burning of a heroic palace or temple and the subsequent escape of Apollo from Delphi to the valley of Tempe: Bourguet 1914, 124-26; Harrison 1962, 425-29; Roux 1976, 166-68; Bommelaer and Laroche 1991, 146-47. On the exedrae, Stoa of the Athenians, and temple terrace as both framing the area and serving as viewing platforms, see Wescoat 2012, 84-86.

[27] Lonsdale 1993, 281, quoted in Wescoat 2012, 86. Wescoat (2012) has shown that the elaborate and mysterious theatral circle in the sanctuary of the Great Gods on

constructed in the Greek world after the end of the fifth century (with one or perhaps two exceptions like the theater at Thorikos, which might be earlier, or the rectangular theater at Calydon) has a circular or semicircular orchestra seems to confirm at least some connection between circular space and performance.

Recently, the connection between circularity and performance in the ancient Greek world has been more carefully defined and developed.[28] Luigi Polacco, for example, has stressed the long-abiding interest among the ancient Greeks in geometry and geometric forms, and the relationship of these particular forms to performance, psychic harmony, and physical health.[29] The Pythagoreans, in particular—for whom the most beautiful figures were the circle and the sphere—explored the interconnections among music, mathematics, and the health of the soul; for them, circular space, music, and well-being were deemed to be utterly interdependent. In the first half of the fourth century, the Pythagorean Archytas described astronomy, geometry, arithmetic, and music as "sister studies" (fr. 1 Diels-Kranz = fr. 1 Huffman).[30] His work, and that of the earlier Pythagorean Philolaos,

---

Samothrace, with its host of over forty life-sized bronze statues standing in attendance, was "a theatron, literally a place of watching; in particular, [a place for] watching performed actions" in which "concentrically placed circles shape both the space of performance and the place of witness." Wescoat connects the theatral circle on Samothrace to the ritual reenactment of the search for Harmonia, her safe return, and her joyous wedding to Kadmos, all of which suggest that dancing and music formed an important part of this celebration.

[28] E.g., the panel dedicated to "Circular Space and Performance in Ancient Greece," organized by Bonna Wescoat, 107th Annual Meeting of the Archaeological Institute of America, Montreal, January 2006.

[29] Polacco 1998. See also Wiles 1997, 72-77, on the importance of circular space to the organization of Greek society and culture.

[30] On Archytas: Huffman 2005, which includes extensive discussion and bibliography in addition to the fragments and testimonia; also Schofield 2014.

gave rise to the influential idea of the "music of the spheres." Archytas's friend Plato, in his account of the creation of the cosmos in the *Timaeus*, privileges the circle, which he defines on several occasions as that form "whose extremes are everywhere equally distant from the center" (*Prm.* 137e, *Epistle* 7.342b, *Ti.* 33b). Finding the circle and sphere "the most perfect and self-similar of all shapes" (*Ti.* 33b), Plato has the "world soul" (νοῦς) circulate within it even as it perfectly encircles the heavens (36d).[31] Pythagoras himself is said to have employed circular formations together with musical performance for the purpose of healing the body and the soul: he would arrange individuals in a circle, place a lyre player in their center, and have them sing hymns and/or dance in order to calm and cheer them via a kind of "medicine through music" (Iambl. *VP* 110-11; cf. also Porph. *Pythag.* 32-33; this passage is discussed in greater detail below, in Chapter Four).[32]

Given the many connections between circularity and performance in both ancient Greek praxis and the ancient Greek imagination, the circular design of the thymele suggests that this building, too, may have been used for musical performance (Figs. 17-18). When we pair this possibility with the conclusions presented in Chapter Two, that the word *thymele* can

---

[31] On the organizational, literary, symbolic, and functional roles of music in Plato's dialogues, especially in relation to Pythagorean theory: Kennedy 2011. Kennedy (250) suggests that the dialogues, when read aloud, may have exerted a psychological or emotional effect on audiences, due to the musical scales embedded in the texts.

[32] It is perhaps not coincidental that the Pythagoreans had a community in Phlius (Diog. Laert. 8.46; cf. also Pl. *Phdr. passim*), a town in the northern Peloponnese between Sicyon and Nemea, not far from Epidauros. Among Pythagoras's possible followers in Phlius was a certain Echecrates, an associate of Socrates (he is present in the *Phaedo*) who believed that the soul harmonizes the various properties that hold the body together. On Echecrates and other Pythagoreans who believed the soul to be an attunement (*harmonia*), see Zhmud 2014, 105-6. On the many traditions of Pythagoras and his teachings, see Huffman 2014.

be defined as "a ritual space wherein worshippers communicated with the gods through performance of sacrifice, prayer, and/or song and dance," the idea that some kind of musical performance took place in or around the thymele becomes even more attractive.

THE LABYRINTH AND THE ACOUSTICS OF THE THYMELE

Due to its puzzling and intricate labyrinthine foundations, the design of the thymele is much more complex than that of other enclosed Greek tholoi. Recall, also, that the thymele's cella has a hole in the center of the floor that opens into the unique, hollow corridors of the building's foundations (Figs. 4 and 14-15). As noted above, Svolos published the remains of the 1.23 m marble capstone that sat in the middle of the cella floor and that rested above the center of the labyrinth (Fig. 12).[33] This capstone had a ca. 0.38 m hole in its center, not much smaller than the size of a modern manhole cover. As suggested above, a hole of such diameter could have been covered with a marble cap or a bronze grille to prevent worshippers from stepping through it—a necessary precaution in a building with heavy foot traffic.[34] In either case, a substantial hole in the thymele's floor suggests that the spatial volumes of the labyrinth and cella were intended to communicate with one another in some way on at least some occasions.

In the context of the present argument, this puzzling hole becomes especially significant. The hole at the center of the thymele's cella allowed the building's interior space to be opened onto the building's labyrinthine foundations in a manner superficially reminiscent of the drum of a guitar.[35]

---

[33] Svolos 1988b, 280-81; above, pp. 40-42.

[34] On foot traffic, and lack thereof, in Greek temples: Hollinshead 1999 and Mylonopoulos 2011, with comprehensive bibliography.

[35] The thymele's design—a large cella that leads through an opening to labyrinthine foundations—is somewhat analogous to the anatomical structure of the human

Indeed, it was this analogy that first inspired us to think about the thymele as a potential site for musical performance; we believed that this complex, hollow space beneath the cella's floor may have somehow amplified, or otherwise modified, sounds in the thymele's cella—especially sounds made near the opening in the floor.[36] The only way to test this theory, however, was through acoustical analysis. In 2011 and 2012, Andrew Fermer and his engineering team at Hann Tucker Associates Ltd built a virtual model of the thymele and ran the model through CATT Acoustic software.[37] CATT is a ray tracing prediction program used by sound engineers to design and test the acoustical properties of theaters, orchestra halls, and other public spaces.

Fermer and his team concluded that the opening and/or closing of the hole in the center of the thymele's floor would have had a noticeable, if subtle, effect on music played within the building proper. "Specifically," Fermer writes, "the labyrinth at some positions appeared to 'absorb' some reflections, possibly directed into the labyrinth from the shape of the ceiling, resulting in a more pleasant, a more soothing, and a more controlled listening experience than when the labyrinth was closed off,

---

ear. This may not be coincidental. Alkmaeon of Croton (associated by some with Pythagoras) was among the first Greeks known to have studied the anatomy of the human ear and believed that sounds made near the hollow chamber of the outer ear were taken in by the inner ear where they resonated until the brain perceived them (frags. A5 and A6 DK). For discussion of this passage, and of other ancient theories about sound and the ways that the human body senses it, and about ancient views of auditory affect, see Gurd 2016, Ch. 2, esp. 89-96.

[36] Luigi Polacco has theorized a similar effect at the ancient theater at Syracuse: he argues that a rectangular trench cut into the floor of the orchestra functioned as a resonance chamber for a wooden platform, or θυμέλη, which stood above it. Polacco identifies this platform with the various platforms on which citharodes and other musicians are depicted as standing on Greek vases. Polacco et al. 1990, 81-113.

[37] See below, Appendix.

i.e. when it reflected sound energy directly back up into the thymele's cella."[38] Although acoustical analysis of the building did not reveal any amplificatory effects per se that can be connected to the building's labyrinthine foundations, it seems equally clear that, when the hole was open, an ancient listener within the thymele's cella would have experienced a noticeably *unique* kind of soundscape.

How would the thymele's soundscape have been experienced and interpreted by ancient Greek audiences and communities? This is impossible to say. And yet, archaeoacousticians Steven Waller, Miriam Kolar, Graeme Lawson, and many others have conducted careful documentation of similar phenomena throughout the ancient world with fascinating results.[39] Although not dealing with the formal composition and reception of sacred music in early Greece, their work does show how numerous ancient sites were designed to create divine and transcendental effects by way of sound. In sum, a spectacular variety of ancient buildings and locales—from Stonehenge, to Chavín de Huántar, Peru, to the Horseshoe Canyon of Utah, U.S.A.—functioned as "ritualized sound environments" that elevated worshippers and produced the near magical effects aimed at connecting ancient communities to their ancestors, their spirits, and their gods.[40]

Was this kind of subtle, sonic effect the result of conscious planning and experimentation on the part of the thymele's architect? Was the thymele designed to allow priests, musicians, or healers to alter the acoustical

---

[38] The full text of Fermer's results appears below, in the Appendix. We cannot know the precise shape and composition of the ceiling; too little of the superstructure remains, see above, p. 39.

[39] Waller 2006; Kolar 2013a; 2013b; 2014. See also: Scarre and Lawson 2006, Garfinkle and Waller 2012; Eneix and Zubrow 2014; Mills 2014; Blake and Cross 2015; and Eneix 2016.

[40] Kolar 2013a; 2013b; 2014. See also below, Conclusions and Beginnings.

properties of the building in response to sacred concerns, to divine mandates, or in the service of therapeutic effects? If so, then it might explain why the architect did not choose to fashion a traditional foundation for the thymele with solid, easy-to-cut, rectangular stone but instead chose to pursue a new, much more costly and time-consuming method of construction. As we have seen, there is no doubt that the building was innovative on a number of levels. Acoustical innovation fits well with the building's other novelties, especially if Polykleitos the Younger—the master architect responsible for the revolutionary acoustics at Epidauros's nearby theater—was responsible for this building's design, as ancient sources claim he was.[41]

One other feature of the thymele's basement may be relevant in this context: an enigmatic set of marks in the building's foundations. These marks, inscribed on the euthynteria of the thymele's basement foundations, were originally documented by Svolos, who identified them as contractors' initials or monograms (Figs. 19-20).[42] Might these marks, instead, have served some sort of musical function?

---

[41] The diameter of the thymele at stylobate level (ca. 20.15 m) is close to the diameter of the orchestra of the fourth-century theater at Epidauros (ca. 19.5 m)—a difference of only ca. 0.6 m. This kind of dimensional continuity seems to strengthen any possible ties between performance within the orchestra of the theater and within the nearby thymele. Might Polykleitos have discovered a specific acoustical effect towards which he worked in both structures, and might he have seen the two architectural "instruments" playing counterpoint in a more complex song?

[42] Svolos 1988b, 251-56, with plans 37, 41 and fig. 6-7. Burford (1969, 68) relates the thymele's marks with the masons' marks in Shrine V (Enclosure Y) and argues that the two structures are contemporary on the basis of the marks' similarity. The marks on Enclosure Y, however, are clear pairs of letters that occur on adjoining blocks of the krepis, on either side of the joint, from A (alpha) to T (tau): A-A, B-B, Γ-Γ,...T-T; Lempidaki 2003, 31-33 and fig. 9. It is quite interesting that though Enclosure Y, like the thymele, dates to the mid-fourth century, the marks are entirely different and in the case of the thymele they are rotated in various directions. See also below, Chapter Five.

In typical masonry practice, letters or characters of this kind were used to assign each block to a different workshop or to indicate the position of blocks within any given structure. The only contractor known from the accounts to have worked in the walls of the labyrinth is Eunikos from Epidauros, and yet there are more than seven different types of marks preserved.[43] It is also difficult to accept that, following the position of these marks, every ring was manufactured by four or five different workshops laboring simultaneously across and between building zones.[44] Moreover, one block has two such characters carved on its sides, which suggests that the marks may not function to indicate placement order. Thus, while it is quite possible that these are "masons' marks," they do not appear to correspond either to masons' names or to a build order.[45]

Given that the only structural element on which these marks occur is the lowermost course of the labyrinth's foundations, perhaps another explanation for these marks can be found. Here, the Roman architect Vitruvius may give us a clue as to one potential purpose for these marks. In his discussion of the architecture and acoustics of theaters, Vitruvius speaks of the Greek tradition of using bronze resonating vessels (*echea*) to amplify and modulate sound.[46] According to Vitruvius, the Greeks installed these vessels within the infrastructures of theaters (5.5.1-2). He also asserts that these vessels were especially useful in buildings constructed of materials that do not resonate, like marble or stone as opposed to wood (5.5.7). Might the

---

[43] Burford 1969, 155. Of course, other contractors may have worked on the building, but their names have not survived.

[44] See below, Chapter Five.

[45] As confirmed by Svolos, personal communication. See also below, Chapter Five.

[46] Recent analysis by Godman (2006) demonstrates that the material of the resonating vessels does not greatly affect acoustics: terracotta vessels seem to work as well as those made of bronze.

thymele's strange basement have been designed to hold bronze echea, like those described by Vitruvius? If so, then it is tempting to identify the marks on the thymele's euthynteria as symbols representing ancient musical notation or other signs indicating the position of a set of resonating vessels.

Vitruvius instructs that, in order to produce the best possible acoustic effects in a theater of medium size, an architect must "mark out a horizontal range half the way up the height of the theater, and within this create thirteen arched niches with twelve equal spaces between them" (5.5.2).[47] John Landels explains in laymen's terms how this system works. In each niche, a bronze jar was placed upside down on a small platform; some of the jars were propped on wedges so that they could collect sound from the stage. These jars were arranged in a mirrored scheme to articulate a system of acoustics based on seven notes: corresponding pairs of jars were then tuned to each of the seven notes except the lowest note (2 x 6 + 1), yielding thirteen jars.[48]

Within the thymele, the marks inscribed on the building's foundations look roughly like the following Greek letters: Α, Γ, Δ, Ε, Λ, Π, and Ι

---

[47] Vitruvius 5.5.2: designationes autem eorum, quibus in locis constituantur, sic explicentur. si non erit ampla magnitudine theatrum, media altitudinis transversa regio designetur et in ea tredecim cellae duodecim aequalibus intervallis distantes confornicentur, uti ea echea quae supra scripta sunt in cornibus extremis, utraque parte prima conlocentur, secunda ab extremis diatessaron ad neten diezeugmenon, tertia diatessaron ad paramesen, quarta ad neten synhemmenon, quinta diatessaron ad mesen, sexta diatessaron ad hypaten meson, in medio unum diatessaron ad hypaten hypaton.

[48] Landels 1967; Landels 1999, 192-95. Illustrations of how these vessels may have been positioned in a theater: Landels 1967, 86, fig. 6; Rowland and Howe 1999, 246, fig. 82. Archaeological evidence for resonating vessels: Plommer 1983, and below, Chapter Five. Analysis of the acoustic effects of resonating vessels: Godman 2006, and below, Chapter Five. On the echea described by Vitruvius: Hagel 2010, 251-55, and below, Chapter Five. On resonating vessels and the acoustic theories of Aristotle, Aristoxenos, and others: Saliou 2009; and below, Chapter Five.

(Figs. 19-20).⁴⁹ The fact that these characters are seven in number is striking given that there are seven notes in one of the most common musical scales used in the fourth century (a heptachord, based on the conjunction of two tetrachords, described by Aristoxenos in his fourth-century treatise *Harmonics* 58-59).⁵⁰ Seven is also the traditional number of strings on Apollo's lyre.⁵¹ Perhaps the seven marks in the thymele's foundations are traces of an innovative musical system. Letters such as those found in the thymele's basement were used for musical notation in hymns of the second century BCE at Delphi, as well as in fragments of a hymn to Asklepios from Epidauros that was inscribed in the third century CE, but their use is

---

⁴⁹ Published in Svolos 1988b, 251-56, with plans 37, 41 and fig. 6-7.

⁵⁰ Two tetrachords could also be combined disjunctively (eight notes rather than seven), also described by Aristoxenos (*Harm.* 58-59). On the theories and writings of Aristoxenos and their influence on later theorists, see Mathiesen 1999, 287-344; Gibson 2005; Barker 2007, 113-259; Barker 2009; the contributions to Huffman 2012; and below, Chapter Five.

⁵¹ By the fifth century some musicians were playing lyres and citharas with more than seven strings (e.g. Timotheos, among others, was criticized for playing an instrument with twelve strings, [Plut.] *De mus.* 1141d-1142a, quoting Pherecrates, *Cheiron*); however, as Barker (2007, 276) comments, "…we know from vase-paintings and allusions in poetry that there were only seven [strings] on the traditional tortoiseshell lyre, on which schoolboys still learned the rudiments of the art." A good visual example of Apollo's seven-stringed lyre is a white-ground kylix from Delphi (ca. 480-470 BCE) depicting the god pouring a libation and holding his tortoiseshell lyre prominently in the foreground (Delphi Museum, Inv. no. 8140). There are many depictions of seven-stringed instruments on Greek pottery; see Maas and Snyder 1989; Bundrick 2005. On seven as the traditional number of strings for the lyre and cithara, see also West 1992, 62-4; Landels 1999, 47-68, esp. 54-55; Mathiesen 1999, 247. We use the term "lyre" to denote the genre of stringed instruments more broadly, of which there were several, including the cithara and barbitos. As others have observed, these terms, especially lyre and cithara, could be used interchangeably in antiquity, especially by poets; see Mathiesen 1999, 235; Battezzato 2009, 144 with n. 33.

almost certainly centuries older.⁵² In one of the Delphic hymns, by the poet Limenios, the notations—represented by symbols that look like Π, Λ, C—are rotated in different directions in a manner similar to that evidenced by the marks in the thymele's foundations (Fig. 21).

These examples of musical notation are quite a bit later than the construction of the thymele (and such systems of notation undoubtedly changed over time), but the similarities between the sets of marks are interesting.⁵³ In Vitruvius's acoustic scheme, as we have seen, bronze vessels were manufactured to resonate the seven principal notes of Greek music and were then positioned within thirteen niches of a theater's infrastructure in a mirrored formula, but we can easily imagine how a musical genius like the architect Polykleitos the Younger (if he was the thymele's architect) may have developed his own acoustical plan. Indeed, every architect may have contributed a variation in the arrangement of bronze echea.⁵⁴

Although Vitruvius was writing about these resonating vessels in the first century CE, it is clear from his text that the use of resonating devices derived from an older, Greek tradition. Vitruvius notes that such vessels are

---

⁵² The inscribed hymns from Delphi: Pöhlmann and West 2001, nos. 20 and 21; Marsá 2008; illustrated in Bélis 1992. The inscribed hymns from Epidauros: Pöhlmann and West 2001, no. 19. For discussion of both, see also Furley and Bremer 2001; Barker 2007; Hagel 2010, 280-85; and below, Chapters Four and Five.

⁵³ By the third century BCE, there were two systems of musical notation, one vocal and the other instrumental, each with its own sets of symbols. Instrumental notation may have been in use as early as the fifth century BCE. See West 1992, 254-76; Landels 1999, 206-63; Mathiesen 1999, esp. 593-607; Hagel 2010; and below, Chapter Five.

⁵⁴ Such vessels must have required "tuning," moreover, as the building was brought into line with different performances, compositions, and instruments. Thus it is likely that our hypothetical vessels in the thymele did not remain always in a fixed position; rather, the echea may have been moved and/or rotated around the basement as circumstances necessitated. See also below, Chapter Five.

found in theaters within Greece and Italy, but not in Rome, and he cites one prominent example: a theater at Corinth (5.5.8). Most importantly, he also states that an architect who wishes to place the resonant vessels properly must consult a diagram drawn up in accordance with Aristoxenos's laws of music (5.5.6).

Aristoxenos, born ca. 370 BCE, was the first Greek musical theorist of note. His treatise, *Stoicheia Harmonika*, is considered to be the earliest substantial textbook on music theory that has been preserved. His writings epitomize the revolution in music that had been underway since the fifth century, when composers like Melanippides, Kinesias, and Timotheos— many of them citharodoi—were introducing radical changes to musical performance: the so-called "New Music."[55] The fourth century also marks a period of profound interest in acoustic theory, with treatises on the subject attributed to both Aristotle and Euclid, and another treatise by Archytas at the beginning of the fourth century. Might there be a direct link between such developments in Greek music, meter, and acoustics, and the construction of the thymele, which took place just after and even alongside these developments? Given the lengthy building history of the thymele—it took more than twenty-five years to complete—we may well imagine that any scheme for resonating echea within the building would have been "retuned," revised, and reorganized as theories of harmonics shifted over the course of the thymele's long period of construction. If this was the case,

---

[55] West 1992, 356-85; Wallace 1995; Musti 2000; Richter 2000, 1-41; Barker 2004; Csapo 2004; Hagel 2010; D'Angour 2011, 184-206; Power 2012; LeVen 2014; and below, Chapter Five. LeVen (2014, 5-6) emphasizes that this "New Music" was part of a much wider culture of innovation: "...the 'new musicians' lived in a cultural context in which they would have rubbed shoulders not only with 'new architects,' 'new vase painters,' 'new scientists,' and 'new rhetoricians/educators,' but also with 'new banker-financiers,' 'new military strategists,' 'new politicians,' and a whole class of nouveaux riches [all during] an intellectual 'innovation hype.'"

then the apparently random scattering of notation in the thymele's basement might not be random at all, but rather might be the remains of an ancient experiment in musical innovation.

THE INTERIOR DECORATION OF THE THYMELE AND THE QUESTION OF THE LYRE

Further hints of this kind of innovation, and of musical performance generally, are suggested by another aspect of the thymele's interior decoration and design. Pausanias (2.27.3) mentions two paintings in the interior of the thymele, both by the famous fourth-century artist Pausias: one was a painting of Methe (Drunkenness) drinking out of a crystal phiale, with the neat trick that you could see her face through the crystal as she held it up to quaff; the other was a painting of Eros setting aside his bow and arrows to pick up and play a lyre (*lyra*).

We will return to the painting of Methe in Chapter Four, but the significance of the lyre within the thymele and within the sanctuary should not be overlooked. The lyre had strong cultic associations with Apollo, Asklepios's father, who shared the sanctuary at Epidauros with his son, and the lyre was a primary instrument for the performance of paeans, hymns sung often in worship of both Asklepios and Apollo. The lyre also produces a comparatively small sound, one that benefits from amplification and clarification. Indeed, hearing stringed instruments in an outdoor venue was so difficult that Vitruvius mentions these instruments specifically in his discussion of resonating vessels within theaters (5.5.7).[56] He observes that

---

[56] Vitr. 5.5.7: hoc vero licet animadvertere etiam ab citharoedis, qui, superiore tono cum volunt canere, avertunt se ad scaenae valvas et ita recipiunt ab earum auxilio consonantiam vocis. cum autem ex solidis rebus theatra constituuntur, id est ex structura caementorum, lapide, marmore, quae sonare non possunt, tunc echeis hae rationes sunt explicandae.

singers who accompany themselves on the cithara or lyre (*citharoedi*) often benefit from turning towards the wooden folding doors on a theater's stage to gain amplification for their music. He goes on to suggest, moreover, that theaters made of non-resonant materials in particular, such as stone or marble (like the thymele), ought to be fitted with bronze vessels to produce the necessary clarification and inflection.[57]

Might we imagine then that when Pausias's painting of Eros taking up his lyre was installed inside the thymele, it would have been understood as a deliberate reference to one of the building's functions? Given what we have seen in this chapter regarding the thymele's circularity, which can readily be connected to musical performance, and the thymele's labyrinthine basement, which may have been designed with some kind of acoustical concern in mind, Eros's lyre would seem to suggest an intentional orchestration of decoration and musical function.

---

[57] Similar to these bronze vessels, ceramic pots were used for amplification in medieval churches. Graeme Lawson has studied how the architecture of churches in northwestern Europe appears to have been adapted in the Middle Ages to improve the sound produced by, above all, lyres, instruments that, as Lawson (2006, 89) observes, "…hardly output a dramatic volume of sound, considering the milieu in which they are said to have been employed." One adaptation on which Lawson focuses is the insertion of resonating jars beneath the choirs of medieval churches.

Chapter Four
Paeans And Healing

Indeed the gifts of the Muses and Apollo are gentle and comforting. For Apollo is addressed as Paieon—Healer—and as Averter of Evil, inasmuch as he steers men away from misfortunes and instills health, rather than illness or madness, in their souls and bodies....Moreover, music is believed to have been discovered by men as a form of therapy for the emotions, especially for altering souls in a rough and savage state. For this very reason, some philosophers attune themselves to the lyre at dawn.
Dio Chrysostom 32.56-57

If we accept, for the moment, that the thymele at Epidauros may have functioned as a locus for musical performance on at least some occasions, then we should ask questions about the specific nature of those performances. For instance, what sorts of music did this elaborate structure frame and thereby enhance?[1] Where within the space of the building were the performers who generated this music, and where was the audience who experienced it? What might the effects of this music have been both on the performers and on other worshippers? In this chapter, as we explore answers to these questions, we will propose that one genre of music

---

[1] The theories of Alfred Gell and Jane Bennett offer another promising lens through which to explore the impact of the thymele on ancient worshippers. Gell (1998) and Bennett (2010) argue that objects continue to shape their surroundings through social interactions. Carolyn Laferrière (2016) has recently applied, and expanded, the theories of Gell and Bennett to an analysis of the Cave of Pan at Vari in Attica in order to take into account its sonic elements (alongside its primarily visual features, such as its famous carved reliefs). Laferrière comments, "Both scholars [Gell and Bennett] have re-focused traditional archaeological research on the many ways that objects and spaces may have an impact upon their beholders. Yet both of their theories overlook the range of sensations and perceptions that are provoked when one ascribes agency to an object or a place." The sensations and perceptions created among worshippers by of the sacred space of the thymele, whose visual and sonic dimensions were not just innovative but even unique, must have been profound. For sensory archaeology generally, see Hamilakis 2013 and 2017.

performed within the thymele was the paean, a type of hymn sung often in worship of Asklepios and his father Apollo. Moreover, we will suggest that this sacred music was thought to confer potent therapeutic benefit; this music could heal.

Of course, we do not suggest here that paeans were the only form of worship, musical or otherwise, associated with the building. Nor do we suggest that the thymele functioned exclusively as a space for musical performance. Rather, we hope to show how the texts of the paeans and the conditions of their performance complemented the design and function of the thymele as we have interpreted it. We also hope to demonstrate how these hymns correlate to well-documented ancient Greek theories and practices of musical therapy—ἡ διὰ τῆς μουσικῆς ἰατρεία—literally, "healing through music."

Music and Asklepios

When we visit ancient sanctuaries today, especially those located in rural areas, one of their most striking and immediate attributes tends to be a relative silence, a quiet that we might embrace as reverential and calming. But that silence can be misleading.

Music played an enormous role in ancient worship and would have permeated these sanctuaries often, from large-scale, formal performances such those of the City Dionysia in Athens—which involved hosts of professionals, a sizeable theater, populous choruses, and hefty sums of money—to hymns sung in a much less public context, much like the paean that Euripides imagines Ion singing alone at daybreak while sweeping the steps of Apollo's temple in Delphi (Eur. *Ion* 82-183, which includes, curiously enough, reference to a thymele, the precise meaning of which remains difficult to interpret in this context, as we have seen in Chapter Two). The sound of all of this music is largely lost to us, yet its impact is felt when, for instance, throngs of tourists sit in the ancient theater at Epidauros and test its acoustics. These tourists marvel and we continue to wonder at the music that filled these sanctuaries, music that, as Ludwig Edelstein comments, might have meant more to the Greeks than the words that accompanied it.[2]

Music played an especially prominent role at Epidauros as well as at other sanctuaries of Apollo and Asklepios. At Delphi, for instance, Apollo himself is said to have established a tradition of hymnic performance there as soon as he had finished building his temple (*Hymn. Hom. Ap.* 514-19), and the Pythian games from the earliest years included competitions in music (Strabo 9.3.10; Paus. 10.7.7). Indeed, hymns were so central to worship at Delphi that they became part of the visual and even tangible landscape in addition to the aural: the south face of the Athenian Treasury, for instance, situated conspicuously along the Sacred Way, bears inscribed texts of hymns that were performed in the sanctuary (Fig. 21).[3]

This same tradition of publishing hymns on stone flourished in

---

[2] Edelstein 1945, 2:199; Edelstein here paraphrases Plato's remarks at *Resp.* 401d about the power of rhythm and harmony on the soul. On the therapeutic role of music in Plato's *Republic* and *Timaeos*: Provenza 2006. On music in Greek cult, especially its ability to create context: Lind 2009. A recent essay by Angelos Chaniotis (2009) elucidates just how much attention the Greeks paid to music and musicians during the Hellenistic period when musical competitions and associations blossomed. We can easily imagine this same level of enthusiasm, and indeed fervor, over musical performances and performers at Epidauros with its exceptional theater and thymele. On the significance of song, and especially choral performances, in ancient Greek culture in relation to laws, customs, and the preservation of communal memories, see recently Gurd 2016, esp. 33, with bibliography.

[3] For discussion of the performance context of one of these inscribed hymns, a paean composed for the Athenian Pythais festival at Delphi in 138 or 128 BCE, see Furley 1995, 33-37. On inscribed hymns at Delphi and Epidauros being in dialogue with their "ritual, material, and mythical surroundings," see LeVen 2014, ch. 7, who contends that, "to read these songs out of context is to miss one half of a dialogue between site and sound" (329).

sanctuaries of Asklepios. At Epidauros, stelai erected in the very center of the temenos near the god's temple, altar, and the thymele itself displayed these hymns for all to see.[4] A cluster of such hymns preserved on a single stone with instructions for performance at specific times of day may even have been, Jan Bremer has suggested, a "'breviary-on-stone' for daily worship" (*IG* 4² 1, 129-34).[5]

The importance of musical performance at Epidauros can be traced back to the early history of the sanctuary. According to Plato, rhapsodic and other musical competitions were taking place in the Asklepieion already in the fifth century BCE (Pl. *Ion* 530a). Over time the importance of music is evident also in the architecture of the site, as demonstrated both by the large fourth-century theater, located southeast of the central area of the sanctuary, and by the later Odeion, which sits adjacent to the thymele and may thereby suggest the continuity of musical performance in the center of the temenos.[6] This intense interest in music might also be reflected in the

---

[4] The group of inscribed hymns at Epidauros has been studied by Maas 1933; Wagman 1995. See also Furley and Bremer 2001, 2:161-205. *IG* 4² 1, 129-34 were inscribed together in the second or third century CE, though the texts of the hymns are much older. Wagman 2012 argues that they were inscribed on the walls of a Classical or Hellenistic monument, and suggests the so-called "gymnasium" (Hestiatorion) within which the Odeion was constructed in the second century CE. Isyllos's paean, recovered east of the temple of Asklepios, has received close attention by, e.g., von Wilamowitz-Moellendorff 1886; Kolde 2003.

[5] Bremer 1981, 210. Bremer's argument suggests that these inscriptions were read, perhaps carefully; yet these inscriptions may have served symbolic and monumental roles in addition or instead (so Thomas 1992, 84-88).

[6] Tomlinson (1969, 111) argues that the central court of the "gymnasium" at Epidauros, into which the Odeion was later built, may have been used "for the performance of a part of the ritual for which the 'Odeion' was subsequently constructed in Roman times," or as a staging area for processions to or from the temple (which helps explain the "gymnasium's" imposing propylon and ramp). Tomlinson's conjecture suggests that long before the Odeion was constructed, the area just southeast of the thymele was well integrated into the performance dynamics of

impressive number of freestanding exedrae at the site, mentioned earlier. These semicircular seating areas were invented (as a type) in the third quarter of the fourth century BCE, contemporaneously with the construction of the thymele, and seem to have served both a votive function and as a means by which conspicuous elite display might have been projected within the ritual spaces of the Greek world.[7] While the architectural motifs and types of these exedrae have been studied extensively by Susanna von Thüngen, the connection between smaller exedrae designed for seating, known as the *Schalensitz*-type, and sacred musical performance has never been discussed in detail. At Delphi, for instance, five of the seven known exedrae there surround the circular halos in the center of the Sacred Way in front of the Stoa of the Athenians (von Thüngen, nos. 8, 9, 10-12). In this case, it is clear that these seats were used as venues from which various performances, such as the Stepterion, might be witnessed.[8]

At Epidauros, we see a similar grouping of *Schalensitz*-type exedrae in the immediate area of Asklepios's temple, altars, and, perhaps most importantly, his thymele. The fact that Epidauros boasts more than twice the number of exedrae of any other major panhellenic sanctuary on the mainland deserves some thought within this context.[9] The only other major Greek sanctuary that shows more interest in exedrae is the sanctuary of Apollo on Delos (with thirty exedrae) and it too, not surprisingly, is a space where ritual and performance—especially the performance of sacred music—played a key role.

---

the sanctuary.

[7] von Thüngen 1994, 44-46.

[8] On exedrae and performance at Delphi, especially in conjunction with the Stepterion, see above, p. 72.

[9] Number of exedrae at Epidauros: 18; at Delphi: 7; at Olympia: 4; at Nemea: 0; at Isthmia: 0.

At Epidauros, within this architectural framework so conducive to musical performance, the Greeks sang countless hymns. Ludwig Edelstein summarizes succinctly the vital role played by music at Asklepieia, especially Epidauros: "In all the ceremonies, be they daily exercises or solemn festivals, one feature recurs: the singing of hymns. They were recited in the temples morning and night; they were chanted during processions; they were accompaniment for sacrifices. The song characteristic of the Asklepios worship was the paean."[10] We must imagine, then, that the sanctuary of Asklepios and his father Apollo at Epidauros resounded often with music, especially the paean, whether as part of major festivals or of daily rituals, performed by large groups, small ensembles, and even solo musicians, and that this music would have transformed the experience for all who witnessed it.

Paeans

Recent discussions by Lutz Käppel (1992), Stephan Schröder (1999), Ian Rutherford (2001), and Andrew Ford (2006) demonstrate quite clearly that the genre of the paean is frustratingly nebulous, even to ancient commentators, and seems to have encompassed almost any utterance, from battle cries to celebratory songs at symposia, that included the word "παιάν."[11] Paieon,

---

[10] Edelstein 1945, 2:199. Edelstein's larger discussion of the role of music in sanctuaries of Asklepios remains valuable (1945, 2:199-208).

[11] In addition to the major surveys of the genre mentioned above, all undertaken within two decades of one another (although one should not overlook the still valuable although now dated study by Arthur Fairbanks [1900]), there has been a flurry of scholarship on Pindar's paeans in particular, including, in addition to the monographs by Käppel and Rutherford, studies by Giacomo Bona (1988) and numerous articles by Giovan Battista D'Alessio, some of which are listed in Rutherford's bibliography. The reason for this surge in paean studies is an intriguing matter in itself, one that Käppel touches on in a succinct overview of modern academic interest in Greek lyric poetry (part of his review of Rutherford 2001: BMCR 2002.10.38). Käppel writes, "A fruitful discussion of these texts demands a

an early healing god later assimilated to Apollo and Asklepios, seems to be the namesake of the genre, but almost any god could be addressed as Paieon, especially when appealed to at a time of crisis. For the purposes of this book, we will limit the term paean to what might be called cultic paeans: that is, paeans performed in sanctuaries or at festivals. Here we hasten to emphasize that our analysis could (and should) apply to genres beyond the paean; in classical antiquity genre classification almost certainly had more to do with performance context than the strict taxonomies of Hellenistic scholars would lead us to believe, and even within the Hellenistic period, the application of these genre labels was often disputed.[12] Thus while we imagine that paeans were performed often at Epidauros (a label due as much to performance context perhaps—in a sanctuary of Apollo and Asklepios—as to any set of formal characteristics in the texts of the hymns themselves), we believe that other genres of music too would have been performed within the thymele proper.[13]

---

multiple and complex methodology indeed: The single poem as well as the whole genre has to be considered as an act of oral communication in a very elaborated system of literary, linguistic, and social interactions. After Calame [1997] had cut the Gordion knot it was merely a natural development that scholars took up the neglected material and a real boom of studies of the lyric genres ensued...." A spike in scholarship on Greek hymns has ensued indeed, much of it consisting of studies that, à la Calame, are not strictly textual but more broadly contextual, situating the hymns in the occasions and locations of their performance; e.g., Furley and Bremer 2001; Hinge 2006; Kowalzig 2007; Hinge 2009; LeVen 2014; the many essays in Budelmann 2009, and in Kowalzig and Wilson 2013. On the contexts of musical performance in the Hellenistic period, see: Martinelli 2009 and Ford 2011.
[12] The discussion of Ford 2011, esp. Ch. 5, on these points is accessible and illuminating, and worth reading by anyone interested in the development of classifications of lyric poetry from Plato and Aristotle to Alexandria.
[13] Nor are paeans the only genre of lyric poetry that is difficult to define and isolate. In 1950, Amy M. Dale remarked presciently: "To determine accurately the special characteristics of the various lyric types is an impossible task for us, and the more our store of fragments is added to the more irretrievably mixed the

Sources from Homer on indicate that the song-dances known as paeans enjoyed a wide currency, especially in sanctuaries of Apollo and Asklepios.[14] Delphi in particular had a long and thriving paean tradition. The *Homeric Hymn to Apollo* describes Apollo leading a chorus of Cretan priests who sing paeans to the tune of the god's lyre (514-19) and a paean by Alcaeus describes how the Delphians composed a paean for Apollo and organized dances of youths around the tripod to lure him back to Delphi from the land of the Hyperboreans (Alc. fr. 307c Voigt).[15] Paean performances also featured among the earliest events of the Pythian Games (Strabo 9.3.10),[16] and by the fourth century paeans were being inscribed on monuments at Delphi and poets were being granted privileges, such as *promanteia* (the right to consult the oracle before most other pilgrims), for the

---

categories appear" (quoted in Ford 2006, 279, from *The Collected Papers of A.M. Dale*, edited by T.B.L. Webster and E.G. Turner [Cambridge 1969] p. 38).

[14] It is important to remember that most hymns in Greek antiquity would have been accompanied by dance; Walter Burkert (1985, 102) remarks, "Dancing and music are inseparable. Even the simplest musical form, the song, leads to dancing." We borrow the term "song-dance" from Rutherford (1995, 2001) as a way of foregrounding both aspects of choral performance.

[15] In Alcaeus's hymn, which survives only in a prose summary by Himerios, we learn that Apollo then agreed to return to Delphi because it was time for the Delphic tripods to resound (ἐπειδὴ καιρὸν ἐνόμιζε καὶ τοὺς Δελφικοὺς ἠχῆσαι τρίποδας). See Furley and Bremer 2001, 1:99-102, 2:21-24, for text and discussion. Might these early traditions of music and dance around tripods at Delphi—tripods that were perceived as resounding/resonating—have helped to generate the design of the round thymele with, as we are suggesting, its bronze resonating vessels? Furley and Bremer 2:91 note that when the tripod made noise, moreover, it was thought to be the voice of the god speaking his prophecies (e.g., Ar. *Eq.* 1015-16, Eur. *IT* 976).

[16] According to Strabo 9.3.10, paeans performed by citharodes dominated the games before their reorganization in 576 BCE; afterward, these performances expanded to include instrumental-only paeans; cf. Paus. 10.7.7. On paean performance also at the Delphic Theoxenia, especially of Pindar's sixth paean, see Kurke 2005, Hedreen 2010.

quality of their paeans.¹⁷ Paeans were popular, too, at sanctuaries of Asklepios where they played a role not only in worship but also in healing, as will be discussed in greater detail below. An inscription from the Asklepieion at Erythrae, for instance, specifies that those who seek healing should first sing paeans to Apollo (*PMG* 933), and Aelius Aristides, a devotee of Asklepios at Pergamon in the second century CE, describes writing paeans and other hymns as part of therapy as well as worship of the god (e.g., Aristid. *Or*. 47.30, 47.33, 49.4, 50.4, 50.38, 50.43).

Despite the cultic paean's prevalence at Delphi, Epidauros, and elsewhere, surprisingly few examples of the genre survive. We have only fragments by such noteworthy poets as Pindar and Sophocles, and only two complete cultic paeans survive before the fourth century (Ariphron's hymn to Hygieia [813 Page] and Bacchylides 17, although scholars debate whether these should in fact be classified as paeans).¹⁸ Beginning in the fourth century, the evidence for paeans is better because inscriptions at Delphi, Epidauros, and Erythrae preserve six complete or nearly complete paeans, and

---

[17] Rutherford (2001, 144-46) discusses the publication of paeans on stone, a phenomenon that seems to have been especially strong in the fourth century. On the close association between paeans and Delphi, see also Rutherford 2001, 24-29. Philodamos, whose paean was performed at Delphi in 340/39 BCE, was awarded, along with his brothers and their descendants, a proxeny, promanteia, proedria, prodikia, immunity from taxes, and every other civic honor enjoyed by the Delphians (*Coll. Alex.* 170). Aristonoos of Corinth, whose paean was performed at Delphi in 338 or 334 BCE, was awarded, along with his descendants, a proxeny, title of εὐεργέτης, promanteia, proedria, prodikia, asylia, immunity from taxes, and every other civic honor enjoyed by the Delphians (*Coll. Alex.* 164).

[18] See, e.g., Schröder 1999, 50-61, for discussion and bibliography. Ariphron's hymn is called a paean by Ath. 701f, one of several sources for the text; on these sources, see Furley and Bremer 2001, 2:175-80. A fifth-century date for this hymn is uncertain, moreover; it depends upon identifying Ariphron with the tragic poet. Furley and Bremer 2001, 1:224-27, argue that elements of the text are Hellenistic and suggest the late fourth or third century BCE.

we have epigraphic and literary evidence for at least two more.[19] The texts of these fourth- and early third-century paeans provide valuable clues as to their performance. For ease of reference, we have included a table listing cultic paeans of the fourth and early third century (Table 1).

Table 1.
Cultic paeans of the fourth and early third century BCE (*Coll. Alex.* = Collectanea Alexandrina, ed. by J.U. Powell; Käppel = Käppel 1992; Furley and Bremer = Furley and Bremer 2001, Vol. II: Greek Texts and Commentary; *FGrHist* = Die Fragmente der griechischen Historiker, ed. by F. Jacoby).

Number	Description	Editions / Sources
P1	Inscribed paean to Asklepios, from Erythrae, inscr. 380-360 BCE (later copies at Athens, Dion, and Ptolemais).	*Coll. Alex.* 136-37; Käppel 37; Furley and Bremer 6.1
P2	Inscribed paean to Apollo, from Erythrae, inscr. 380-360 BCE.	*Coll. Alex.* 140; Käppel 36
P3	Inscribed paean to Dionysos (Dithyrambos Bacchus), from Delphi, composed by Philodamos of Skarpheia for initial performance at the Theoxenia in 340/39 BCE.[20]	*Coll. Alex.* 165-71; Käppel 39; Furley and Bremer 2.5

---

[19] For recent discussion and bibliography of many of these inscribed hymns, see LeVen 2014, Ch. 7. We might also include among the fourth-century cultic paeans a hymn to Pan inscribed at Epidauros (*IG* 4² 1, 130), which Rutherford (2001, 70) suggests is a paean because its closing refrain (ὢ ἰὴ Πὰν Πάν) sounds much like a typical paean refrain, and the hymn to Hygieia by Ariphron (fl. ca. 400 BCE), if it is indeed a paean as Ath. 702a claims. The latter hymn was also inscribed at Epidauros (*IG* 4² 1, 132).

[20] For discussion of this paean, see Rainer 1975; Stewart 1982; Käppel 1992, Ch. 5; Furley and Bremer 2001, 1:121-35, 2:52-84, with bibliography; Rutherford 2001, 131-136; LeVen 2014, 304-17. Rainer dates the hymn to 340/39 BCE.

P4	Inscribed paean to Apollo, from Delphi, composed by Aristonoos of Corinth for performance ca. 338 or 334 BCE.	*Coll. Alex.* 162-64; Käppel 42; Furley and Bremer 2.4
P5	Inscribed paean(?) to Hestia from Delphi, composed by Aristonoos of Corinth for performance ca. 338 or 334 BCE.[21]	*Coll. Alex.* 164-65; Furley and Bremer 2.3
P6	Inscribed paean to Asklepios and Apollo, from Epidauros, composed by Isyllos of Epidauros, inscr. ca. 300 BCE.[22]	*Coll. Alex.* 132-36; Käppel 40; Furley and Bremer 6.4
P7	Paean to the deified Demetrios Poliorketes, performed in Athens in 291 or 290 BCE.[23]	Ath. 7.253; *FGrHist* 76 F 13
P8	Inscribed paean to Apollo and Asklepios, from Athens, composed by Makedonikos of Amphipolis, ca. 300 BCE(?).[24]	*Coll. Alex.* 138-40; Käppel 41; Furley and Bremer 7.5

Formal characteristics of fourth- and early third-century paeans include the following. First, the paeans often indicate performance by a group of singer-dancers: "Sing Paieon, young men," (Παιᾶνα κλυτόμητιν ἀείσατε κοῦροι, *Coll. Alex.* 136-7, lines 1-2; *Coll. Alex.* 140, line 1); "Sing, young men of

---

[21] This hymn is not certainly a paean, but its composer is Aristonoos who wrote a paean to Apollo (Coll. Alex. 162-64; Käppel 1992, Pai. 42; Furley and Bremer 2001, 1:119-21, 2: 45-52; LeVen 2014, 296-299).

[22] A Philip is mentioned in this hymn ("when Philip was leading his army against Sparta," 63-64), but his identity is debated (Philip II and III are the most likely candidates, though Philip V has also been suggested); see Kolde 2003, 257-301. Furley and Bremer (2001, 1:227-40, 2:180-92) make a strong case for Philip II; if it is Philip III, however, the hymn may date to the early or mid third century BCE.

[23] For bibliography and discussion, see Chaniotis 2011; on the performance context of this hymn, see esp. 161-66.

[24] Inscribed in the Roman imperial period, but Fairbanks (1900, 36) suggested that the hymn may be contemporary with Isyllos's paean. Other scholars place its composition in the first century BCE or CE, as noted by Furley and Bremer 2001, 1:267.

Athens," (εὐφημεῖτε…κοῦροι Ἀθηναίων, *Coll. Alex.* 138-40, lines 1-4), and so on.[25] We do not know how many singer-dancers performed any given paean, and the number almost certainly varied depending on exigencies of performance such as its occasion and location within a sanctuary.[26] A second general characteristic is that these song-dances were accompanied by a stringed instrument, a lyre or phorminx whenever indicated in fourth-century paeans (*Coll. Alex.*162-64, line 15: lyre; *Coll. Alex.*164-65, line 7: phorminx). As discussed above in Chapter Three, such stringed instruments are notorious for being difficult to hear, especially in an outdoor setting, and this difficulty in turn seems to have prompted architects to introduce innovations in theater design so that these instruments might be more audible. Third, the singer-dancers stood or moved in a circle. In Philodamos's paean, for instance, Apollo arranged a circling contest (ἔταξε…κυκλίαν ἅμιλλαν) of many choruses in honor of Dionysos (*Coll. Alex.*165-71, lines 131-4; cf. also lines 58-62 and 123-5, where the image of a circling chorus is repeated). In other paeans, the performers circled around the god or some means of communicating with the god such as an altar. The paean from Erythrae specifies performance three times around the altar of Apollo before incubation (933 Page, *PMG*). In the hymn to Hestia from Delphi, the chorus dances around Hestia's rich-throned thymele (λιπαρόθρονον ἀμφὶ σὰν θυμέλαν χορεύειν,

---

[25] *Coll. Alex.*162-64, *Coll. Alex.*164-65, and Ath. 7.253 also indicate performance by a group. That a cultic hymn was sung by a group is hardly surprising, but with paeans, as with all hymns, there was room for variation in performance. According to Strabo 9.3.10, for instance, some paeans performed at Delphi were instrumental only. Rutherford (2001, 58-63) discusses the predominance and significance of male as opposed to female choruses in paean performance; Swift (2010, 64-66) provides evidence for female performance, especially in tragedy.

[26] We do have indications of the size of some later paean choruses; for instance, Bremer (1981, 199) observes that a second-century BCE paean from Delphi mentions 39 singer-dancers, another of the same century mentions 50.

*Coll. Alex.*164-65, lines 16-17; discussed also in Chapter Two, above), a text that further reinforces associations between *thymelai* and both song and dance.²⁷ And the paean to Demetrios Poliorketes posits the deified Demetrios, savior of the Greeks, in the very center of his friends, as if he were the sun and they the stars encircling him (οἱ φίλοι πάντες κύκλῳ, ἐν μέσοισι δ' αὐτός, ὅμοιον ὥσπερ οἱ φίλοι μὲν ἀστέρες, ἥλιος δ' ἐκεῖνος, Ath. 7.253e).²⁸

It is clear from the latter example in particular that paean performances ideally incorporated an epiphany; the god was thought to be present in the midst of a circle of performers.²⁹ Relevant to this point, some paeans include an appeal to the god to hear the paean—not to see it, but to *hear* it. The paean to Demetrios Poliorketes states: "The other gods do not hear us: they are far away or have no ears or do not exist or fail to give us their attention; but we see you here among us, not made from wood or stone, but real" (ἄλλοι μὲν ἢ μακρὰν γὰρ ἀπέχουσιν θεοί, ἢ οὐκ ἔχουσιν ὦτα, ἢ οὐκ εἰσιν, ἢ οὐ προσέχουσιν ἡμῖν οὐδὲ ἕν, σὲ δὲ παρόνθ' ὁρῶμεν, οὐ ξύλινον οὐδὲ λίθινον, ἀλλ' ἀληθινόν, Ath. 7.253e).

---

²⁷ Gaston Colin (*FdD* III.2, p. 220) has observed that Hestia's altar is never called a thymele but a ἑστία, βωμός, or ἐσχάρα. Given that "thymele" is the name of the tholos at Epidauros, that the term thymele has distinct associations with music, and that the tholos at Delphi has a bench within its interior, we believe that the tholos in the Pronaia sanctuary could be the "rich-throned thymele" in which Hestia's paean was performed. We shall explore this and other connections between performance and the fourth-century tholoi at Delphi, Epidauros, and Olympia in a future publication.

²⁸ As the lines between gods and mortal rulers began to blur with Philip II, Alexander, and their successors, the paean genre expanded to celebrate these new rulers as savior figures; see Cameron 1995, 291-95; Schultz 2007a, 233 n. 160; Ford 2011. The earliest known paean in honor of a mortal is that for Lysander in 404 BCE (Duris, *FGrH* 76 F26, 71; see Cameron 1996, 292, no. 1, for additional testimonia).

²⁹ Aelius Aristides in the *Sacred Tales*, an account of Aristides's many illnesses and the help that he received from Asklepios at Pergamon in particular, mentions worshippers singing paeans before a statue of Asklepios (*Or.* 50.50).

Simply put, the words and the music matter; the paean, as with any prayer, only succeeds if the god can hear it. Lutz Käppel (1992) has argued that paeans function as a dialogue between the performers and the god; the paean, a sacrifice of sorts, is exchanged for divine aid, an attractive theory that helps explain the physical and symbolic centrality of the altar in the paean from Erythrae and of the deified Demetrios. Moreover, as Joseph Day, Mary Depew, and others have argued, hymns were crafted to be so pleasing that they would entice the god to join the performers and audience and to grant them pleasure, often in the form of some benefaction.[30] The synesthetic experience of paeans—the combination of well-chosen words, pleasing rhythms, and graceful movement—would, if successful, result in an epiphany that would include divine aid (often healing or protection) for performers and audience alike, whether in the present moment or at some future time.

To summarize, we have observed that the texts of surviving cultic paeans indicate the following formal characteristics of performance: song-dance in a circular formation by a group of performers to the accompaniment of a stringed instrument. All of these features of paean performance together were designed carefully to convey highly pleasurable music directly to the ears of the gods and thereby delight them, enticing the gods into the company of their worshippers where the gods might ultimately confer some divine benefaction upon their suppliants. We must imagine, then, that this music that

---

[30] Depew 2000; Day 2000 and 2010 (esp. Ch. 6 on hymns, as well as epigrams, as part of the ritual exchange of χάρις). Day 2010, 262-63: "Performers and audiences of hymns sought to entice the god into coming, enjoying, and giving joyful blessings in return. Cultic epiphany was the goal. Hymnic charis articulates this goal in petitions for the god's presence (to receive or give charis) or assertions that the god is present…" On the role of epiphany in Asklepios's cult, see Platt 2011, Ch. 1, which includes discussion of votive reliefs and hymns as frames for understanding epiphanic experiences; also Platt 2011, 260-66, on dreams as instances of epiphany in the cult of Asklepios.

was believed to be capable of pleasing the gods would have contained carefully crafted, even striking, lyrics and melodies. Unfortunately, our data for both is limited, especially with respect to the music of late Classical paeans. But we can still make several observations and venture several hypotheses.

With regard to the lyrics, no set format for their content is evident. Many included a mythological narrative about the god and addressed the god as Paieon. Most fourth- and early third-century cultic paeans, furthermore, beseeched the god to protect the polis represented by the performers. The best example is Philodamos's paean performed at Delphi, asking the god eight times in the course of the hymn to "protect our city" (τάνδε πόλιν φύλασσ', *Coll. Alex.* 165-71, lines 11-13, 23-26, 37-39, 51-52, 63-65, 101-3, 115-17, 128-30).[31] Ian Rutherford has argued that all paeans of all periods and varieties "[promote] the safety and stability of the polis," whether by beseeching the god for help or celebrating a victory or otherwise affirming the security of the city-state.[32] Scholars have criticized Rutherford on this point, especially regarding fifth-century paeans, which contain little evidence for it, but there seems little doubt that he has hit upon one of the key

---

[31] Most of the cultic paeans examined here include some such appeal. E.g., *Coll. Alex.*136, lines 19-20: "visit my city with its wide dancing places" (ἐπινίσεο τὰν ἀμὰν πόλιν εὐρύχορον); *Coll. Alex.*162-64, lines 47-48: "may you follow us and preserve us" (σώιζων ἐφέποις ἡμᾶς); *Coll. Alex.*132-36, lines 59-61: "may you increase your maternal city Epidauros and send health [Hygieia?] in manifest form to our minds and bodies" (τὰν σὰν Ἐπίδαυρον ματρόπολιν αὔξων, ἐναργῆ δ' ὑγίειαν ἐπιπέμποις φρεσὶ καὶ σώμασιν ἀμοῖς); Ath. 6.253e: "bring peace" (εἰρήνην πόησον); *Coll. Alex.* 138-40: "may you preserve the Attic city of Kekrops" (σώζοις δ' Ἀτθίδα Κεκροπίαν πόλιν). We find many of the same sentiments in both earlier and later paeans, such as Pind. *Pae.* 6, which includes an appeal to "love your fatherland and this welcoming people and cover them with garlands of always-blossoming health" (178-81); and Athenaios's paean performed at Delphi in 138 or 129 BCE (*Coll. Alex.* 141-48), which mentions the Gauls' failed attack on the city.

[32] Rutherford 2001, esp. 85-90.

functions of fourth- and early third-century cultic paeans.³³ Emphasis on the safety of the polis is particularly apparent in these latter paeans given that seven of the eight address Apollo or Asklepios, or are from the sanctuaries of these two gods, healers of the body politic as well as of the physical body (the sole exception being Demetrios Poliorketes, who presented himself as a savior nonetheless).³⁴ Such divine assistance must have been at a premium in the fourth century when the threat of Macedon loomed and hegemonies rapidly shifted; Isyllos's paean, for instance, specifically thanks Asklepios for protection against Philip (*Coll. Alex.* 132-36, lines 62-82).³⁵

The music that accompanied these paeans is largely lost to us. Although the best examples of musical notation from antiquity happen to come from two paeans inscribed on the Athenian treasury at Delphi (*Coll. Alex.* 141-48, 149-59; also below, Fig. 21), these paeans were inscribed in the second century BCE, by which time the traditions of paean music may have changed.³⁶ What we do know of paean music of the late Classical period is this: there existed great variety in the use of lyric meters. Käppel (1992, 75-82, 286-90) has observed that some fourth-century paeans demonstrate a complexity of meter greater than those of the fifth, a trend that is almost certainly a reflection of contemporary innovations in music. One of the most famous innovators of the late fifth century, the poet Timotheos in his *Persae*, even called upon Paieon to aid his hymns to which he had given new life with eleven-stroke cithara meters and rhythms (Page, *PMG* 791, esp. lines 229-33).³⁷ Given such innovations in meter and rhythm, it may well be that the

---

[33] E.g., Glenn T. Patten, in his review of Rutherford 2001 (*BMCR* 2002.10.41).

[34] On Asklepios and the body politic, see Wickkiser 2008, Chs. 4-6.

[35] On the identity of this Philip, see above, p. 96 n. 22.

[36] Pöhlmann and West 2001, nos. 20 and 21, for text, discussion, and bibliography; also Furley and Bremer 2001, 2: 84-100.

[37] Csapo and Wilson (2009) observe that several innovations ascribed to Timotheos

music itself, as opposed to the words that accompanied it, was far more important for late Classical paeans than it had been for earlier, highly literary paeans by poets like Pindar and Bacchylides.

In terms of innovation, there is one other characteristic of the music of fourth- and early third-century paeans that deserves special mention in the context of this study: the use of stringed as opposed to wind instruments. Fifth-century cultic paeans—as well as other types of hymns, most notably the dithyramb—were performed typically to the aulos rather than to stringed instruments. Auloi are much more audible than lyres and hence more conducive to performance in large outdoor venues. By the fourth century, the instrument used in cultic paean performance seems to have reverted to the lyre or phorminx.[38] The scantiness of the evidence makes it dangerous to press this distinction, but it is plausible that in the fifth century, concerns over audibility motivated paean composers and performers to depart from Apollo's traditional instrument in favor of the aulos, while in the fourth century this same concern was met by an architectural solution (the thymele) rather than an instrumental one.[39]

---

by the ancient sources predate Timotheos by at least a generation. On the meter of paeans, see also Rutherford 2001, 76-79; on the meter of Hellenistic paeans: West 1992, 383.

[38] The prevalence of the aulos for paean accompaniment: Rutherford 2001, 79-80. Although fourth-century paeans mark a striking and significant exception to this apparent trend, we should remember that the instrument traditionally associated with the paean was the lyre, as indicated by, e.g., the *Homeric Hymn to Apollo*.

[39] As discussed (above, p. 75 n. 35; and below, p. 125 n. 18) the structure of the thymele mimics in key ways the anatomy of the human ear as it was understood by the Greeks of this time: sound travelled via an opening from a cavernous outer ear (~ the thymele's cella) to an inner ear (~ the thymele's labyrinth, resembling the semicircular canals and especially the cochlea of the human ear). Alkmaeon of Croton, associated by some with Pythagoras, believed that sound echoed in the inner ear until it was perceived by the brain. This would seem to add credence to our hypothesis that the designers of the thymele believed that its labyrinthine sub-

None of the formal elements of paean performance discussed here—singing-dancing by a group, in a circular formation, to a stringed instrument, with an appeal to the god to be present and to confer some benefaction upon the worshippers—is unique to the paean genre. Many ancient hymns, which were essentially forms of prayer and thanksgiving set to music and dance, contain many if not all of these same features. Nevertheless, all of these elements together, in conjunction with the fact that the paean was especially common in sanctuaries of Asklepios and Apollo, suit performance within the thymele quite well. The circular shape of the building was appropriate for the paean's circling choruses (Figs. 17-18), and the acoustic properties of the thymele would have modulated both the weak sound of the lyre and the words of the chorus so that—an ancient worshipper may have hoped—the music reached directly to the ears of the gods and prompted a divine epiphany.

THE PERFORMANCE OF PAEANS WITHIN AND AROUND THE THYMELE

We turn now to the question of how the performance of paeans might have been enacted within and around the space of the thymele. At Epidauros, as we have seen, the ornate thymele stands in the very center of the sanctuary. It is located close to and on roughly the same axis as the temple of Asklepios. Just as significantly, it is oriented towards the older altar ca. 38 m due east, which is also on the same axis as the thymele and is identified often as an altar of Apollo (it was part of the sanctuary before Asklepios's role was clearly prominent, and an inscription found in the vicinity records a dedication to Apollo Pythios, *IG* 4^2 1, 142).[40] Exedrae frame the "altar

---

structure increased the perceptibility of sounds created within the cella.

[40] The inscription, altar, and evidence for Apollo in the early stages of the sanctuary: Burford 1969, 47-50; inscribed dedications to Apollo at Epidauros: Melfi 2007, 148-209 *passim*; identification of the altar, also LiDonnici 1995, 7.

court" in front of the thymele and thus mark this area apparently too for performance (Fig. 9).[41] The exedrae not only would have served as prime seats from which to view choral dances and other rituals performed in the area, but it seems quite plausible that the high backs of these exedrae would have afforded sitters better "ears" with which to hear the music.

Inside the thymele, the space enclosed by the Corinthian colonnade is quite large (9.08 m diam.) and could easily have accommodated twenty-five people in a circle with arms partially extended, not to mention concentric circles of singer-dancers, and, of course, the musician(s) (Figs. 17-18). The musicians would have stood near the hole in the center of the cella floor, where, as we will recall from Chapter Three, the labyrinth appears to have best absorbed sonic reflections, producing thereby a more pleasant and more soothing experience for the audience.[42] As to the location of the audience, it is likely that some worshippers would have stood or sat within the thymele, perhaps in the space between the Corinthian colonnade and the walls of the building (a space 1.05 m wide), especially if the chorus was large. The most important audience, the god(s), would have been present ideally in the very center of the performers, as the paeans themselves articulate. The immediacy of this epiphanic experience — of the god coming into the very presence of his worshippers within an enclosed space — accords well with Asklepios's typical mode of healing whereby he visited the sick in dreams that only they, as individuals, experienced. The structure of the thymele, with its protective walls, would have added to this sense of sacred mystery.[43]

---

[41] Free-standing exedrae: von Thüngen 1994; exedrae and the monumental and ritual development of Epidauros: Melfi 2007, 60-63.

[42] See above, Chapter Three, and below, Appendix. A musician accompanying circular choral song stood traditionally in the center of the circle of performers; see Chapter Five; see also below, p. 125 n. 18.

[43] It is entirely possible that the visual boundary created by the walls enhanced the

Such a scenario in which performers and audience together occupy the space within the thymele may describe many paean performances, but the "altar court" just outside the thymele suggests that on at least some occasions such as major festivals, the performers traveled between the interior and exterior spaces or occupied the two spaces simultaneously (Figs. 7-9). If the paean from Erythrae is indicative of ritual at Epidauros (933 Page, *PMG*), then paeans were performed around an altar, perhaps the altar located directly east of the entrance to the thymele. Some paeans even

---

epiphany for those outside of the building as well. (The practice of obstructing or withholding views of Asklepios in order to heighten the expectation of epiphany is a point made, albeit with different evidence, by Petsalis-Diomidis 2010, 172-73, 222-38; Platt 2011, Ch. 1.) We came to this realization when we heard ethnomusicologist Tore Lind speak on "Music and Cult in Ancient Greece" (Aarhus University, Jan. 2004, at the conference "Aspects of Ancient Greek Cult"; a version of this talk is published as Lind 2009). Lind began by playing the opening track of a CD by Atrium Musicae de Madrid, a group that reconstructs ancient Greek music and acknowledges in the booklet that accompanies the CD that the sounds of this music are largely unknown to us (*Musique de la grèce antique*, Harmonia Mundi, 1978 [CD: 2000]). The first track of their CD is a brief explosion of noise (all of the reconstructed instruments play *fortissimo*) followed by silence. Only after this silence, which lasts for several seconds, does the music begin. Those moments of silence in which our minds are encouraged to explore how we think ancient music must have sounded are among the most moving of the CD. The purpose, Lind commented, is to "tune us in, to play with our expectations and sharpen the ear for what is to come." In much the same way as the absence of sound at the start of this CD frees the mind to imagine music, the lack of a view inside the thymele for those gathered outside of it would have freed the mind to imagine the god—a revelatory experience perhaps just as intense and real as for those within. It is useful to consider also how the sounds of music produced inside the thymele would have worked alongside dreams and other epiphanies marked by a striking visual element that took place elsewhere in the sanctuary, such as those described in the Epidaurian healing inscriptions (published with translation in LiDonnici 1995). The discussion by Chion (2000) of "audio-vision"—of the ways that audio enhances what we see—is provocative in this regard, though Chion focuses on the value that audio adds to the experience of cinema per se.

include a prosodion, a short processional piece well suited to accompany movement between, for instance, the altar and thymele.[44] As we have noted above, this altar may have been sacred to Apollo as well as Asklepios, and if the dedication to Apollo Pythios found nearby it indicates the importance of Pythian Apollo at Epidauros, we should not be surprised that paean performances in particular, with their rich tradition in the sanctuary of Apollo Pythios at Delphi, took place around this very altar and within the thymele that seems to have been aligned intentionally with it.[45]

There may have been occasions, too, when part or even all of the mortal audience remained outside the thymele to hear performances enacted within the building. While the walls of the thymele created a visual barrier that prevented an external audience from seeing what was taking place inside the building, these same walls did not necessarily constitute an aural boundary. The comments of Barry Blesser and Linda-Ruth Salter regarding aural architecture apply with particular resonance to the thymele:

> Because visual and aural boundaries are independent means of enclosing a space, our visual and aural experience of size, the space between boundaries, may not be consistent....With two kinds of spatial partitions, we also have two kinds of spatial areas—aural and visual. Only physical boundaries impermeable to both light and sound produce a consistent experience. But consistency is more the exception than the rule.[46]

Although the walls of the thymele provided a visual boundary, they would, at the same time, have helped project the sound of paeans and other music

---

[44] E.g., Pind. *Pae.* 6 and Limenios's paean from Delphi (*Coll. Alex.* 149-59).

[45] Burford (1969, 32) suggests that the earthquake at Delphi in 370 BCE may have helped motivate the flurry of construction at Epidauros beginning at about the same time. Following Burford's line of argument, we wonder whether construction of an innovative new venue for musical performance at Epidauros came about in part as a result of the destruction of the temple of Apollo and other areas in the upper sanctuary at Delphi where hymns were probably performed.

[46] Blesser and Salter 2007, 21.

out of the building's doors and across the sanctuary, thereby pushing the thymele's "aural boundaries" well beyond the physical space of the building. This model is consistent both with the notion that a paean is a form of prayer and with the correlate hope expressed by the paeans themselves that the deity will *hear* them. *Hearing* as opposed to *seeing* a paean may have been of paramount importance, not just for the immortal audience but for mortal witnesses as well. Indeed, the act of hearing paeans was thought to be especially efficacious as a form of music therapy.

The Thymele and music therapy

We should not lose sight in this discussion of the principal function of this and all other sanctuaries of Asklepios: healing the physical body. Here, too, music played a significant role. A close association between Asklepios and the performance of poetry, especially tragedy and comedy, has long been recognized: most Asklepieia contained a theater or, as in the case of the Asklepieion on the south slope of the Athenian Acropolis, were located in close proximity to one. Recently Robin Mitchell-Boyask has examined connections among healing, drama, and the cult of Asklepios in Athens, and Karelisa Hartigan has discussed the use of drama as therapy at ancient Asklepieia as well as among healers in the contemporary United States.[47] Given the nature of the evidence that remains to us, it is understandable that both Mitchell-Boyask and Hartigan focus on the texts of the dramas that were enacted—the narratives—with little attention to the music that

---

[47] Mitchell-Boyask 2008; Hartigan 2009. Mitchell-Boyask (14) refers to passages in Homer, Hesiod, Sophocles, Euripides, Aristophanes, and Gorgias that speak to the power of song to heal physical and emotional disturbances. Hartigan relates her experiences as a participant in the Arts-in-Medicine program at Shands Hospital at the University of Florida, which draws on many forms of "art as therapy," including music, painting, dance, and writing.

was so integral to all Greek drama, to say nothing of other types of performance, such as oratory, instrumental music, and so on, that must also have been performed in these theaters. Another way to reflect on the importance of theater to Asklepios and his cures, then, is to consider the role of music.

Associations between music and healing were deeply embedded in ancient Greek culture—and are enjoying a renaissance in western medicine today.[48] Paeans in particular were tied closely with healing. Thaletas, a paean composer of the seventh century BCE from Crete, is said to have used his compositions to cure Sparta of a plague (*limos*; Pratinas, 713(iii) Page, *PMG*).[49] And Aristoxenos apparently observed that when the women of Locri and Rhegium were suffering from madness, an oracle prescribed as a cure the performance of twelve paeans per day for sixty days, which led, he remarks, to an influx of paean composers into Italy (fr. 117 Wehrli = INC 2 20 Kaiser).[50]

---

[48] On musical therapy in antiquity, see West 2000. Today, programs in music therapy are increasingly common within medical schools. On the variety of ailments that music is used to treat and on the range of medical institutions that employ such techniques, see the website of the American Music Therapy Association (http://www.musictherapy.org/). Apart from formal practitioners of music therapy, there exists also a subset of musicians known as "medical musicians" who play in hospitals, nursing homes, hospices, and the like.

[49] See also West 1992, 33.

[50] For Aristoxenos, other strong connections existed between music and the body; e.g., according to Censorinus, Aristoxenos believed that music resides in the voice and movement of the body (*DN* 12 = III 3 135 Kaiser). In the same passage, Censorinus indicates that the famous Hellenistic physicians Asklepiades and Herophilos both recognized the significance of music to the human body: Asklepiades, like Aristoxenos, used music as therapy for the mentally ill (*phreneticorum mentes morbo turbatas saepe per symphonian suae naturae reddidit*), and Herophilos believed that the pulse of the blood vessels moved to musical rhythms (*venarum pulsus rhythmis musicis ait moveri*). On Herophilos and musical pulsation in the body, which is well attested in sources such as Galen, see Pigeaud 1978; von Staden 1989, 276-88; and Berrey, forthcoming, Ch. 5, who argues that Herophilos adopted his terminology and theory of rhythm from Aristoxenos. On connections

These ties between paeans and healing must relate to the tradition that Paieon was originally a separate healing deity; Homer, for instance, depicts him treating injured gods in the *Iliad* (*Il.* 5.401-2, 899-901). Later, Paieon was assimilated to Apollo and Asklepios. So close was the connection between healing and paeans that Pythagoras, too, is said to have employed a treatment of "medicine through music" (ἡ διὰ τῆς μουσικῆς ἰατρεία) in which he seated those who could sing in a circle, placed a lyre player in their center, and had them sing paeans to calm and cheer the soul; at other times they danced (Iambl. *VP* 110-11; cf. Porph. *Pythag.* 32-33).[51] Martin West remarks, moreover, that the healing paeans employed by Pythagoras included "wordless melodies on the lyre," and therefore that "it was clearly the music itself, independently of any associated text, that was regarded as potent."[52]

---

between Aristoxenos and music therapy, see also West 2000.

[51] According to Iamblichos, moreover, Pythagoras preferred the lyre to the aulos for healing because the latter had a sound that was haughty, ostentatious, and ignoble in every way. Iambl. *VP* 110-11: ἐκάθιζε γὰρ ἐν μέσῳ τινὰ λύρας ἐφαπτόμενον, καὶ κύκλῳ ἐκαθέζοντο οἱ μελῳδεῖν δυνατοί, καὶ οὕτως ἐκείνου κρούοντος συνῇδον παιῶνάς τινας, δι' ὧν εὐφραίνεσθαι καὶ ἐμμελεῖς καὶ ἔνρυθμοι γίνεσθαι ἐδόκουν....χρῆσθαι δὲ καὶ ὀρχήσεσιν. ὀργάνῳ δὲ χρῆσθαι λύρᾳ· τοὺς γὰρ αὐλοὺς ὑπελάμβανεν ὑβριστικόν τε καὶ πανηγυρικὸν καὶ οὐδαμῶς ἐλευθέριον τὸν ἦχον ἔχειν. "He used to seat someone holding a lyre in the center; round about in a circle he would position those able to sing, and thus while the first one played the lyre, they chanted certain paeans in unison, through which they expected to induce feelings of joy, and to become graceful and rhythmical.... They also made use of dances. As an instrument they used the lyre; for Pythagoras believed that pipes had a wanton, showy, and wholly ignoble sound" (translation Dillon and Hershbell 1991, with minor changes). Other healers attributed therapeutic effects to pipes for the treatment of ailments ranging from epilepsy to sciatica and snakebites; see West 1992, 33. On the association of the lyre with healing in Greek antiquity, see Provenza 2014, with bibliography. Nor should we underestimate the significance of dance as part of therapy; on associations between dance and healing within pagan cults as well as in Judaism and Christianity, see Backman 1952.

[52] West 1992, 33. See also Karanika 2005 on the many ways that dance, music, and

Iamblichos and Porphyry specify that Pythagoras used paeans and other types of music to heal not only physical ailments, including the pain caused by these ailments, but also emotional imbalances such as depression, rage, and desire (Iambl. *VP* 111; Porph. *Pythag.* 32-33), much as paeans cured the women of Locri and Rhegium who suffered from madness.[53] Indeed already in the *Iliad* we find Achilles soothing his anger by singing to the lyre (*Il.* 9.185-91). This should not surprise us since many Greeks, including philosophers and physicians such as Plato, Herophilos, and Galen, viewed the health of the body and soul as directly related.[54] Many, too, argued that

---

healing were interrelated in antiquity. Karanika's portrayal of Asklepios's cult is largely one of rituals conducted in silence, however; while silence may have been the norm for some instances of incubation, it is likely that music too played a role in therapy at Epidauros. For additional sources on music and healing, see Dodds 1951, 79-80, although Dodds's anachronistic distinctions between "magico-religious catharsis" and "purely physical treatment" are dubious; also Garber 2008; Woerther 2008.

[53] Iambl. *VP* 111: εἶναί τινα μέλη πρὸς τὰ ψυχῆς πεποιημένα πάθη, πρός τε ἀθυμίας καὶ δηγμούς, ἃ δὴ βοηθητικώτατα ἐπινενόητο, καὶ πάλιν αὖ ἕτερα πρός τε τὰς ὀργὰς καὶ πρὸς τοὺς θυμοὺς καὶ πρὸς πᾶσαν παραλλαγὴν τῆς τοιαύτης ψυχῆς, εἶναι δὲ καὶ πρὸς τὰς ἐπιθυμίας ἄλλο γένος μελοποιίας ἐξευρημένον. "There are certainly melodies created for the soul's emotions, which, in fact, were designed to be most helpful against despondency and mental suffering; and again, other melodies against rages, angers, and against every mental disturbance of a soul thus afflicted; there is also another kind of musical composition invented for the desires" (translation Dillon and Hershbell 1991, with minor changes). The musical innovator and theorist Aristoxenos is said to have remarked upon the Pythagorean tradition of musical therapy for the soul in particular (fr. 21 Wehrli = INC 2 15 Kaiser): οἱ Πυθαγορικοί, ὡς ἔφη Ἀριστόξενος, καθάρσει ἐχρῶντο τοῦ μὲν σώματος διὰ τῆς ἰατρικῆς, τῆς δὲ ψυχῆς διὰ τῆς μουσικῆς ("The Pythagoreans, as Aristoxenos said, effected a purification of the body through medicine and of the soul through music.") On Aristoxenos and music therapy, see Provenza 2012.

[54] The essays by B. Gundert, T.M. Robinson, P.J. van der Eijk, and H. von Staden in Wright and Potter 2000 provide excellent discussion and recent bibliography on the topic; also Jouanna 2009; Holmes 2010. On Plato's and Galen's views regarding the impact of eros in particular on the body and soul, see Rosen 2013. We

music together with dance were ideal therapies for disturbances of the soul in particular (e.g., Pl. *Leg.* 790d, on purifying the souls of Korybantes through music and dance). Galen, when discussing how physicians heal the soul by rebalancing emotions, points to none other than Asklepios as one who treats the soul by prescribing the composition of poetry and music (*De sanitate tuenda* 1.8.19-21 = VI.41-42 Kühn).[55]

It is the use of music to heal both body and soul that suggests another scenario for the thymele in particular: those in need of healing may have convened inside the thymele to play music, dance, and/or sing as a form of therapy. Lutz Käppel has analyzed in detail the convergences among Pythagoras's theories, music, and healing at Epidauros within the context of the theater there, but he does not explore the possibility that the thymele was relevant to these phenomena.[56] The central location of the thymele—close to the stoa where incubation probably took place and where music emanating from the thymele would almost certainly have been audible, and near the temple and altars of Asklepios where suppliants petitioned the god for help and thanked him for his cures—would have made the thymele

---

find a mind-body connection also in Herodotus's account of Cambyses (Hdt. 3.33), where the historian remarks that someone with a serious bodily ailment might well have an unhealthy mind too.

[55] Aelius Aristides (*Or.* 38.24) speaks also about the soul-body connection while under the care of Asklepios. For Aristides's references to music as therapy in Asklepios's cult, see above, p. 94 and p. 98 n. 29; also the discussion of Edelstein 1945, 2:125-27. Edelstein remarks that there is no evidence for treatment of the soul by Asklepios as early as the fourth century, but absent the prolific writings of an Aelius Aristides, who as an orator and writer was especially interested in and underwent such treatments, or a Galen, who commented widely on all sorts of healing practices, it would be unwise to assume that Asklepios did not dispense musical therapy for the soul, and by extension the body too, in the early period of his cult.

[56] Käppel 1989.

an ideal venue for musical therapy.

We can imagine therefore a range of audiences who would have benefitted from the therapeutic sounds of paeans performed within the thymele, from smaller groups of suppliants accommodated by the space of the thymele itself, to larger groups of worshippers participating in rituals in the central area of the temenos, to those individuals who were incubating in the nearby stoa. It is certainly significant in this context that healing inscriptions (*iamata*) detailing cures at Epidauros credit not only Asklepios but also Apollo for their success; it may well be that Apollo, the god of music and the lyre, was believed to be especially efficacious in and around the thymele, even though such therapies are not mentioned in the healing inscriptions.[57] Indeed, this scenario would suggest that far beyond what our current understanding of the rituals of incubation leads us to believe, a rich variety of therapeutic topographies—of spaces for healing as well as methods of healing—may have been operative in this important sanctuary renowned for its cures.

ANOTHER LOOK AT EROS AND METHE

Let us return, finally, to Pausias's paintings within the thymele, which we believe support our hypothesis. We will recall that Pausanias describes only two paintings inside the building, one of Eros setting aside his bow and

---

[57] Iamata: *IG* 4^2 1, 121-24. See also LiDonnici (1995) for text and translation of, as well as commentary about, these healing inscriptions. The inscriptions bear the title "Iamata of Apollo and Asklepios." The aural dimension more generally of the cures of Asklepios and Apollo deserves greater attention. Epidaurian iamata, for instance, often mention conversations between these gods and their worshippers, and votives depicting ears have been recovered in sanctuaries of Asklepios, indicating perhaps that the god listens to the requests of his worshippers, and/or that worshippers listen to the recommendations of the god. For evidence and discussion, see Petsalis-Diomidis 2005, esp. n. 76; Petsalis-Diomidis 2010, Ch. 5, esp. 231-32, 243-44, and 264; also Platt 2016, 167-79.

arrows to pick up and play the lyre, and the other of Methe, or Drunkenness, imbibing from a crystal phiale (Paus. 2.27.3). As noted above, Eros's lyre suggests that music played a role in the ways that the building was experienced. But what of Methe?

Personifications of Methe appear certainly in Greek art and literature for the first time only in the second half of the fourth century. These include a comedy by Menander entitled *Methe* wherein the title character speaks the prologue (fr. 224 Kassel and Austin, *PCG*), and a bronze statue group by Praxiteles that features Methe (Plin. *HN* 34.69).[58] Pausias's painting of Methe numbers among these first secure depictions of her and must have attracted attention for the novelty of its theme. Moreover, Pausanias tells us that one could see Methe's face through her crystal phiale, a neat trick and yet another example of how innovative the thymele was in terms not only of its structural design but also of its decoration.

A phiale, or libation vessel, seems at first glance like a surprising container for Methe to drink from; we might expect her to quaff rather from a kylix or other cup designed for the consumption of wine, as in representations of Dionysos.[59] Here, context may help: the phiale, much as the

---

[58] These and other examples can be found in Gutzwiller 1995, 390-91. Gutzwiller observes (390-91, with n. 24, citing Furtwängler, *Die antiken Gemmen*) that a nude female drinking from a cup appears on a number of ancient gemstones and that, due to Pausias's painting in the thymele, she is identified often as Methe. See also A. Kossatz-Deissmann, *LIMC*, sv. "Methe." Rosen 2002, 26 suggests that Methe may be an allegorical character in Cratinus's comedy *Pytine* of 424 BCE; if so, she was personified well before Pausias.

[59] The significance of Methe's phiale may relate also to the exterior adornment of the thymele: the building's metopes, carved in relief, feature what appear to be phialai within the rosettes (Roux 1961, 140; see also above, p. 35). Moreover, a bronze statue of Asklepios that stood next to the entrance of his temple featured the god holding a phiale out of which water poured into a basin below (Lambrinoudakis 2014, 22). In addition, there is evidence from other sanctuaries of Asklepios

bow and lyre, are typical of the iconography of Apollo. Attic vase paintings depict Apollo holding (and even playing) a lyre with one hand while pouring a libation from a phiale with the other.[60] In the paintings of the thymele, then, the prominence of the lyre and the phiale, along with the bow and arrows, might have been understood by some worshippers as hallmarks of the divinity and power of Apollo in particular, who cured the sick in this sanctuary alongside his son.[61]

It is the juxtaposition of the figures of Methe and Eros, moreover, that is particularly striking in light of the therapeutic effects of music on the soul. Eros and Methe, Desire and Intoxication, were representative of emotional imbalances for the Greeks. The two were linked often in ancient thought, frequently by cause and effect. For instance, the poet Posidippos professed that he could fend off Eros only when he was not drunk (*Anth. Pal.* 12.120 = Posidippos 7, Gow and Page). The comments of Claude Calame are apt to this discussion: "In the guise of desire, *erôs* may also be designated by other terms, which enrich its semantic field, a field that may be extended to take in love's affinities with other intense emotional states, such as the madness or intoxication to which I have already referred."[62] These imbalanced, extreme, potentially harmful states required healing, and it is not

---

of worshippers dedicating phialai; see Aleshire 1989, 230, on their presence in the inventory lists from the Asklepieion on the south slope of the Athenian Acropolis. A Posidippos epigram (Austin and Bastianini 2002, 97) mentions a worshipper who dedicates a silver phiale to Asklepios.

[60] Laferrière 2017, Ch. 2.

[61] Inscriptions recovered from the area of the stoa immediately to the north of the thymele narrate worshippers' healing experiences; these narratives bear the heading: "Healings of Apollo and of Asklepios" (*IG* 4² 1, 121.1-2).

[62] Calame 1992, 18-19. Machemer 1993, with particular reference to Pind. *Nem.* 4, discusses the many transitory pleasures of the symposium (e.g., drink, as well as food and arousal) in contrast to the lasting pleasure and curative effect of music.

surprising that in poetry (the words that accompany music) we find many references to music as a cure for just such imbalances. For instance, Theokritos's eleventh *Idyll* describes the song that the lovesick Cyclops Polyphemos sings as a *pharmakon*, or cure, capable of removing his intense desire for the nymph Galateia. He sings this song, moreover, to the accompaniment of his lyre. And later, the poet Ovid mentions that Cheiron taught Achilles to play the cithara and calmed his fierce anger (*animos feros*) by means of soothing skill (*placida arte*; *Ars am.* 1.11-12), almost certainly a reference to *Iliad* 9.185-91 where Achilles sings to a lyre as he struggles to control his rage against Agamemnon. In the mythological tradition it is remarkable that Cheiron tutors not just Achilles but also Asklepios, and that the two arts most often imparted by Cheiron are music and medicine (hence there is some ambiguity in the Ovid passage about which *placida ars* Cheiron uses to calm Achilles—medicine, music, or perhaps both).[63]

Even more remarkable is the fact that we find music functioning as a cure for emotional imbalance already in the earliest Greek literature, and in the very figure of Apollo. At the opening of the *Iliad*, the Greeks sing and dance paeans to soothe Apollo's anger over a grave insult to his priest (*Il.* 1.472-74). This very anger, we should underscore, had prompted Apollo to send a rain of plague-inducing arrows down upon the Greek army, producing a major medical emergency. Thus in Homer, Apollo's *bow* represents both physical disease and the emotional dis-ease that results from it, while his *lyre*, to which the Greeks almost certainly performed their paeans in the hope of diminishing both the anger and illness expressed by his bow, represents healing.[64] These are the same two instruments—bow and lyre—represented

---

[63] On Cheiron's mythology, M. Gisler-Huwiler, *LIMC*, sv. "Cheiron." On song as a cure for lovesickness in Hellenistic poetry: Faraone 2006; Rynearson 2009.

[64] The tension of these two instruments of Apollo is apparent in other poetry, such

in Pausias's painting of Eros. Herakleitos believed that these two instruments constituted a παλίντροπος ἁρμονία (a framework [ἁρμονία] that turned back on itself [παλίντροπος] and thereby expressed unity; fr. 51 DK).[65] This same idea is paraphrased in Plato's *Symposium* by the physician Eryximachos while he delivers an encomium of Eros (Pl. *Symp*. 187a-c)—a speech, moreover, that compares balance in music to balance induced in the body through the art of medicine.

There are many ways to interpret Pausias's paintings. One interpretation suggested by the evidence gathered here is that Methe and Eros personify two types of imbalance, specifically intoxication and desire, which often go hand in hand.[66] The bow that Eros sets aside itself represents a wide range

---

as Callim. *Hymn* 2 and *HHom* 3. See Bassi 1989, esp. 224-26; Cheshire 2008. On the opposition of bow and lyre as they relate to Apollo, see also Burkert 1985, 145-48. Homer opposes the destructive force of the bow with the healing force of the lyre also in the figure of Odysseus: comforted by the songs of Demodokos at the banquet of the Phaeacians, eventually he exacts vengeance upon the suitors using a bow (*Od*. books 8 and 22; the comparison between bow and lyre is made explicit at *Od*. 21.405-9).

[65] Our interpretation of the Herakleitos fragment follows closely the discussion of Snyder 1984; Snyder notes, moreover, that the lyre as well as the bow is a curved instrument that when viewed from the side describes the arc of a circle. On Plato's use of dualities throughout the *Symposium* that seem to relate to an overarching theme of harmony, and on Apollo's role in the dialogue, see Ziolkowski 1999. Ziolkowski (19) views the bow and lyre, both stringed instruments, as innately opposed due to the capability of the one to produce higher tones and the other lower.

[66] The lyre, a common element in the iconography of Eros, was thought capable also of inciting desire. Would the ancient audience have interpreted the lyre in Pausias's painting, then, as counteracting desire or as arousing it? Perhaps the ambiguity was intentional. Later sources pair Hygieia (Health) with Eros: e.g., Proklos identifies Hygieia as a daughter of Eros (*In Ti*. 3.158e); on the relationship in Greek literature and art between Hygieia and Eros—as well as other instantiations of desire—see Stafford 2000, 147-71. There seems to have been a widespread idea that love, wealth, and all other of life's "goods" are worthless without health

of imbalance and even destruction; a bow and arrows in the hands of Eros can incite ardent desire, while in the hands of Apollo, who inhabits this sanctuary alongside Asklepios, these same weapons can inflict plague and death, and they represent Apollo's intense anger. But in Pausias's painting, Eros does not hold onto these weapons. Rather, the god lays down his bow and takes up an instrument that has the power to heal.

(cf. Ariphron's paean to Hygieia, a copy of which was inscribed at Epidauros, *IG* 4² 1, 132).

Chapter Five
Response: A Musical Maze For Asklepios?
An Archaeoacoustic Assessment
of the Thymele at Epidauros

Harmonia is a dark and difficult musical literature—
and very much so, indeed, for those who do not know Greek.
Vitruvius 5.4.1

The preceding chapters have proposed that the thymele at Epidauros was a venue for musical performances in honor of Asklepios, and that these were specifically therapeutic in nature. The authors struck upon this idea independently of a similar thesis advanced over a century ago by Thiersch, who argued that the thymele was in fact a kind of concert hall or odeion.[1] This theory, after winning some support, largely disappeared from the literature after J. Charbonneaux aptly criticized the analogies which Thiersch had drawn with the Skias at Sparta and the Odeion of Pericles, and his discredited thesis that a round form normally indicated a concert space.[2] Thus, when G. Roux came to review competing theories in 1961, he characterized Charbonneaux's critique of Thiersch as "objections décisives…

---

[1] Above, p. 26 ns. 15-16. Thiersch 1909; note also further references in Roux 1961, 189 n. 3.

[2] Charbonneaux 1925, esp. 168–71, but see above, pp. 66-75. That the Skias, built according to Spartan tradition in the seventh century, was the site of the Karneian musical contests has been deduced from Paus. 3.12.8, in whose time one could see hanging there a κιθάρα, allegedly the famous offending instrument of Timotheos (for the sources of this legend, see recently Prauscello 2009, 172–88, who analyzes how and why Timotheos's performance was later transferred in legend to the shrine of Eleusinian Demeter). But the Skias was evidently not round, since Pausanias troubles to specify a round building adjacent to it: Dinsmoor and Anderson 1950, 119 n. 2. As to the Periclean Odeion, Thiersch's belief that it was round (on the basis of Plut. *Per.* 13.7) was of course disproven by excavation (references in Sear 2006, 389–90).

contre la thèse de la tholos-odéon" and did not revisit the case.³ Yet while Thiersch's comparanda were themselves perhaps uncompelling, Charbonneaux hardly *disproved* a musical thymele; for nothing prevents the building from being so assessed on its own merits. In fact, Thiersch's argument was bolstered by many further details concerning Asklepios's cult and the performance of ritual music, including the paean. Schultz, Wickkiser, Hinge, and Kanellopoulos have developed attractive new arguments in support of a musical thymele, adding the further suggestion that the mysterious, labyrinthine substructure may have served some complementary acoustical purpose. Moreover, they wonder whether the letter-like signs inscribed on some foundation stones of the labyrinthine substructure, long interpreted as masons' marks, might rather be an early form of musical notation—perhaps marking the placement of bronze resonating vessels of the sort which Vitruvius attributes to some Greek theaters both of his own day and times past.

The authors have invited me to contribute a response to these last hypotheses. I shall not address in detail their contextual arguments regarding circularity, choral performance, and mystical healing: on the whole I find the proposed scenario of paeanic and other cathartic music rituals in the thymele satisfying both for what is known of Greek musical therapy and musical mysticism generally, and because it offers a plausible role for a prominent element of the sanctuary whose precise function has hitherto remained elusive.⁴ My principal focus will be rather the proposed

---

³ Roux 1961, 189.

⁴ For an overview of Greek music-therapy: Provenza 2007. Musical mysticism: Burkert 1972; Godwin 1987; Franklin 2006b. I would, however, offer an organological observation. The hypothesis that the thymele housed lyre-performances specifically is based on the familial connection of Asklepios and Apollo; on the instrument's prominence in sources relating to musical healing (e.g. the famous story of Pythagoras); and on iconography associated with the thymele itself. Similar powers were also attributed to the αὐλός; besides explicit testimonies, one

interpretation of the labyrinth and its signs.

Three main issues must be considered, to be treated in turn.

First is the problem of ancient resonating vessels generally. I shall defend the reliability of Vitruvius—our main source for what he presents as a widespread Greek practice going back at least a century and a half before his own time—by appeal to archaeological evidence and further literary sources. This material strongly suggests that resonators were well known in theaters of the Hellenistic world, whether ubiquitous or not. That they were available as early as ca. 370–360, for deployment in the thymele, is in principle quite credible. I therefore close this section with observations on the thymele's possible position within the development of Greek acoustical thinking and its practical application to performance spaces.

Next is the question of an acoustical interface between the cella and the labyrinth, since the hypothesis of resonators only makes sense if the two areas enjoyed significant sound communication. So before appealing to detailed acoustical modeling via software, one should present arguments in favor of the labyrinth per se (i.e. leaving resonators aside) as having had an acoustical purpose—whether this was its primary function, or only one of several simultaneously operative. I shall suggest that this hypothesis may indeed find some support in the archaeological record, and deserves continued consideration.

Finally, I will examine the idea that the labyrinth contained resonators,

---

should not overlook the instrument's fundamental role in the cathartic art of tragedy (Provenza 2009; Provenza 2010). It may be unnecessarily restrictive, therefore, to concentrate solely on the lyre, especially given that the αὐλός had reached great new heights of popularity in the two generations before the thymele was built. See e.g. Wilson 1999; Franklin 2013. One should also note that αὐλός and paean are connected as early as Archilochus fr. 121 W; further evidence in Rutherford 2001, 79-80; see also above, p. 102 n. 38 and p. 109 n. 51.

with signs serving to mark their positions. Here a closer examination will suggest that this part of the hypothesis should probably be abandoned. In my view, the signs accord rather better with the larger class of so-called "masons' marks," known from many other sites (even if the precise functions of these often elude interpretation). Conversely, the signs do not conform well to the standard system of Greek notation, which was already quite developed by the time of the thymele. Still, for the sake of thoroughness, I shall lay out the special concessions one would have to make to keep this part of the hypothesis open.

THE THYMELE'S POSITION IN THE DEVELOPMENT OF GREEK ARCHITECTURAL ACOUSTICS

Archaeoacoustics is enjoying an efflorescence as a field of investigation, with many conferences held in the past decade to examine abundant material from around the world.[5] These studies call for a greater sensitivity to the sonic potential of ancient sites—largely ignored in past archaeological work—and propose new criteria for assessing intentionality. They raise stimulating questions about how ancient cultures may have experienced sound and soundscapes differently from ourselves, constructed purposeful acoustical environments, and manipulated sound and space to induce various psychoacoustical effects for purposes ranging from the ritual and mystical to the spectacular and entertaining. A central point of interest has been natural or artificial resonance effects—various forms of sound-reflection which can modify the amplitude, duration, and timbre of a sound-source, for instance the human voice.[6] While there is now very convincing statistical evidence for the exploitation of natural cave-resonance as early as the Paleolithic period,

---

[5] Scarre and Lawson 2006 and above, pp. 27-28 n. 17; also below, pp. 176-70 ns. 2-6.
[6] E.g. Reznikoff 2006.

the literary record begins only much later, in Greek and Roman sources.[7]

An early fascination with musical resonance (of which the consonant fifth and fourth are a subspecies) is attested by a rich body of musical mythology, from heroic lyre-kings reflecting Late Bronze Age palatial music down to the *musica speculativa* credited to Pythagoras.[8] The transition of such ideas to writing begins in the fifth century; an interest in resonance specifically is attributed to Lasus of Hermione and Hippasus of Metapontum—if they did indeed conduct experiments with vessels (ἀγγεῖα), as a later text seems to suggest.[9] A more general interest in acoustics is implied by Demokritos's contemplation of the cognitive interface between perception and knowledge (fr. 11 D-K). And Peripatetic sources offer very rich evidence for sustained engagement with the phenomena of sound, including resonance (see below). But it is Vitruvius who enjoys pride of place in modern studies, with his famous discussion of how theaters "in parts of Italy and many cities of the Greeks" (in Italiae regionibus et in pluribus Graecorum civitatibus, 5.5.8) used bronze sounding-vessels (*echea* < Gk. ἠχεῖα) to reinforce musical performance. Lesser theaters with smaller budgets, he says, might substitute ceramic jars (*fictilibus doleis*) with good effect.[10] Vitruvius cites, as a well-known event, L. Mummius's "retrieval" of bronze echea during his sack of Corinth in 146 BCE: these were brought back to Rome and dedicated in the temple of Luna (5.5.8), where perhaps they continued to serve a musical purpose in their new home, reinforcing whatever cultic music transpired there.[11] Mummius's action must be seen as part of his larger depredation of

---

[7] Reznikoff 2002, et al.
[8] See Franklin 2005, 9–22; Franklin 2006a.
[9] Theon Smyrn. 57.6–7, 59.4–15, although the corrupt text precludes certainty.
[10] The *v.l. Italiae regione*, recently defended by Saliou 2009, may have somewhat different geographical implications: see her discussion of the passage.
[11] Mummius's choice of this particular god as recipient has been plausibly con-

major Corinthian artworks.[12] In other words, these vessels were not merely valuable for their bronze, nor again solely for their undoubted utility as a complete sounding-set: they were crafted to the highest specifications, and perhaps adorned with high-quality engravings. These ἠχεῖα were probably some of the finest examples in the Greek world, and may well represent the art of bronze resonators at its peak of popularity.

Vitruvius goes on to present his well-known scheme for the placement of up to three concentric semicircles of resonators, depending on the size of the theater. A small structure might house only one row, tuned to the so-called "standing tones" of the Perfect System (less the lowest, προσλαμβόμενος) — now known to have been current by the early fourth century at the latest.[13] Note that, although the number of distinct tones provided for in the first row is seven, these are *not* themselves the tones of a standard heptatonic scale in any of its forms (Greek or otherwise). Rather, they mark the tetrachord *boundaries* of such scales when extended to the two octaves of the Greek Perfect System; the two intermediate tones of the tetrachords are provided by the second and third rows of resonators. Thus there is no special connection to be made here with the archaic seven-stringed lyre. For small theaters with lower budgets, the minimal one-row configuration would leave unspecified many details of mode and what the Greeks called γένος (enharmonic, chromatic, diatonic), and hence could support many forms of music. This makes perfect sense: funders would desire maximum "bang for buck." In larger theaters further vessels were introduced, corresponding to the

---

nected to two lunar eclipses which are reported for his campaign. Less credible is the connection of this event to a custom of warding off eclipses through the striking of bronze: see with references Saliou 2009, 219–20. Further theories: Gros, et al. 1997, 696.

[12] Cf. Saliou 2009, 219 with ancient references.

[13] Hagel 2005.

characteristic interior notes of tetrachords which generated the chromatic and diatonic genera in their textbook form—that is, without the further specification of microtonal shades (χρόαι). A basic form of enharmonic (without divided semitone) would also be accommodated thereby.[14]

Despite these transparent allusions to musical practice, a persistent factoid seems to have lodged itself in studies by acousticians—namely that Vitruvius's Augustan date makes him an unreliable witness to Greek theory and practice of three centuries earlier.[15] Even some philologists, despite our now quite clear understanding of ancient harmonic theory, persist in supposing that the architect's specific scheme is a theoretical fantasy.[16] But Vitruvius's intimate connection with contemporary music was recently proven by Stefan Hagel, who demonstrated a close correspondence between the architect's varying numbers—some tones of the Greek musical system being represented by more vessels than others—and the note range and distribution in the extant Greek musical scores of the centuries CE.[17] This

---

[14] See the good discussion of Landels 1967.

[15] E.g. Cremer 1975; Barron 1993, 244.

[16] Poule 2000.

[17] Hagel 2009, 251–55. This finding constitutes a sufficient answer to Poule 2000 who, while admitting that Vitruvius's resonators derive from musical practice, asserts that the specific layout he offers was motivated by purely theoretical, and specifically cosmological, considerations. The main argument is far-fetched: from among the various known configurations of the harmony of spheres (Burkert 1972, 350–68; Richter 1999), Vitruvius selected one in which the tone ὑπάτη is equated with the moon; this Poule then connects with the fact that the central vase in Vitruvius's basic first row, and the only one which does appear only once, corresponds to ὑπάτη ὑπατῶν—as if this were identical to ὑπάτη! (too little Greek music theory is never healthy); he finally relates this "deficient" "moon string" to Vitruvius's report that Mummius dedicated the Corinthian vases in the temple of Luna, and the eclipses during Mummius's campaign. More plausible and interesting is his suggestion that Mummius used his resonators in the grand theatrical display which accompanied his triumph (Tac. *Ann.* 14.21.1), and that Vitruvius's scheme

finding has two important implications. First, that Vitruvius did indeed have access to some reliable source, whether hearsay from architects and craftsmen, a technical diagram (by e.g. Aristoxenos: see below), or both. Second, that specific vessel-configurations were probably enacted at different times and places depending on a combination of local, contemporary musical requirements, the physical limitations and opportunities of a given space, and perhaps the aesthetic predilections of architects. Thus Vitruvius presents a single such scheme as paradigmatic. It can hardly be doubted, however, that one of Vitruvius's most notable features will have been a main desideratum in any scheme—a thorough and well-balanced "coverage" of the space in question.[18]

This conclusion is well supported by archaeological evidence. According to recent surveys, varying numbers of ceramic vessels or remains have been found embedded in different parts of theaters at Aezani (Phrygia), Gioiosa Ionica (Calabria), Hippo Regius (Algeria), Nora (Sardinia), and Avaricum Biturigum (Aquitania).[19] At other sites—notably Saguntum (Spain), Nemus Aricinum (near Rome), and Scythopolis (Beth Shean, Israel)—empty niches of no other discernible function have been plausibly identified as housings for bronze resonators long since scavenged.[20] This list is not exhaustive; but

---

reflects the arrangement used on that occasion.

[18] Vitruvius's near contemporary Philo Jud., *De posteritate Caini* 103–4 compares the shape of a theater to that of an ear, and describes both as closed circular spaces optimized for concentrating and collecting sound. When he goes on to discuss the natural basis for the articulation of harmonic space into diatonic, chromatic, and enharmonic structures, it is very tempting to suppose that he still has the theatrical context in mind, and is alluding to resonators (albeit rather obliquely). If this is right, there could be no question of his complete dependence on Vitruvius. Rather, he would be drawing on his own experiences in Alexandria; cf. *De ebriatate* 177 (in a different context): ἤδη γοῦν ἐν θεάτρῳ πολλάκις παρατυχὼν εἶδον κτλ.

[19] Gros, et al. 1997, 686–89; Sear 2006, 8–9; Saliou 2009, 387–99.

[20] See the good discussion of Plommer 1983, also discussing the theater at Caesarea,

while many individual cases remain more or less controversial—with some still questioning the catalogue as a whole—there is now a general consensus that this archaeological evidence is real.[21]

Material evidence for Vitruvius's specific scheme, however, remains ambiguous. At Avaricum Biturigum, thirteen terracotta tubes were found in back of the podium wall and facing the audience; but if the *number* recalls Vitruvius, the *configuration* is entirely different. And the great diversity of possible arrangements is startling.[22] One should therefore treat with great caution the much cited testimony of Onorio Belli, a sixteenth-century Italian physician and botanist stationed on Venetian Crete, who gave descriptions and diagrams of three theaters on the island, attributing to two of them (Hierapytna and Gortyn) a single row of thirteen niches each, and to the Lyttos theater (remains no longer visible) three rows of thirteen.[23] It seems highly unlikely, in the face of so much variation elsewhere, that three theaters in a single region could conform so closely to the Vitruvian scheme— matching even his different requirements for small and large spaces.[24]

The archaeological catalogue might seem to indicate that resonators never caught on widely, or that their greatest vogue was the Hellenistic

---

Palestine; for Scythopolis, see the further references in Segal 1995, 57 n. 80. Hills 1882 mentions niches for the Roman theaters at Nicopolis (Epirus) and Gerasa (Jordan), but I find no confirmation in Sear 2006, 311–12, 413.

[21] Saliou 2009, 387–99; Gros, et al. 1997; Rocconi 2006, 74; Reznikoff 2006.

[22] Sear 2006, 8–9.

[23] Belli in Falkener 1854, 18–19, 31; Hills 1882, 94; Lewcock, et al. 2007–2011; Sear 2006, 298–99. Note that Belli does *not* say, as he is sometimes interpreted, that the bronze vases themselves were still visible: "haveva tredici vasi di rame posti nelle sue celle che si vedono benissimo" (the imperfect *haveva* refers to the theater's own past [i.e. "used to have"], not that of the author's visit, and the antecedent of *che* is *celle*, not *vasi*).

[24] Cf. Saliou 2009, 390–91, also calling for prudence; more optimistically, Gros, et al. 1997, 687.

period and that they were engineered out of later constructions or renovations in the Roman era. Yet it may well be that resonators were often employed *without* dedicated niches, perhaps especially at an early stage. If this sounds like special pleading, consider that at Corinth itself, the one place for which we have explicit literary testimony for the use of vessels, excavation has yielded no evidence of niches. There were, however, remnants of unenclosed blocks which may have served as bases.[25] This would be a considerably less intrusive arrangement, which could have left no clear traces at other sites; and it further suggests that, especially at an early stage, vessels may have been placed with little or no particular accommodation in the stonework.

All told, therefore, resonators were probably once rather more common than the material record would suggest. This is anyway the natural implication of Vitruvius, one of whose main purposes is to renovate Roman architectural practice through emulation of the highest Greek standards.[26] The use of resonators was one of these architectural elements, and it must have been reasonably mainstream for Vitruvius to promote them for Roman stone theaters, which after all were relatively new in his day, beginning to appear only in 55 BCE with the Theater of Pompey.[27]

The main acoustical properties of the mature Greek theater—for instance that of Epidauros, famous and celebrated in both ancient and modern times—are now well understood.[28] These structures were optimized for the recognition of words in the performance of drama (both metrical dialogue and choral lyrics) and, from some time in the fourth century, of

---

[25] Gros, et al. 1997, 687; Saliou 2009, 220–21.
[26] Saliou 2009, 222.
[27] Sear 2006, 133–35; for precedents in other parts of Latium, 44–45.
[28] Canac 1967, esp. 139–47 for Epidauros; Shankland 1973; Cremer 1975; Barron 1993.

concert music. This effect was achieved by a combination of factors. First, the relatively steep grade (from 20–38%) at which the steps rise away from stage and orchestra permitted a quite direct projection of sound across the majority of the audience with minimal interference from the spectators themselves.[29] Second, the orchestra floor reinforced the direct sound by up to 40% through short-interval (40–50 ms) reflections—those which are quicker than "the basic 'grain' of human temporal perception" and therefore blend imperceptibly with the direct sound.[30] Moreover, because the space was not enclosed from above, as in a modern theater, the audience was not exposed to excessive long-interval reflections—those which arrive late enough *not* to blend with the direct sound, and can therefore impede apprehension of speech and lyrics. Finally, it was recently shown, for Epidauros and presumably elsewhere, that the ridged pattern of the seating serves to attenuate frequencies below 500 Hz, effectively eliminating much background noise. Although the fundamental frequency of the human voice typically falls below this range, the brain is able to fill in the missing "information" on the basis of upper partials; and at Epidauros this ability is enhanced by reflective properties of the seats' limestone surfaces.[31]

The "Vitruvian" resonators were well suited to this acoustical environment. Without introducing the more random disturbances of an enclosed space, the ἠχεῖα generated specific, musically relevant tones answering those found in music. It is not unreasonable to consider this a form of

---

[29] Canac 1967, 35.

[30] Cross and Watson 2006. The mature Hellenistic stage-building added some further, lesser support. Canac 1967, 110–13, 124–27; Rocconi 2006, 72–73, with discussion of [Arist.] *Prob.* 11.25 and Plin. *HN* 11.270 (on orchestra reflections) and Vitruvius's own treatment of theater acoustics.

[31] See Declercq and Dekeyser 2007. I owe this reference to Peter Schultz via Garth Whitcombe.

amplification: resonance involves an increase in signal amplitude, as both the direct sound and vessel-tones would oscillate at the same frequency, and therefore reinforce each other. But the modern word hardly accounts for the full range of the effect, which Vitruvius characterizes as *claritas* (Vitr. 5.5.3). This word, as J. G. Landels pointed out, is one of the architect's calques for Greek technical terms (cf. 5.4.1)—here λαμπρότης, implying "loudness, distinctness, and purity."[32] Such vessels would also add an interesting dimension of "surround-sound" which doubtless appealed to an audience's evergreen love of spectacular effects, and had the practical advantage of providing performers with a fixed tonal frame of reference, allowing them always to remain on pitch—or rather no excuse not to.[33]

Theoretical interest in aural λαμπρότης can be traced back at least to the fourth century, when it was discussed in the Aristotelian *De audibilibus* (801b25–802a5). This was but one of a number of works from this period which dealt with the phenomena of sound and hearing.[34] Of these the Aristotelian *Problems* deserve special mention, since they attest an interest in both sound reflection (11.8, 23) and sympathetic vibration—the operative principle of acoustic resonators. Two of the *Problems* discuss the matter in terms of lyre strings (19.24, 42). More revealing is a third (11.8) which deals with the scenario of vessels buried in buildings: ceramic and bronze are both contemplated; the selective nature of the resonance is recognized (the "echo" is an ἀνάκλασις, a "breaking up" or "refraction" of the sound); and

---

[32] Landels 1967, 87.

[33] See generally Comotti 1989, 54. This may be Paul's point in 1 Corinthians, when he compares speaking without love to "ringing bronze or a clanging cymbal" (χαλκὸς ἠχῶν ἢ κύμβαλον ἀλαλάζον, 13:1); but the contrast may rather be between the orgiastic music of Dionysos- or Kybele-cult, and the more rational and abstract "music" of Christian λόγος. Pitch: Landels 1967, esp. 91–94; also Landels 1999, 189–95. Godman 2006 is interesting from a performative point of view.

[34] See further Barker 1984–1989, 2:8–11; Rocconi 2006.

attention is called to the "compactness" of air in a small enclosed space—basic to the operation of so-called Helmholtz resonators.[35] Although theatrical use is not specified here, it is no great leap from this late fourth- or third-century discussion to the exploitation of the phenomenon in the production of professional music.[36]

Indeed it has been plausibly suggested that Aristoxenos himself, on whose harmonic theory Vitruvius spends time so lavishly, is equally the source for his startlingly accurate discussion of sound propagation and resonance.[37] It is perhaps less likely, however, that Aristoxenos ever presented a scheme for the deployment of ἠχεῖα. Not that he would have been unaware of their use. After all, it was in Aristoxenos's own lifetime that Lykourgos revamped the Theater of Dionysos in Athens (ca. 330 BCE), and several of Aristoxenos's fragments reflect the sensational new condition of solo musical performances in theaters.[38] He was thus clearly aware of large-scale performances, of the kind for which resonators were very

---

[35] For discussion, see Harrison 1967–1968, 56; Rocconi 2006, 72. The classic description of such vessels is Helmholtz 1895, 43–45.

[36] That the problem is relevant to theatrical use is reasonably assumed by Gros, et al. 1997, 686–87; Rocconi 2006, 74.

[37] Gros, et al. 1997, 686. The source is presumably the lost *Musical Perception* (Μουσικὴ ἀκρόασις), the one certain notice of which is fr. 90 (Wehrli 1967, Heft 2); other possible candidates are found among fragments 69–89.

[38] Aristox. fr. 70 Wehrli (= Themistius *Orat*. XXXIII) ᾄσῃ, φησί, σπανιώτερον ἐν τοῖς θεάτροις κτλ. That Aristoxenos has in mind not the songs of drama, but solo pieces, is clear enough from his language (τῶν κρουμάτων ... τῆς νέας καὶ ἐπιτερποῦς ἀοιδῆς; σπανιώτερον may well invoke the language of Ion of Chios fr. 32 West, where a citharodic context is clear: cf. Power 2007). This is confirmed by his explicit discussion of aulodic music in fr. 76 (= [Plut.] *De mus*. 1142b) in a similar context: while the "thymelic" nature of this music is problematized by ὑπὸ τῆς σκηνικῆς τε καὶ ποικίλης μουσικῆς, this is balanced by the reference to the songs of Timotheos and Philoxenos. Barbarization of the theater: fr. 124 Wehrli (=Athenaeus 632a).

probably introduced (see below). But for Aristoxenos such music was a "barbarized" state of affairs, and he would probably have despised resonators as sensationalist gimmickry. On the other hand, his διάγραμμα πολύτροπον, whereby thirteen versions of the so-called Perfect System were arrayed in semitone steps, was fully able to accommodate the most complex harmonic modulations of his own day, despite his own obvious distaste for many contemporary specimens of such music.[39] So although there is no very compelling reason to believe that Aristoxenos did treat resonators, all the necessary conditions were present in his time, and the question must remain open.

It has become increasingly clear that, on the whole, early Greek musical theory corresponded quite closely to musical practice.[40] When this is seen against Vitruvius's clear reference to Greek use of ἠχεῖα and the specific case of the Corinthian resonators, his extensive citation of Aristoxenian ἁρμονική, the wide distribution and relatively early dating of some of the archaeological data surveyed above (second century BCE), and the theoretical discussion of embedded vessels in one Aristotelian problem, there can be little doubt that ἠχεῖα were a fixture of the Hellenistic sound-palette, and had probably begun to be developed already in the fourth century. If they were not universally used in the Hellenistic period, they were at least not uncommon. One may safely conclude that their development and increasing use arose, sooner or later, from the general professionalization of Greek music which began in the second half of the fifth century.

The authors have demonstrated above, from their discussion of the term θυμέλη (and related expressions like θυμελικοὶ ἀγῶνες) that, at the

---

[39] See Hagel 2000, 183–88; Franklin 2005, 22; Hagel 2009.
[40] Hagel 2009 has repeatedly shown the intimate interplay between Greek musical theory and practice—much more so than most scholars had suspected.

time the Epidaurian sanctuary was being built, "the term thymele bore a strong and sustained association with both song and dance," and have well argued that the label marked out the building under consideration as a performance hall of some sort.[41] That the lyre especially would benefit from an interior space is indeed an attractive proposal.[42] (Of course, an aulete might be equally keen to enhance his sound.[43]) An instructive analogy is the Odeion of Pericles, apparently (re)built primarily as a new venue for the Panathenaic musical contests, involving both κιθάρα and αὐλός (although this space was available for other functions too.)[44] It is no coincidence that this project was undertaken just when the exciting New Music was reaching a first great peak; it was apparently Phrynis of Lesbos who won the inaugural citharodic contest there, probably in 446/5 with the difficult "bends" which captivated Athenian youth to the dismay of traditional lyre-instructors.[45] Given that the Odeion must have been intended to provide an improved listening environment for audiences that were becoming keen on virtuosity and special musical effects, one may confidently conclude that one of the building's main attractions—beyond its conspicuous display of

---

[41] See above, Chapters 2-4.

[42] Schultz and Wickkiser 2010, 151 and above, pp. 113-17. One might compare the ship-shaped timber buildings used as performance venues for epic poetry accompanied by lyre in the medieval Germanic tradition of northwest Europe, notably Scandinavia: Lawson 2006.

[43] Note that the full Perfect System, with which the Vitruvian scheme accords, grew out of developments in the fifth-century αὐλός (Hagel 2005; Hagel 2009). As I shall suggest, however, the hypothesis of resonators may be rather incompatible, in historical terms, with an interior space: see below.

[44] The Odeion, besides hosting dramatic previews (προαγῶνες) and philosophical debates, doubled as a lawcourt and was used for grain distribution: Sear 2006, 40.

[45] Power 2010, 494–96; Ar. *Nub.* 964–72; Davison 1958, 36–41; Power 2010, 491–500; Franklin 2012, 747–48, 754–55.

wealth and *imperium*—was a greatly enhanced resonant space.⁴⁶ It was in fact the largest roofed structure in Greece.⁴⁷ The effect, as observed by François Canac of the restored Odeion of Herodes Atticus, was probably "une sorte de brassage acoustique."⁴⁸ This stew of sound must have been very impressive, although its detrimental impact on the intelligibility of speech will have done nothing to improve the digestibility of the rich dithyrambic diction of the unpalatable New Music citharodes.⁴⁹

The promoters of cultic music in the ambitious Asklepieion would surely want to enjoy the best sonic advantages that modern thinking could provide. The construction of the thymele as a purposefully resonant space ca. 370–360 (even if it were not *solely* a concert hall) would fit very well with contemporary Greek musical thought. One might see its relatively late dating, by comparison with the Odeion of Pericles, as yet another indication that the Epidaurians, in building the Asklepieion largely with imported talent and materials from Athens, Argos, and Corinth, were attempting to meet contemporary standards of panhellenic grandeur despite limited local resources.⁵⁰

It may be, in fact, that with the thymele one is approaching the end of a century-long trend of indoor performances. While smaller halls did continue to be built (e.g. Rome [Pompey], Ephesus, Athens [Herodes Atticus]), much κιθαρῳδία and other concert music did eventually migrate to the theater, as these reached their mature form, to become "thymelic" entertainment. One reason must be that, as citharodes increasingly enjoyed the status of superstars, theaters became a more practical venue for satisfying consumer

---

⁴⁶ Rocconi 2006, 75; Miller 1997, 232–42; Power 2010, 545–49.
⁴⁷ Power 2010, 495 n. 225.
⁴⁸ Canac 1967, 167.
⁴⁹ Canac 1967, 167.
⁵⁰ See generally Burford 1969.

demand, with some examples able to accommodate audiences of 17,000.[51] The Panathenaic musical contests seem to have been so transferred from Odeion to theater by the second half of the fourth century.[52] For Vitruvius it was a matter of course that citharodes performed in theaters; he describes their technique of projecting the voice against wooden stage-doors (ad scaenae valvas, 5.5.7) to increase amplitude through resonance.[53] And it was in the theater of Naples that Nero famously performed as a citharode.[54]

The increasing use of theaters for professional musical performances was probably further encouraged by, and in turn stimulated, the growing acoustical mastery of Greek architects. And this same trend provides the best context for the evolution of resonators. Given the theater's primary need to minimize *extraneous* reverberations which might compete with comprehension of diction, the advent of ἠχεῖα—offering carefully controlled, strictly *tonal* reverberation—may be seen as a brilliantly practical compromise, emulating the acoustical advantages of a concert hall within the theater's larger, intentionally "dryer" space.

This evolutionary model, conversely, could suggest that ἠχεῖα would have been otiose in highly resonant buildings like the Odeion, or the thymele of Epidauros. What we know of ἠχεῖα, at least as Vitruvius describes their function, does little to support the hypothesis of resonators in the substructure of the thymele. Still, one might suppose that, in an age of acoustic experimentation, ἠχεῖα were deployed in indoor spaces less to augment the

---

[51] For the developing economy of κιθαρῳδία, see now Power 2010.
[52] Frei 1900, 12–13; Kotsidu 1991, 154; Power 2010, 495 n. 222. Demetrios of Phaleron is said to have brought rhapsodic recitations into the theater, Ath. 14.12.10. One of the anecdotes about the fourth-century citharode Stratonikos, a celebrated wit (Gilula 2000), has him performing in a theater on Rhodes: Ath. 8.42.17–21.
[53] For the use of compensatory wooden panels in the σκηναί of stone theaters, see further Rocconi 2006, 73.
[54] Power 2010, 3–6.

overall resonance than to impart greater harmonic articulation and tonal coloration within an otherwise largely amorphous *brassage*.[55] One might further speculate that, once the effectiveness of such resonators had been so appreciated in the proper setting for recital music, someone struck upon the idea of transferring them to the theater, thereby facilitating the presentation of citharodic and other concert music in the much larger venues which had been originally optimized for drama.

In conclusion, then, there is nothing inherently improbable in strictly historical terms (n.b.) about the hypothesis of the thymele as a performing space, nor indeed about the proposed use of resonating vessels at this early stage. Yet neither point is supported by much more than circumstantial evidence and arguments from probability and analogy. To clarify the situation we must turn to the archaeological data. Not that one should expect to find any traces of resonators themselves, of course. If ἠχεῖα were used in the sumptuous thymele, one would naturally suppose them to have been of bronze, a material which rarely survives looting and scavenging, and in any case no trace of ceramics has been found in the labyrinth.[56] So we are concerned rather with, first, the layout of the building itself and its acoustical spaces; and, second, the proposed interpretation of the marks as musical notation.

THE INTERFACE OF LABYRINTH AND CELLA

The great crux in all archaeoacoustical studies is determining whether the acoustical properties of a given space were so intended by its architect, or

---

[55] An important parallel here is the frequent use of resonating vessels in the already highly resonant medieval churches of Europe; apses also had an important acoustic function, sometimes perhaps serving to correct runaway effects of the upper vaulting (Reznikoff 2006, esp. 80–83).

[56] So above, p. 25.

merely a secondary consequence of other design choices.[57] In this section I shall examine the archaeological evidence, relating to the labyrinth and its interface with the cella above, that bears most closely on the question of acoustical intentionality. I shall argue that the evidence does accord fairly well with such an interpretation of the labyrinth, and offer some thoughts on what the structure's purpose may have been.

The acoustics of an enclosed cylindrical space are of a very particular kind, with the circular walls serving to "concentrate" sound, that is, to reflect it in distinctly circular patterns. Michael Barron, a prominent acoustician, offers a succinct and lucid explanation:

The acoustic sensations in a cylindrical space are certainly marked… For a source at the centre of the cylinder, all sound is reflected back to the source. For a speaker or performer this would give the impression of sound appearing to come back from very close to [him]. For a source away from the centre, focusing of sound occurs according to a simple formula.[58]

Many will have experienced a comparable effect at the theater of Epidauros itself, where reflections from the semicircular cavea are concentrated at a central spot in the orchestra.

Certainly the focusing of sound reflections at the center of a (semi)circular or cylindrical space harmonizes well with the hypothesis of a musician standing in this same position, whether or not surrounded by a choral circle.[59] This was after all a traditional position for citharists and auletes

---

[57] See especially D'Errico and Lawson 2006. The basic problem is that "it is not sufficient to demonstrate that a site or structure…possesses acoustic properties for the argument to be made that sound was or must have been an important part of the activities and beliefs associated with that place" (Scarre 2006, 2).

[58] Barron, personal communication. He continues, "The effect of the 14 internal columns would be to disperse some of the sound within the space. To this extent it is counteracting the focussing effects but my guess is that the focussing would dominate."

[59] Schultz and Wickkiser 2010, 153–54; and above, Chapter Three.

accompanying circular choral song; it was an essentially practical arrangement, promoting a well-synchronized performance.⁶⁰ And it was from the central position in an orchestra that competitors in "thymelic" contests would no doubt mainly perform, since this best accounts for the term.⁶¹

The centripetal focusing of sound energy could very well have had the practical advantage of providing a central performer with a kind of monitor system. It is also quite conceivable that it could have been held to enhance the efficacy of any music-therapeutical undertakings in a "magical," circular space (one purpose suggested for the thymele space by the authors).⁶² This would be well in keeping with Greek ideas of divine epiphany, connected with the medium of music already in the late Bronze Age.⁶³ Presumably one would be dealing with a hieratic lyre-player comparable to, say, a member of the Euneidai at Athens, an obscure citharodic genos

---

⁶⁰ See esp. D'Angour 1997.

⁶¹ See esp. Phrynichos *Eclogae* 135 (ed. Fischer): Θυμέλην· τοῦτο οἱ μὲν ἀρχαῖοι ἀντὶ τοῦ θυσίαν ἐτίθεσαν, οἱ δὲ νῦν ἐπὶ τοῦ τόπου ἐν τῷ θεάτρῳ, ἐφ' οὗ αὐληταὶ καὶ κιθαρῳδοὶ καὶ ἄλλοι τινὲς ἀγωνίζονται, and cf. id. *Praep. Soph.* 74.9 (ed. de Borries): θυμέλη. νῦν μὲν θυμέλην καλοῦμεν τὴν τοῦ θεάτρου σκηνήν (though note the late date—second century CE). Cf. also the somewhat confused Isid. *Orig.* 18.47.1: Thymelici autem erant musici scenici qui in organis et lyris et citharis praecanebant. Et dicti thymelici quod olim in orchestra stantes cantabant super pulpitum, quod thymele uocabatur. These and other relevant passages are discussed by Gow 1912, 233–38; cf. Thiersch 1909, 39 n. 2.

⁶² Schultz and Wickkiser 2010, 153–56; and above, Chapter Four.

⁶³ Above, p. 25 n. 14, p. 71 n. 18, and p. 122 n. 8. See also Barron, personal communication: "The idea that paeans are directed towards a god at the centre of the space would be substantiated by the acoustic behaviour of the cylindrical form." Birds are often regarded as a sign of divine epiphany in Minoan/Mycenaean art, and appear in complex scenes containing lyrists, and as decorative elements on stringed-instruments themselves (as represented): Nilsson 1968, 330–40; Anderson 1994, 4–7, 12, 22. The special value of the Chania pyxis (Chania XM 2308, LM IIIB, c. 1275: Maas and Snyder 1989, 2, 16 and fig. 2b) is to isolate the two elements, lyre and divine, in a single composition, making the connection crystal clear.

from whose number the priest of Dionysos Melpomenos was drawn.[64] Kinyras, the early Cypriot lyre-god / lyre-priest, permits a very detailed case-study of how hieratic lyrists instantiated the god in whose service they performed; he is aptly depicted, by Pindar, as receiving praise at the center of a Cypriot chorus (*Pyth.* 2.15–17).[65] All of these suggestions may be made on the strength of the cylindrical cella itself, although they must remain inconclusive in the absence of corroborative evidence.

Let us now turn to the proposed acoustical function of the labyrinth and its hypothetical ἠχεῖα. According to Vitruvius's scheme, resonating vessels, though placed beneath seats or within niches, were nevertheless not strictly subterranean, as is suggested for the thymele: being positioned among the *rising* seats, they were able to receive the same direct sound energy that reached the audience. Yet the placement of resonators *beneath* a musical source is not inconceivable, since sound is propagated in three dimensions, as the Greek acousticians were well aware ([Arist.] *Prob.* 11.8: see above). It has been suggested, for instance, that the low wooden stage of the early Greek theater may have functioned thus as a "resonant chamber," and the analogous pit in the orchestra at Syracuse was noted above. One may compare the abundant evidence for ceramic vessels placed both beneath floors and in walls of medieval chapels and church choirs, well documented for France, England, and many other parts of Europe, including the Greek and Russian orthodox traditions.[66]

---

[64] Kearns 1989, 79; Burkert 1994.

[65] See further Franklin 2015, esp. Ch. 10.

[66] Lewcock, et al. 2007–2011. See, with further references, Hills 1882; McKenny Hughes 1915; Biddle 1962; Harrison 1967–1968; Lawson, et al. 1988, 188–89; Lawson 2006; Reznikoff 2006, 80–81, citing a recent unpublished dissertation. Because such practices are not mentioned in literary sources before the fifteenth century, some attribute them to the direct inspiration of Vitruvius and his survival through the monastic scribal tradition (McKenny Hughes 1915, 76; Harrison 1967–1968,

For vessels in a subterranean position to function, of course, there must be communication with the sound-producing agents, as was evidently the case in the relevant medieval contexts. Unfortunately the evidence of the thymele is not unambiguous on this point. The basic problem is to establish the nature of sonic interface—if any—between the cella and the labyrinth.

The cella floor was comprised of ornamental lozenges (17 cm thick) set upon a further layer of slabs (30–31 cm thick) resting directly upon the labyrinth walls, although the main weight-bearing work was performed by the circles beyond the maze.[67] Obviously such an arrangement would permit no direct passage of air between cella and labyrinth. While the impact of dance steps might still be transmitted into the labyrinth, the only possibility for the passage of music per se would be if there were some kind of aperture at the center of the floor.[68] Here three scenarios have been suggested:

1) Svolos's theory that the central capstone, plausibly identified from two surviving pieces, contained a hole in its center, of about 0.38 m in diameter.[69] Although his reconstruction was probably motivated by a desire to accommodate those who would see some definite function for the labyrinth, it is made plausible by the apparent absence of any remains

---

55–56). But the distribution of finds between churches east and west makes it very likely that we are dealing with a continuous tradition going back to antiquity (Reznikoff 2006, 80–81). Thus Vitruvius is not the source, but a common practice throughout the Greco-Roman world, almost certainly rooted specifically in theater architecture—the original "place of assembly." Yet another early method of "assisted resonance," anecdotally attested for secular buildings in early modern England, is the placement of horses' skulls beneath the floor of e.g. a house of musicians (Hills 1882; McKenny Hughes 1915).

[67] Roux 1961, 132–34; Tomlinson 1983, 65; Svolos 1988b, 278–81.
[68] Kanellopoulos and Lawson, personal communications.
[69] This figure, Fig. 12, is approximated from Svolos 1988b, 279 plan 25, in which the central capstone is restored from its remains.

belonging to the centermost position, combined with the fact that the two extant pieces exhibit a thinning towards, and apparently a slight curve around, the presumed center of the capstone.[70] At first glance, the reported thinning might suggest a purposeful "funneling" of sound, reminiscent of the "acoustic ports" in Wells Cathedral in Somerset, the "steeply conical" sides of which served as "a horn-mouth into which to sing."[71] But the 3–4 mm incline of the thymele capstone is probably too slight to have had any significant acoustical impact—nor even carry much weight in the argument for a central hole (Svolos himself recognized that the incline may not have been intentional).

2) The entire capstone was a later addition to an original opening of 1.236 m in diameter, covered perhaps by an ornamental grille.[72] While this would provide a significantly larger opening, it is probably ruled out by the beveling of the capstone, which was carefully shaped to fit the 4% grade of the surrounding ring of black marble, represented by seven pieces. In other words, the two elements were probably built at the same time and form an integral unit. By this arrangement the capstone was "simply slipped in"; it may or may not have then been clamped to the surrounding ring.[73]

3) The entire capstone was periodically raised for musical performance, once again giving an opening of 1.236 m. This does seem impractical, given the 700 kg calculated by Roux, who therefore rejected the idea that it was regularly removed.[74] It is hard to imagine that regular musical events were necessarily

---

[70] Svolos 1988b, 280–81.
[71] Lawson 2006, 89–93, quotation 91.
[72] Above, pp. 41-42 and 75.
[73] Svolos 1988b, 280.
[74] Roux 1961, 135–36: "Il est donc exclu qu'on ait soulevé cette dalle, étroitement

preceded by an adjustment which could not be effected "without a crane, or a tripod scaffold and pulley."[75] There is also the somewhat undignified problem of where and how to store such a large capstone during performances. For Roux, the immovability of the central stone led to his view that the sole function of the labyrinth was to support the ceiling slabs; its lighter-weight construction, by comparison with the three outer rings, would then be explained by the different loads each was designed to bear. It is true that concentric rings would be a natural shape for such a substructure to take within a circular building, with the doors simply a temporary means for workers to pass from one part to another. But Roux's hypothesis cannot explain why the "corridors" were not filled in, as was the case with the outer rings, in order to give additional support; this would certainly have been possible if laying of the lozenges proceeded from outwards in, as was evidently the case.[76]

So of the various scenarios permitting the flow of sound between cella and labyrinth, it is the first which best accords with the available evidence. That the labyrinth corridors were not filled after construction does suggest that some kind of continuous "access" was desired between cella and labyrinth. Yet with the most probable opening of 0.38 m, any regular descent by humans would have been very awkward at best, and impossible for many.

A potentially crucial point which has been overlooked is that the vertical faces of the labyrinth stones were further worked after extraction to obtain quite smoothly curved corridor walls.[77] This must be read against the fact,

---

ajustée au reste du dallage par un bandeau d'anathyrose, chaque fois que l'on devait descendre dans le labyrinthe." Note too that Roux believed there was the further impediment of a ceiling slab beneath the capstone (136); for this Svolos found no conclusive evidence (1988b, 281).

[75] Kanellopoulos, personal communication.

[76] Svolos 1988b, 248: "For greater stability the spaces between the rings were filled with scraps of bedrock, earth and porous limestone working chips."

[77] Svolos 1988b, 250.

established by Burford, that stone-work which would ultimately not be visible—notably foundations—was carried out by Epidaurians using local materials.[78] Money was thereby saved for the exterior decorative work in fine stone which was executed by highly skilled specialists brought in from Argos, Corinth, and Athens. If this principle was consistently applied, it should follow that the labyrinth was *never meant to be seen*. This would seem to exclude Kavvadias's theory of a maze used for mystic initiations.[79] One might counter that the chthonic gloom appropriate to catabatic wandering or incubation would excuse the absence of fine stone-work. But neither of these scenarios can account for the vertical smoothing of the walls, any better than that of Roux's.

Therefore the most economical interpretation of the physical evidence seems to indicate that (1) the labyrinth had a definite and ongoing purpose; (2) this function is inextricably related to its relatively costly shape; and (3) involved no significant *visual* experience. This combination of factors does accord rather well with an acoustical function—noting especially that dressed walls would benefit the propagation of sound.

Two complicating factors must be immediately noted.

A couple of horizontal cavities on the central ring wall were interpreted by F. Robert as beds to support a flight of wooden steps joining cella to labyrinth. Such a staircase would obviously partially obstruct the flow of sound between labyrinth and cella. Still, the interpretation is far from

---

[78] Burford 1969, 191–206; for the thymele itself, 155–56
[79] Kavvadias 1900, 75; see above, p. 24 n. 10. For Roux (1961, 136), the idea of a maze which began at the center and terminated in a cul-de-sac was improbable. That is hardly a fatal objection, however, since one's progress away from the light (and sound?) of the cella could be imagined as a *katabasis*, a descent, followed by a return to light and life. That said, if the labyrinth served such an important mystic function, it would surely have been constructed more monumentally.

certain.[80] The idea that it provided regular access to the labyrinth seems incompatible with the most plausible scenario canvassed above, that the capstone featured an aperture no larger than 0.38 m in diameter. One could also suppose that a staircase was part of the temporary arrangements during the construction of the labyrinth and laying of the lozenged floor, and was dismantled just before the capstone was inserted.

A second, similar issue is the idea of a musician straddling a central sounding hole, since some superstructure would have been needed to prevent his falling through. This is rather awkward for the hypothesis that the circular space was intended to concentrate sound reflections so that they might enter the labyrinth, as sound would necessarily be somewhat obstructed. Still, the problem is perhaps not fatal if the βῆμα were made sufficiently tall and/or permeable. The ornamental bronze grille proposed above by the authors might serve this purpose well.[81]

With this we come at last to the question of what specific effect the labyrinth may have had on the acoustics of the cella above. The two salient features are that the labyrinth maximizes corridor length, hence overall time and distance of sound propagation; and that it introduces a series of "kinks" into the sound-path. Initially this made me think a useful analogy could be a spring-reverberator, in which an audio signal, in the form of electrical oscillations, is sent down a length of wire which prolongs and alters it,

---

[80] Roux (1961, 135) believed them to be gouges left by metal-seekers. Tomlinson (1983, 61) was overly confident: "it is thus certain that it was intended that there should be access at the centre of the building through a hole in the floor (which may have had some form of trap door or cover over it)"; Svolos (1988b, 251), is more prudent, although he may also have in mind several further vertical bands mentioned by Roux when he refers to "discernible but difficult to interpret traces, obviously related to a construction whose form and purpose we continue to ignore."

[81] So above, pp. 41-42 and 75; wooden platform, Schultz and Wickkiser 2010, 154.

creating the illusion of a larger space.[82] But the acoustical models developed by Andrew Fermer of Hann Tucker Associates (whose sound files I have auditioned) indicate a rather different effect.[83] From various simulated positions within the space, and with the models for both the larger and more probable smaller openings (described above), there is a kind of damping effect on early sound reflections, so that a sound source (the models used male voice, female voice, and guitar) seems less "awash" in the space ("there are less early loud reflections which could be considered to disrupt the listening experience," as Fermer puts it).

It may be, therefore, that the labyrinth was intended to attenuate the acoustical effects of the circular space. These effects may have been desirable on the whole—hence the choice of a round building in the first place—but perhaps tended to "cloud" any music performed there, and so undermine the desire for λαμπρότης. Alternatively, a circular building may have been motivated more by a concern for sacred geometry or other esoteric reasons relating to Asklepios's cult; in this case, the labyrinth may have been introduced as a kind of acoustical corrective.

THE MARKS IN THE MAZE

The hypothesis of the labyrinth as an acoustical device does not depend on the existence of resonating vessels, since the structure may be so interpreted in its own right. But it would be very neatly proven if one could show that

---

[82] Cf. Nisbett 1965, 409: "The metal is differentially etched and notched along its length, so that its transmission characteristics change, with the effect that at each discontinuity there is a mismatch, and part of the sound is reflected. Each such reflection fathers its own family of subsequent echoes from all the other irregularly distributed discontinuities, and so the characteristics of reverberation are produced."

[83] See below, Appendix . One must bear in mind that the models could not account for the unknown design and construction of the thymele's ceiling.

the marks in the labyrinth were indeed a form of musical notation, as has been proposed.[84] One must consider first the case for and against the signs as masons' marks, the standard interpretation. Then they must be compared with the Greek notational system—which is now very well understood—to see what harmonic sense they might make, if any. Unfortunately, I feel, the evidence tells against the hypothesis.

A partial survey of the signs, which are confined to the lowest course of blocks in the inner three rings of the labyrinth, was offered by G. Roux, who interpreted them as "masons' marks." A more thorough collection was possible for Svolos, and confirmed the accuracy of Roux's initial observations.[85] The signs are presented here in Fig. 19, a map of the labyrinth upon which I have positioned Svolos's hand-copies of the signs, giving each an upright orientation for the reader's convenience (i.e. this is how each would look if one were facing the wall at the appropriate spot).[86] I also present them in tabular format, giving each an alphanumeric equivalent, for ease of reference in what follows.[87] Although the placement of signs gives a very random impression, they may have been more thoroughly distributed, some not surviving the erosion and weathering that may be observed both here and in other foundations of the Asklepieion.[88] Unfortunately it is now

---

[84] Schultz and Wickkiser 2010, 150; and above, pp. 78-83.
[85] Svolos 1988b, 253.
[86] Svolos 1988b, 310 plan 41.
[87] The letters in the top row (C, D, E, F) indicate the four rings progressing inwards; the outermost rings of the foundation (A and B) are not part of the labyrinth; I follow Roux's labeling: Svolos's Greek number-letters are potentially confusing since most of the *signs* are also Greek letters, or variations thereon, as are many of the music-notation symbols. My numbering of the signs proceeds from the door of each ring in a counterclockwise direction. Question marks indicate either Svolos's own insecurity, or fairly certain deductions required by omissions or inconsistencies in Svolos's own diagrams.
[88] For Sanctuary Y, see Roux 1961, 279–82.

impossible to double-check, since the labyrinth has been "fully reconstructed and capped with ceiling and paver."[89] Still, there is no reason to doubt the thoroughness and accuracy of Svolos's collection per se (beyond a few minor typographical slips: see below).

So-called "masons' marks" occur in five main categories—"quarry marks, contractors' marks, suppliers' marks, marks for inventory purposes, assembly marks."[90] Very often these marks are epichoric letter forms. Their form is sometimes archaic compared to contemporary monumental forms, due to provinciality and/or conservatism within a workshop. They may also be abstract symbols.[91] On the whole, the labyrinth signs appear to be letters (some apparent exceptions may be ligatures: see below). It is indeed quite clear that the labyrinth signs are not "assembly marks," indicating the order blocks were to be placed, and typically following an alphabetic sequence.[92] That practice may be seen in many Greek monuments—extensively and spectacularly in the ceiling of the Hephaisteion in Athens—and is found in Sanctuary Y of the Asklepieion itself, where the letters are neatly carved, carefully placed, and consistently oriented.[93] But such a system would not have been necessary in the labyrinth, since the blocks of each ring were of uniform size, and thus largely interchangeable.[94] It is certainly inaccurate to call the marks in Sanctuary Y "very similar" to those in the labyrinth: not only do the latter not follow any clear alphabetic order, they were only

---

[89] Kanellopoulos, personal communication.
[90] Cooper 1995, 354; see generally Martin 1965, 221–31.
[91] Martin 1965, 222; Wyatt and Edmonson 1984, 143, 146, 156; similarly at Pompeii: see e.g. Marriott 1895, 62–85.
[92] Above, p. 79 n. 45.
[93] Wyatt and Edmonson 1984, esp. 141–66; Roux 1961, 280 and fig. 80; and above, p. 79, n. 45.
[94] Roux 1961, 133; Svolos 1988b, 251.

roughly gouged into the stones.⁹⁵ And their placement on each block varies very considerably.

It is this last feature especially which has prompted comparison with the Greek musical notation.⁹⁶ But many of the specific "rotations" in the labyrinth signs are not found in the canonical notation, on which more in a moment. Moreover, retrograde letters are quite common among masons' marks. At the temple of Apollo at Bassai (Arcadia, ca. 427–400 BCE), for instance, one finds among the roof tiles a number of forms which parallel those of the labyrinth, e.g. retrograde E and rotated Δ — to choose only examples of letters also found in the thymele.⁹⁷ Furthermore, some apparent labyrinth rotations would disappear if the blocks were flipped over, as might naturally have occurred since this would make no practical difference given the blocks' uniform shape and size. Although other rotations cannot be so eliminated, if the signs are interpreted not as assembly marks but suppliers' initials (see below) one may readily suppose that they were applied with only partial consistency as to position and alignment, since those dimensions would not introduce any meaningful information.⁹⁸ This too would

---

⁹⁵ So Burford 1969, 68. One might try to read F3-2-1 as sequential if F3 could be taken as Γ; but that this is random is strongly suggested by the absence of any other three-sign sequence. See also Roux 1961, 134 n. 5.

⁹⁶ See above, pp. 78-83.

⁹⁷ Cooper 1995, 357–60; Π, Λ, and perhaps I are also found, though not rotated.

⁹⁸ Thus for instance if the block containing F4 were flipped, both rotation and position on block would become the same as the F1 block, and the same may be said of D8 and D6 which contain the same letter in the same position as F1/F4 (all being varieties of epsilon; F5 would exhibit the same orientation and placement at block-end, but its vertical positioning would be slightly different). On the assumption of contractors'/suppliers' marks, this seems to suggest a fairly consistent practice by the owner of this particular initial; yet it would not be absolutely consistent, since it does not work for D2 and E9, where the initial position is 90 degrees off from F1, F4 and F5. C1, C4 and C5 (variations of Π) are equally inconsistent. E1 and F3 (variations of Λ) are consistent in rotation but not placement.

accord with their rough gouging. The Bassai tiles also contain letters modified by diacritics, e.g. an E with a stroke is perhaps a ligature of E and Λ, and a Γ is similarly modified. Compare signs E4, 6 and 7 (see Figs. 22-23), which appear to be ligatures of Δ and perhaps I; and D9, which Roux interpreted as a ligature of A and P (for possible identifications, see below).[99]

When such letters are clearly not assembly marks, it is often possible to interpret them as the initials of contractors and suppliers. They were typically applied to blocks at the moment of extraction, in order to verify work and ultimately to facilitate accurate collection of payment from commissioners.[100] There is a clear case at Delphi, where names from the accounts of the temple builders (*naopoioi*) can be well matched to initials on the blocks of the fourth-century temple to Apollo.[101] These initials can be found on blocks scattered throughout the site. A revealing diagnostic case is an Argive supplier named Pangrates, recorded as delivering stones for three different projects and clearly identifiable among the marks since he used the first three letters of his name. Because his siglum is found alongside those of other suppliers "within the same category of architectural members," it is clear that, in some cases, "a need for contractors' marks arises when *multiple suppliers* contribute stone or finished blocks for specific parts of the building."[102]

The Delphic material thus offers a useful control for the multiple marks in the labyrinth. We are not necessarily dealing with multiple contractors *working* side-by-side, but multiple contractors supplying materials, the

---

[99] Roux 1961, 134 n. 5. Letters modified by diacritical "flags" are found at Pergamon; but there the letters are certainly assembly marks, and the flags serve to distinguish one alphabetic series from another: Bohn 1896, 58–62, with plate before 59.

[100] Martin 1965, 222.

[101] Martin 1965, 222.

[102] Cooper 1995, 359, my emphasis.

assembly of which was then supervised by a single contractor.[103] The latter was presumably the Eunikos who was fined for some reason related to the horizontal dressing of stone for the foundations of the thymele (*IG* 4² 1, 103 A 19: παρ' Εὐνίκου ἐπιτιμὰν τᾶς στοιβᾶς ἐπιξοᾶς ἀπήν[ικε). On the other hand, Roux has plausibly conjectured that this event was related to a hold-up in work on the outer rings.[104] If this is right, Eunikos may have had nothing to do with the labyrinth per se (as Burford believed), the construction of which (materials, technique) shows that it was built at a slightly later stage than the weight-bearing outer rings.[105] As Svolos pointed out, this chronological discrepancy, and the differences in material, may well explain why three of the letters found in ring C (Π, Γ and I [?]) do not reappear in rings D–F.[106] This would also, perhaps helpfully, reduce the number of simultaneous marks to a maximum of four (although there may have been further marks which do not survive on other stones). And as we shall see, the concentration of signs into several recurring groups also favors the hypothesis of "masons' marks" over musical notation.

More precise understanding of the contracting for the thymele's foundation is maddeningly elusive, given the state of the building accounts. Years two through eight, and possibly one or two more, are lost in a lacuna of 100 lines.[107] This is precisely the period in which the substructure was executed by local Epidaurian contractors (see above); when the inscription

---

[103] Although note, for instance, that Cooper 1995, 1:364 identified six master craftsmen (and crews) working together on the pteroma ceilings at Bassai.

[104] Roux 1961, 173, connecting it with the penalty against Arisophanes, a Corinthian contractor, for retarding work on the peristasis (*IG* 4² 1, 103, A 49; Burford 1969, 238).

[105] Burford 1969, 66.

[106] Svolos 1988b, 251, 257 n. 19.

[107] Burford 1966, 278; Burford 1969, 220.

resumes the project has moved on to quarrying, transport, and assembly of Corinthian and Argive stone (A 9–15)—that is, the finer materials and work which were used for the upper, conspicuous structure—followed by two penalties for work on the substructure (A 16–19), including the one against Eunikos. The gap leaves space aplenty for the specification of contracts to stone suppliers and carters, and the two separate phases of ring-work.

One can hardly hope to offer unambiguous matches between the labyrinth marks and the known names of Epidaurian contractors. Comparison of the accounts for the various buildings of the sanctuary shows that it was fairly common—as one would anyway expect—for contractors to work on different projects, or different phases of the same project, at various times. It is also clear that the career of a given contractor might span twenty-five years and more. The pool of potential contractors therefore becomes quite large, and of course it is likely enough that other contractors listed in the lacuna did not appear elsewhere in the building accounts. Nevertheless, one may offer the following observations and informed speculations by way of example, and to demonstrate the general viability of interpreting the marks as name-initials.

With the exception of Γ, and leaving aside the uncertain reading I, most of the letters—that is, A, Δ, E, Λ and Π—are among the best represented initial letters in the Greek onomasticon. These five fall within the more "productive" half of the alphabet, to judge from the prosopography of the Asklepieion building accounts themselves.[108] Although this is a very small sample by comparison with the total prosopographic material so far assembled for the Greek world, it has the advantage of eliminating geographical and temporal variables; it may also help account for local naming fashions

---

[108] Following the very nearly complete catalogues of Burford 1966, 324–28; Burford 1969, 237–45.

prevalent among men of the appropriate professions and positions.[109] This "coincidence" of initials and name-distribution, by itself, provides strong support for the interpretation of the marks as name-initials.

Moving on to specific identifications, note first that the use of local contractors for foundation work (see above) lets us exclude the proposal of Roux to see two Corinthian stone suppliers, Euterpidas and Archikles, behind respectively the various forms of E and the sign D9, which he interpreted as a ligature of A + P (see above).[110] While both are mentioned in the Asklepios temple accounts (IG 4² 1, 102, A 12–14, 14–16), in each case the contracted stone was destined *specifically for the temple cella*—thus nicely confirming Burford's principle that visible stonework was entrusted to foreign specialists. Conversely, it was an Epidaurian, Mnasikles, who was contracted "to quarry, cart, and set in place the foundation core of the colonnade" (A 1–3, trans. Burford). An easier identification for E is therefore Eunikos himself, if one can suppose that his work on the foundation did indeed extend to the labyrinth proper, as is likely enough; and if he, like Mnasikles on the temple, was also contracted to supply stone.

It is equally tempting to connect Λ (signs E1 [?] and F3) with the Lysikrates who sat on the "finance board" for the thymele (IG 4², 1 103 A 6). As Burford maintained, discussing Lysikrates specifically, "a man influential enough to become head of the finance board (as priest) would in many ways be well qualified to act as entrepreneur for a big supply contract."[111] On this basis she convincingly identified him with the Lysikrates who had

---

[109] Fraser and Matthews 1987–2010. But there is a counteracting factor: as noted by Burford (1969), contractors were in general of lower social status than guarantors, katalogoi, members of finance boards, and building commissioners; and these social distinctions were partially reflected in naming trends.

[110] Roux 1961, 134 n. 5, followed by Svolos 1988b, 257 n. 21

[111] Burford 1969, 223, cf. 120

been contracted "to quarry, cart, and set in place the foundation core of the pavement" for the Asklepios temple (*IG* 4² 1, 102, A 31–3, trans. Burford). If this is the same Lysikrates who managed finances for the thymele, nothing would be more natural than for him to supply for the new building the same materials he had for the temple foundation. To be sure, there is a potential conflict of interest here, the avoidance of which is basic to Burford's methodology when attempting to identify two instances of the same name.[112] Yet here the lacuna offers a helpful escape: the gap of six to eight years would allow Lysikrates an easy transition from finance board back to contractor. Indeed one might reasonably speculate that it was his successful execution of the contract for the temple foundation, perhaps only five years earlier, which secured him the honor of overseeing the initial stages of this next important building project.

Further identifications must begin from known contractors, who should in general take precedence over the various attested building commissioners, finance board-members, guarantors, and κατάλογοι. While administrative officers are sometimes found elsewhere as contractors (for instance the Lysikrates just discussed), such "cross-over" was relatively infrequent (20% or less), a predictable symptom of class distinctions.[113] For convenience and *exempli gratia* we may restrict ourselves here to those contractors connected with other phases of work on the thymele itself, and on the nearly contemporary Asklepios temple. Eliminating those not concerned with stone-work, and those whose initials are not represented by the labyrinth marks, we are left with only the following candidates. From the thymele, besides the Eunikos already discussed, one finds an Episthenes (*IG* 4², 1 103 A 23, B 98) receiving stone from a Phylios, presumably a

---

[112] For the case of Charikleidas, see Burford 1966, 278 (ad l. 8c); Burford 1969, 133.
[113] Burford 1969, 222–36, esp. 230–31.

Corinthian or Argive supplier.[114] There is also a Glaukos who was paid for "unloading stones at the harbor" (Γλαύκωι παρκαλίσιος τῶν λίθων ἐπὶ λιμένι, A 63), and presumably transporting them to the site. Neither figure is here a supplier of stone, only a handler; but that is expected at this stage of the project, when the substructure was complete. Clearly a local contractor skilled in transporting stone had prior experience, and this must have come from delivering stone locally. Perhaps we need not assume that such handlers were invariably quarriers too; could Epidauros have supported seven such entrepreneurs? Some stone-carters may have been rather middle-men who put their own initials on a load. From the temple, one may note (H) ektoridas (*IG* 4² 1, 102, B I 89) and Eudamos (A I 47, B II, 258), although their activities—pediment sculpting and stele-work—perhaps put them a notch higher than needed here.[115]

Further possibilities come from attested administrative officers who may have served as contractors at other times. For convenience, I limit myself here to officers appearing in the records of the thymele itself, with names whose initials may match the letters of the labyrinth (of names in A-, I include only those in Αρ-, following Roux's interpretation of D9 as a ligature of A + P: see above.) Many known as contractors from other projects are readily disqualified for not having worked in stone.[116] A second round eliminates individuals known to have served two administrative roles, since this indicates a qualification of civic prominence

---

[114] Burford 1969, 245.

[115] The temple's stone-workers are discussed as a group by Baunack (1890, 49–51), although one must beware outdated readings. There is also Asphaltos, who supplied stone for a threshold (B II, 247: Ἀσφάλτωι λίθων ὑπὸ τὸν ὀδόν, omitted from Burford's translation [1969, 218]). But D9, as noted above, is probably a ligature of A + P. For an appropriate identification, see below.

[116] Aristodamos, Damagetos, Damophanes, Euainos, Eubolos (via family connection to timber contractor), Eukrates.

rather than contracting experience.[117] Another, Damokritos, can be ruled out for being a building commissioner when fines were issued for the foundation-work: presumably he was not himself implicated. One viable candidate may be Eukles, a member of the thymele finance board whom Burford identifies with a homonymous stone contractor from the building account for a fountain house.[118] There is also the katalogos Archias, if he is indeed the father of the homonymous akroterion-worker on an unknown project a generation later.[119] If one may interpret sign E4, 6 or 7 as a ligature of Δ and Ι, one could see here Dionysodoros, the only name in Di- connected with the thymele (*IG* 4², 1 103 A 147). There remain, beside these, six candidates in Ἀρ-, two in Δ-, seven in Ε-, four in Λ-, and four in Π.[120] So there are very many possibilities for connecting the labyrinth signs to Epidaurians involved in the project.

The local nature of the foundation work is also helpful for narrowing down the analysis of letter-forms. The early Epidaurian repertoire exhibits sympathies with those of Argos, the eastern Argolid (Methana, Troizen and Hermione, which do not use the Argive alphabet), and Lakonia (which influenced the eastern Argolid scripts).[121] Leaving out the potential ligatures, and ignoring rotations, comparison with the relevant tables in

---

[117] Alexikles, Aristandros, Aristokrates, Aristokritos, Aristomedes, Damokrines, Damopeithes, and Damophilos.

[118] Comprised of several fragments, which she groups as her text IV in Burford 1966 and Burford 1969. For Eukles, A 19 (ἀγωγᾶς λίθων), though note the alternative reading of Peek 1969.

[119] See Burford 1969, 232, Table XX.

[120] These are: Aristaichmos, Archeleidas, Arist—, Aristainos, Aristoteles, Aristolochos; Damaretos, Damastas; Eudamos, Eukles (2), Eumenon, Eurymedes, Eusthenes, Euchares, Echetimos; Lakritos, Lentinos, Lysicrates (see above), Le—; Pantakles, Polykles, Pyrrhen, Pythôn.

[121] Jeffery 1990, 179–81.

Jeffery reveals nothing that cannot be paralleled. Some of the forms do belong on the earlier end of the scale, yet as noted above, such archaism can indeed be the case with conservative "masons' marks."[122]

That the signs only appear on the lowest course of stones is explicable by the fact that only these blocks were covered by earth, while the vertical faces of the upper courses all received on-site finishing, effacing any initials applied at time of extraction.[123]

There remains, admittedly, the puzzle that two signs (F2/3) were carved on a single block. Pairs of letters are not uncommon among masons' marks elsewhere, although typically they are the first two letters of a name, comparable to the ligatures just discussed, or a double alphabetic sequence for locating blocks on an X-Y grid.[124] Still, the two letters in question are also found among the identifications just proposed, including the likely Lysikrates. As suggested above, a stone-carter might apply his own initial to a shipment of stone which he did not himself quarry; conceivably this might lead to two separate initials. I shall refrain from contriving further scenarios. But since we are still so ignorant about processes underlying the field of "masons' marks," it would be rash to reject the present interpretation of the signs as a whole on the basis of a single enigmatic case, in the face of so much else that makes sense. Given the complex interconnections of contractors, suppliers, and other agents involved in such large building projects, one should not be surprised if marks appear in a variety of baffling configurations. Fred Cooper, for instance, although able to prove

---

[122] Comparison is somewhat hindered, especially in the case of delta, by the "rotated" forms of the labyrinth. Note also that the pis in the labyrinth have the full shape of Π, whereas those in the official thymele accounts have a shortened right leg.

[123] Svolos 1988b, 251–53.

[124] See e.g. Cooper 1995, 355, 359 and Wyatt and Edmonson 1984, 144.

that the marks on the pteroma ceiling at Bassai were not assembly-marks but suppliers' initials, still could not discern any clear system, and concluded: "A random mason's mark on a foundation block, or architectural member, therefore, can represent, at this stage of our understanding, almost anything."[125]

All told, then, the labyrinth signs can be well accounted for by their usual interpretation as masons' or suppliers' marks. For the sake of completeness, however, and for those not yet convinced, let us now compare the signs' behavior with that of the Greek musical notation, as presently understood (which is very well).

Vitruvius complained that "*Harmonia* is a dark and difficult musical literature—very much so, indeed, for those who do not know Greek."[126] After some twenty-five centuries it is still more obscure. Nevertheless, the basic principles of Greek musical notation have been well grasped now for many generations; and the past thirty years have seen increasingly detailed and exhaustive study of Greek musical theory and practice, culminating in a spate of useful handbooks and now an exhaustive, ground-breaking study by S. Hagel.[127] So we now understand fairly well the diachronic development not only of the notation, but the underlying tonal structures of the music, with which the notation itself co-evolved. The evidence indicates clearly that the formative period of both the notation and the musical system for which it was designed was the fifth and early fourth centuries—as the tonal resources of the "modern" αὐλός, and its ability to effect modulations, expanded in the hands of innovators like Pronomos of The-

---

[125] Cooper 1995, 359 and 365.

[126] Vitr. 5.4.1: harmonia autem est musica litteratura obscura et difficilis, maxime quidem quibus graecae litterae non sunt notae.

[127] Esp. West 1992; Hagel 2009.

bes (ca. 470–390).[128] It is impractical here to present even the most concise introduction to these matters. I shall simply lay out the principal arguments for and against seeing the signs as musical notation. Those for whom my (mainly negative) conclusions remain opaque must wrestle with the standard works on the subject.[129]

We may observe first that even if the signs *are* drawn from the musical notation, their physical placement rules out an interpretation as music per se. The great majority of the Greek musical documents are vocal scores, in which poetic texts are accompanied by melodies more or less syllable-by-syllable, with the appropriate notation symbol being positioned over the text.[130] A few brief instrumental pieces survive, but these comprise a continuous stream of symbols on a manuscript page; that is, they are intended to be read in steady sequence. With a single sign placed on a single block, one could only be dealing with some sort of tonal "map."

Given this, the proposed hypothesis that they mark the placement of resonators is not in itself unreasonable. Yet the arrangement in three concentric corridors, which at first seems a striking reminiscence of Vitruvius's triple-tiered scheme, is a red herring. The problem is not that we have here a full circuit, versus a semicircular cavea: the archaeological evidence for niches and acoustic jars, such as it is, indicates considerable variety, so that one readily expects a site-specific installation. It is the labyrinth itself which invalidates the analogy. Vitruvius arrays his resonators in an evenly spaced and widening cone, so that the whole audience could enjoy the resonant effects

---

[128] Pronomos: Paus. 9.12.5; Ath. 631e; for his dates, see now Wilson 2007.

[129] For an introduction to the notation and key systems, West 1992; Landels 1999; for the evolution of both, Hagel 2009; for primary theoretical texts upon which the constructions are based, in English translation, with commentary and cross-references, Barker 1984–1989; for the extant scores, Pöhlmann and West 2001.

[130] Pöhlmann and West 2001.

as sound traveled outwards (subject of course to the lottery of actual tones played or sung by a musician). The maze, however, despite its circular shape, presents a sound-source in the cella with a single continuous corridor down which to travel. While this might produce an interesting effect in itself, it invalidates a strict analogy with the Roman architect's tripartite scheme.

Also problematic is that the marks, on the lowest course of stones, would have been beneath the level of the soil (see above) and thus invisible after completion of the thymele. Therefore musical signs so placed could not have served any *long-term* purpose. One would then have to presume that they marked an initial placement, intended to be unchanging. Yet how could the vessels be placed before the ground level was itself established— at which point the marks would be hidden? This problem disappears if the signs are regarded as contactors' marks.

Let us now compare the labyrinth signs to those of the Greek notation, in both its vocal and instrumental versions (Figs. 22-23).[131] One should stress first that, because the vocal notation is based upon the alphabet, all "masons' marks" which use Greek letters—i.e. the vast majority—have the potential to resemble the musical notation, at least superficially. By contrast, the oldest core of the older instrumental notation, as Hagel has recently shown, is rooted in the simplest signs which may be rotated with the least potential for ambiguity; but because of the limited number of simple stroke combinations, some of these also resemble (and may sometimes derive from) Greek letters. So it is no surprise that some of the labyrinth signs can be mapped onto the notation, both vocal and instrumental. The question is whether any coherent pattern emerges.

---

[131] The underlying notation diagram in the figures is taken from Hagel 2000, a revised version of which (with a few minor corrections) may now be found in Hagel 2009.

With a newly discovered musical score, one must first determine which kind of notation is being used, vocal or instrumental (some signs are shared, with different tonal values). With the labyrinth signs, no consistent identification is possible. Many have no counterpart in either system. Others seem initially promising, yet the specific rotation is not found among the notation. One can hardly get around this difficulty by appeal to flipped blocks (a likely enough procedure per se, posited above in support of "masons' marks.") While interchangeable blocks might be installed pell-mell for building a wall, the notation system permits no such flexibility. One would have to suppose the careless handling of blocks and signs precisely in a context where care was most needed. Considering the sumptuousness of the thymele as a whole, and the high cost which would be incurred by a large system of bronze resonators, no chances would have been taken with such an installation.

Matters are not much improved when one considers only those labyrinth signs which *do* have a counterpart in the notation (whichever set). One looks first to see if they fall within a single pitch-key, as is the case with the majority of the surviving musical documents (from the Roman-era); similarly, Vitruvius's placement scheme supposes resonators corresponding to the tones of a single key, the central Lydian which was the most commonly used by musicians through the history of the notation.[132] Yet for the thymele signs no single key emerges, in either vocal or instrumental notation.

Still, pieces from the Classical and Hellenistic periods were more complex, and typically involved some amount of modulation between keys. The best example is the first Delphic hymn by Athenaios, though the same tonal diversity is evident even in quite small fragments from the Hellenistic

---

[132] Hagel 2009, 291–95.

period.¹³³ Once one widens the net in this way, it does become possible to accommodate the subset of labyrinth marks which do match the notation symbols in various more or less plausible combinations of keys (for example Lydian and Hypodorian or Dorian in the instrumental system.) Yet since so many cannot be matched *at all*, the only way to save the hypothesis is to suppose that the labyrinth signs represent an earlier stage in the development of notation, and/or some epichoric variant. Such a retreat position is both uneconomical and would require special pleading. Still, for the sake of completeness, one may note the following.

First, the thymele is early enough that the scenario of alternative notation and key systems is not inconceivable. Our earliest specimen (the *Orestes* fragment of Euripides) goes back only to a third-century BCE papyrus.¹³⁴ Although much of the standard notation system had evolved by the time of the thymele, it is possible that some shapes and conventions of rotation were not yet fully crystallized.¹³⁵ The most tangible example here would be the set of three rotated symbols, marked in Fig. 22 with a larger circle and question mark. There is general scholarly agreement that these evolved from an earlier, more ambiguous sign featuring an acute angle. This sign, it has been plausibly suggested, was some form of delta, originating as an abbreviation of διάτονος (sc. λιχανός)—the degree below the central tone μέση—in the basic Lydian key.¹³⁶ How difficult it would be to give delta, in its normal triangular form, three unambiguous rotations may be judged from the considerable variety found in the deltas of the labyrinth. Similarly, one might attempt to match the various diacritics which modify

---

¹³³ Pöhlmann and West 2001, no. 20. See analysis in Hagel 2000; Hagel 2002; Hagel 2009, 256–324.

¹³⁴ Pöhlmann and West 2001, no. 3.

¹³⁵ Hagel 2009, 1–52.

¹³⁶ Hagel 2009, 367; cf. West 1992, 38.

the labyrinth-deltas by appeal to the strokes which appear in the notation, which originated probably as a means of designating octave harmonics on the lyre (since these symbols stand an octave apart from the same ones without strokes).[137] Finally, it is known that, prior to Aristoxenos, there were several competing tonos-systems, in which keys were positioned at different relative intervals than they occupy in the canonical Aristoxenian scheme. Given a fixed notation system, these could be unambiguously represented. But since the key and notations systems certainly co-evolved, one may easily imagine a time in the later fifth and early fourth centuries when there existed divergent systems of notation, answering to competing representations of modern modulating music. Both of the known obsolete key systems did involve the incorporation of keys which in the later canonical system occurred immediately "to the right" of the basic Lydian (i.e. Hypophrygian, Phrygian, Hypodorian, Dorian). This might in turn give some distant hope for the thymele signs, since some of them find matches in this same area of the standard notation.

Still, Epidauros seems an unlikely location to posit a semi-independent epichoric key/notation system. Political and musical sympathies with Athens (see above) would suggest conformity with the Attic paradigm, which proved to dominate the notation's evolution (as one may reasonably infer from the facts of Greek musical history in the fifth and fourth centuries.) A more attractive contender for a vigorous epichoric system would be nearby Argos, an important center of musical innovation in the later sixth century (probably involving Lasus of Hermione among others.)[138] Moreover, this was the home of Polykleitos the Younger, the probable thymele architect; he, if anybody, would have assigned resonators to their posi-

---

[137] Hagel 2009, 32, with older references.
[138] Cf. Hdt. 3.131–32; Franklin 2013, 222–26.

tions. And yet the letter-forms themselves rule out a purely Argive or Attic origin, whereas they are consistent with signs that would be used by local stone-contractors, as noted above.

The relative weighting and distribution of the signs also tells against the hypothesis. In the Vitruvian scheme, we have seen, the resonators are deployed so that the most important tones of contemporary music would be equally emphasized, while their arrangement provides even coverage of the space. Neither tendency may be inferred for the labyrinth marks. There are, first, suspicious clusters of the same sign (e.g. C4–C5, and the many delta variants in ring E). Then, if one were to suppose that this installation was designed to meet the requirements of some early, lost modulating system, one would expect an increased variety of signs by comparison with a single key installation (à la Vitruvius), since two keys would introduce further tones needing resonator coverage. In other words, as one attempts to accommodate the data by introducing more flexibility in matching signs with keys, the solution becomes proportionally less likely due to the limited repertoire of the given signs themselves. Moreover, according to Vitruvian logic, one would expect that the standing tones of whatever keys were involved would be best represented; but again, no such pattern emerges from the standard notation.

One might attempt to avoid this crux by supposing the selection of resonators to be highly idiosyncratic, suited to the very particular requirements of some one form of music, presumably some specific cult repertoire. Yet even this is unlikely, since what hints of specific tones there might be in the labyrinth signs (when interpreted as standard notation) suggest nothing like anything that we know about Greek music in this period—which after all is now not inconsiderable. And while what Aristoxenos (fr. 83 Wehrli = [Plut.] *De mus.* 1135a) tells us about the intervallic and modal structure of traditional libation music might indeed support the idea of a limited, static cult repertoire, there is a powerful counterexample in Pindar, one of the great old masters of paeanic composition, who regularly promoted the progressive novelty of his music.[139]

◫ ◫ ◫

All told, therefore, the hypothesis of resonators placed in the labyrinth according to the marks is probably not viable. The standard interpretation as "masons' marks" finds good parallels, and even if one cannot fully grasp the logic of their distribution (especially the two signs appearing on a single block), such obscurity is commonly encountered in similar cases where one is certainly not dealing with musical notation. On the other hand, that the labyrinth itself had an intentional acoustic function does seem to accord fairly well with the thymele's position in the development of Greek acoustical theory and design practice, and with the more concrete archaeological evidence of the structure itself. This latter conclusion here is based on a line of argument independent of the more general considerations that the authors have offered in support of the thymele as a performing space. When the material is taken all together, the hypothesis of a musical function for the building, and an acoustical role for the "labyrinth," does seem more cogent and compelling than any other interpretation yet offered.

---

[139] Franklin 2013, 225–26.

Conclusions and Beginnings

The end is the beginning of all things, suppressed and hidden,
awaiting to be released through the sacred rhythms...
Jiddu Krishnamurti

Sometime around 300 BCE, a young woman named Andromache and her husband, Arybbas, arrived at the sanctuary of Asklepios and Apollo in Epidauros. She was having trouble conceiving a child and had traveled from the town of Epirus, more than a month's journey distant, to seek aid from Asklepios and Apollo. As Andromache and Arybbas walked through the temenos, they marveled at the amazing buildings and monuments they saw, from baths, fountain houses, and hostels, to a stadium, temples with gilded statues, a magnificent theater, and a luminous round building, a large tholos unlike any they had ever seen before. They smelled the smoke and burning flesh of animals being sacrificed on an altar. Water splashed from a bronze statue of Asklepios standing in front of his temple. They also were careful to stop and inspect the wide range of votive reliefs dedicated by grateful worshippers who had been healed by the gods. One that especially fascinated Andromache showed a woman with her newborn son bathing in a fountain. Andromache and Arybbas felt more hopeful seeing how powerful and wonderful the healing gifts of Asklepios and Apollo could be. They just might have a child after all!

A robed priest greeted them and explained that it was time for Andromache to enter the stoa where she would sleep and begin her sacred therapy. Andromache knew that Asklepios or Apollo might come to her in a dream, if she was lucky. Her heart fluttered, not knowing what to expect, but she was hopeful and grateful for the opportunity. She had tried almost everything else to become pregnant.

As she prepared for sleep, Arybbas remained outside the stoa to worship and pray. A group of women, perhaps two dozen of them, dressed in rich, colorful fabrics, processed to the center of the temenos and formed a circle around the altar across from the tholos—the thymele, as it was called, Arybbas had learned. A musician began plucking the strings of his lyre, and the women started singing, moving around the altar in unison, circling it several times before they made their way into the thymele. In wonder, Arybbas listened to this beautiful music and noticed that many other worshippers, some of them clearly suffering and searching for a cure, were now following the chorus towards the thymele. He recognized among these worshippers a certain man whom he had met earlier, named Hagestratos, who had explained that he suffered from debilitating headaches and hadn't been able to sleep well for years. So great was his distress that he had decided to travel to Epidauros from Knidos, on the other side of the Aegean Sea.

Arybbas decided to follow Hagestratos, the chorus, and the other worshippers into the thymele. What would happen next? he wondered. The music continued as the lyre player walked towards the center of the building. Arybbas found a spot to stand just beyond the chorus, who had formed a ring again, this time around the musician. A swirling pattern of black and white tiles on the floor mesmerized him as he watched the dancers circling the musician, moving back and forth around him, singing all the while. The sound of the music was indescribable; Arybbas felt it resonate deeply within him. He glanced towards Hagestratos and saw a radiant smile spread across his face. Asklepios was indeed in their midst!

Next door to the thymele, Andromache lay on a pallet in one of the stoa's rooms, waiting anxiously for sleep to come. Her body shook with expectation. An attendant came by, patted her arm, reassuring. Andromache willed her eyes to shut. Eventually the dulcet sounds of the lyre and the soothing voices of the singing women began to drift over her. It seemed as if this music was coming from some place nearby, close but distant—a sound of unsurpassed tranquility. She had never heard anything like it. Little by little, she relaxed and fell into a deep sleep….

When day broke, Andromache awoke with great joy and rushed outside the stoa to find her husband and to tell him what had happened: she had dreamed! In the dream, the gentle god had visited her and touched her with his healing hand. Andromache and Arybbas rejoiced, thanking Asklepios and Apollo profusely by offering more sacrifices, singing hymns alongside other grateful worshippers around the gods' altars, and dedicating a votive plaque in celebration of Andromache's encounter with Asklepios, that would be placed near the stoa and thymele. Within a year she gave birth to a son.[1]

---

[1] The scenario described here is based in large part on healing narratives recovered from the sanctuary. A certain Andromache and Arybbas from Epirus did visit Epidauros in the hopes of conceiving a child; Andromache dreamed that the god came to her and touched her with his hand, and within a year she gave birth to a son (IG 4^2 1, 122.60-63). Another woman, Kleo, gave birth to a son immediately after a dream in the sanctuary (though in this case she was pregnant for a very long time rather than trying to conceive), and she dedicated a votive plaque (*pinax*) in thanks to the god (IG 4^2 1, 121.3-9). A man named Hagestratos came to the sanctuary seeking a cure for severe headaches accompanied by chronic insomnia (IG 4^2 1, 122.50-54); we do not know where his hometown was, but it was not uncommon for worshippers to travel great distances. For example, another devotee (Antikrates) did travel to Epidauros from Knidos (IG 4^2 1, 122.63-68) in the fourth century. The monuments mentioned are attested in the archaeological record, including the statue of Asklepios that poured water from a phiale held by the hand of the god (Lambrinoudakis 2014, 22). The part of the scenario described here that remains conjectural is how music might have been performed in and around the thymele and how this music in turn might have affected or enhanced cures for worshippers like Andromache and Hagestratos. Highly relevant to this scenario is the fact that some modern therapies for infertility, for insomnia, and for headaches incorporate music.

◫ ◫ ◫

Sometime around 2500 BCE, the ambitious members of a Bronze Age community in what we now call south central Wiltshire hauled thirty enormous stones from the quarries at Marlborough Downs to an imposing burial mound near modern Amesbury. There, atop centuries of detritus, these massive blocks were erected to create what would later become known as Stonehenge. While the theories and evidence regarding Stonehenge's "original function" are conflicting and complex, recent archaeoacoustical studies leave no doubt that the pattern and disposition of the henge's circle of stones created an intentional, dynamic soundscape—a soundscape that would have produced a distinct and mystical effect in the ears and minds of ancient peoples—a soundscape that would have served to connect ancient listeners to higher powers.[2]

Over a thousand years later, on the other side of the world, at Chavín de Huántar, Peru, cultural elites likewise manipulated space and sound to cultivate acoustical effects that evoked the mysterious and the divine. Using sound-producing instruments—decorated *strombus galeatus* marine shells, known in the Andes as "pututus," many of which were excavated on site—along with carefully designed architectural galleries, the authorities of Chavín's most active period of development (1100-600 BCE) influenced

---

[2] Watson and Keating 1999; Waller 2006; Till 2010; Fazenda 2013; Fazenda and Drumm 2013. Tim Darvill (2012) and his team have further suggested that Stonehenge in the middle third millennium was the site for ritualized healing, while Paul Devereux and his team with RCA *Landscape and Perception Project* (2007-16) has shown that the so-called blue stones of the henge are lithophones. Mills (2014) and Eneix (2016) give energetic introductions to the general religio-acoustical patterns that may have guided the design of this kind of prehistoric soundscape; see also above, p. 28 n. 17.

human experience through the creation of elaborate soundscapes. The power of these environments and how they were produced seems to have been both technologically innovative and shrouded from the understanding of most worshippers by the "clergy" of Chavín's famous oracle. The effects of these soundscapes, famously documented by Miriam Kolar and her teammates, would have dramatically reinforced the authority of the "priesthood" and confirmed Chavín's status as a cultural, commercial, and religious center. How these environments would have affected worshippers or other participants remains a mystery, but there can be no doubt that sound played a fundamental role in connecting early audiences to superhuman and divine agents.[3]

In 2012, a fragment of a burned lyre's bridge was excavated by Steven Birch, Graeme Lawson, John Purser, and their team in a limestone cave located about a kilometer southeast of the Scottish village of Torrin.[4] In addition to confirming the presence of sophisticated stringed instruments and their attendant songs among the Western Celts in the fourth century BCE, this cave seems to have been chosen intentionally to bring visitors into a sphere that was fundamentally removed from the mundane. "Descending [the cave's] steep and narrow steps," John Purser notes, "the transition from light to dark transports you out of one world and into a completely different realm, [one] where human senses are accentuated. Within the cave, sound forms a major component of this transformation…"[5]

---

[3] Kolar, et.al. 2012; Kolar 2013a; 2013b; and 2014.

[4] The so-called High Pasture Cave, or the *Uamha an Ard Achadh*, as the cave is called in Gaelic. The date and context of this lyre fragment have yet to be fully published. The most detailed information can be found in Purser 2014, 211-12.

[5] Purser quoted in "Skye cave finds western Europe's earliest string instrument," BBC News 28 March 2012. http://www.bbc.com/news/uk-scotland-highlands-islands-17537147.

Over the past fifteen years—and across the world—the interplay among music, ritual, space, religion, and the human sensorium has received increasing attention by scholars.[6] What was once niche scholarship, conducted on the edges of archaeology, has now taken center stage, and rightfully so. The common threads that bind these studies together are important, interdisciplinary, international, and possessed by a series of linked imperatives: a regard for human intentionality and agency; a common interest in embodied cognitions, perceptions, and values; and a respect for the shared aspects of human communities that transcend mere essentialism. By encompassing the study of shared human senses, archaeology has embraced the study of the individual, the subjective, the fleeting, the ephemeral—the study of human experience, broadly imagined. We hope to have demonstrated that it is possible to add the thymele at Epidauros to this growing list of ancient sites that were designed, constructed, and/or used with sensual, spiritual, and transformational effects in mind.

When we look at larger trends within Greece at the time of the thymele's construction, this makes especially good sense. In the fourth century BCE, Greece was a locus of radical innovation. A concern with "the new" permeated all spheres of public and private discourse, spanning the fields of architecture, art, philosophy, theater, medicine, and music, among many others. It was a time, too, that witnessed a rapid rise in the popularity of the healing god Asklepios and his cult, with some scholars estimating over two hundred sanctuaries of Asklepios being founded in the fourth century BCE alone.[7] The god's cures were in great demand; there is no doubt that his cult centers around the Aegean blossomed during this period of unrivaled growth, prosperity, and "modernism." We might well expect

---

[6] See above, pp. 27-28 n. 17 and p. 31 n. 19.
[7] *PECS*, sv "Epidauros"; also Wickkiser 2008, Ch. 2, with bibliography.

that Epidauros in particular, the epicenter of Asklepios's cult, would have led the way in innovations related to the god's rituals and therapies.

And yet, if what we have argued here is true—that in addition to other functions, the thymele was used for musical performances, and that these performances were therapeutic—then what do we ask next? Many questions come to mind. For instance, how were musicians commissioned to perform in the thymele? What was the role of Asklepios's priesthood—or the role of other intellectual elites—in the selection and integration of sacred music into therapeutic ritual and practice? Were solo instruments the only sort performed in the thymele? What about larger, symphonic productions? Healing and music have a long, intertwined connection throughout the ancient Greek world; had something like the thymele been conceived and executed earlier? Did Epidauros host competitions for the composition of therapeutic music, much as festivals of Asklepios in other parts of the Mediterranean would host medical competitions?[8] With regard to the building's construction, was the thymele's design kept a secret to further enhance the mystical effects produced by the building's structure? Did fourth-century philosophers—musical theorists, like Aristoxenos or other fourth-century Pythagoreans—take an active role in the acoustical design of the thymele? If Polykleitos the Younger was indeed the designer of both the thymele and Epidauros's great theater, what effect did these acoustical projects have on each other? And why were no other hollow basement systems designed after the thymele? Might the thymele have been a "failed" acoustical

---

[8] Inscriptions from Ephesos document medical competitions held during the festival of Asklepios there in the second century CE. These included competitions in surgery, instruments, problems (apparently, a single problem to solve: πρόβλημα), and composition (σύνταγμα, which probably entailed writing a treatise or compounding drugs, though the term could extend also to arranging musical notes). See Zimonyi 2014, with references and bibliography.

experiment? These are but a few of the questions that spring to mind. Hopefully they inspire more.

Of course, questions like these must remain open-ended for the moment, due to the current state of the surviving evidence, but they do hint at the wide range of enquiry now available. Even more importantly, these questions point once again to the goal of this project. Our purpose has not been to "crack the code," to provide the "definitive answer" to the thymele's mysteries, or to otherwise limit the interpretative possibilities that surround the thymele at Epidauros. Rather, it has been to open these types of questions and these possibilities more fully to the discussion, the criticism, and the imagination of our friends, our colleagues, and our students—to open the debate to anyone with interest and passion. It is through this kind of dialogue that this extraordinary building and its makers can continue to enrich our minds, communities, and our world. It is through this kind of conversation that we can allow this ancient structure—and those who made it—to sing to us once more.

APPENDIX
Acoustical Report on the Thymele at Epidauros
Andrew Fermer, Hann Tucker Associates Ltd

The firm of Hann Tucker Associates Ltd has been commissioned to undertake a geometrical room acoustic study of the thymele at Epidauros, the results of which are presented below.

OBJECTIVES

The project had the following four objectives:
- To construct a three-dimensional geometrical acoustic model of the thymele of Epidauros, based on drawings and information received;
- To predict the reverberation time and early reflection response of the interior space for a selection of source and receive locations by means of ray-tracing simulation within the constructed model;
- Upon receipt of a dry musical recording, to use auralization software within the model to produce an audio file simulating the response of the space;
- To model listener and performer acoustical effects, where possible, relating to various source and receiver types and locations.

METHODOLOGY AND SURFACES

The CATT Acoustic software is a ray tracing prediction program. The 3D model of the thymele was created and each "plane" assigned acoustic absorption and diffusion properties. "Source" and "Receive" positions are selected. When the model is run a pre-set number of rays are sent from the source. Each time a ray comes into contact with a plane on its path to the receiver, the absorption and diffusion properties of said plane alter the sound energy and direction of the ray until the receiver is reached. The time taken and energy associated with the ray at the point of reaching the receiver is used by the model to predict the reverberation time and subsequently the auralization of the space.

The CATT Acoustic software is based on geometrical acoustic theory, which handles the diffusion and energy transmission of sound geometrically; it does not consider the physical wave nature of sound (i.e., wave acoustics). Wave acoustics quickly become complicated in larger, real room situations with varied surface angles and finishes; they are also less relevant for spaces with dimensions which are large when compared to the wavelength. Geometrical acoustics can be reliably used for large, complicated spaces to predict and to model the acoustic environment. The limitations of the theory are that a space's modes and resonances (a factor of wave theory) are not considered. Also, with larger, more complicated spaces, a high number of rays are required to produce accurate models; this can lead to restrictively high processing requirements that limit the number of models that can be efficiently generated.

Using CATT Acoustic V8.0 software, an acoustic computer model was built of the thymele in order to analyze its acoustic parameters. The model was based on dimensions and surface finishes detailed on drawings received. Typical absorption and scattering coefficients were used for each surface material.

To summarize, we understood the proposed surface finishes to be comprised of the following:

Location	Finish
Walls, columns, floor	Smooth Stone/marble
Ceiling, door	Wood
Labyrinth	Porous Stone/limestone

Sound source and receiver positions were located within the computer model so as to simulate the typical source and receive positions which are likely to be associated with the thymele's space. The software was then used to predict reverberation times, echograms, and auralized audio files for various source and receive locations.

RESULTS

Reverberation Times

The CATT Acoustic model was used to predict the likely reverberation time within the thymele, based on finishes described in the table above. The predicted octave band reverberation times are presented in the following table. The predictions were run with a 1.23 m diameter hole, a 0.38 m diameter hole, and a closed hole positioned at the center of the thymele's cella with the understanding that the hole opened into the building's "labyrinth." The sizes of the hole were dictated by preserved diameters of the capstone block and its central hole as recorded by Svolos. Various locations for source and receive positions were run through the model. A model was also run for "Locations 2" with the interior columns of the thymele removed for the purposes of comparison.

	Predicted Reverberation Time (Seconds) at Octave Band Centre Frequency (Hz)							
	125	250	500	1k	2k	4k	8k	16k
Locations 1, Large Hole, Receive 1	6.24	6.51	5.44	5.17	4.67	2.17	0.90	0.37
Locations 1, No Hole, Receive 1	5.97	6.00	5.32	5.29	4.74	2.53	1.19	0.58
Locations 1, Small Hole, Receive 1	6.18	6.54	5.54	5.30	4.67	2.20	0.84	0.35
Locations 2, Large Hole, Receive 1	6.20	6.50	5.45	5.41	4.81	2.63	1.21	0.57
Locations 2, Large Hole, Receive 2	6.01	6.48	5.67	5.29	4.74	2.58	1.26	0.56
Locations 2, Large Hole, Receive 3	6.27	6.64	5.52	5.30	4.78	2.61	1.31	0.64

Locations 2, No Hole, Receive 1	6.26	6.67	5.48	5.42	4.84	2.56	1.19	0.57
Locations 2, No Hole, Receive 2	6.28	6.51	5.46	5.33	4.80	2.62	1.24	0.60
Locations 2, No Hole, Receive 3	6.22	6.34	5.52	5.43	4.74	2.72	1.29	0.66
Locations 2, Small Hole, Receive 1	6.27	6.50	5.52	5.42	4.78	2.55	1.23	0.55
Locations 2, Small Hole, Receive 2	6.26	6.69	5.59	5.44	4.83	2.57	1.23	0.61
Locations 2, Small Hole, Receive 3	6.42	6.55	5.51	5.32	4.75	2.70	1.32	0.64
Locations 3, Large Hole, Receive 1	6.36	6.59	5.49	5.29	4.70	2.31	1.04	0.45
Locations 3, Large Hole, Receive 2	6.35	6.58	5.42	5.36	4.74	2.51	1.19	0.59
Locations 3, Large Hole, Receive 3	6.27	6.67	5.50	5.36	4.76	2.69	1.37	0.72
Locations 3, No Hole, Receive 1	6.24	6.46	5.07	5.16	4.68	2.29	1.05	0.44
Locations 3, No Hole, Receive 2	6.28	6.36	5.40	5.45	4.77	2.56	1.21	0.60
Locations 3, No Hole, Receive 3	6.21	6.46	5.53	5.46	4.78	2.71	1.40	0.71
Locations 3, Small Hole, Receive 1	6.05	6.46	5.16	5.28	4.68	2.30	1.02	0.45
Locations 3, Small Hole, Receive 2	6.37	6.62	5.46	5.38	4.80	2.56	1.17	0.58
Locations 3, Small Hole, Receive 3	6.17	6.49	5.53	5.33	4.86	2.67	1.37	0.70
Locations 4, Large Hole, Receive 1	6.19	6.48	5.49	5.35	4.66	2.52	1.12	0.58
Locations 4, Large Hole, Receive 2	6.11	6.43	5.48	5.23	4.74	2.81	1.16	1.66
Locations 4, Large Hole, Receive 3	6.24	6.47	5.47	5.29	4.78	2.67	1.30	0.65
Locations 4, No Hole, Receive 3	6.21	6.67	5.53	5.39	4.85	2.70	1.31	0.69
Locations 4, Small Hole, Receive 1	5.89	6.28	5.10	4.82	4.26	1.96	1.07	0.72
Locations 4, Small Hole, Receive 2	5.67	6.20	5.21	5.39	4.08	2.05	1.31	-

Locations 4, Small Hole, Receive 3	6.50	6.70	5.48	5.28	4.82	2.70	1.28	0.66
Locations 2, Large Hole, Receive 1 NO COLUMNS	7.24	7.62	6.43	6.24	5.46	2.93	1.36	0.66
Locations 2, Large Hole, Receive 2 NO COLUMNS	7.13	7.60	6.39	6.27	5.43	2.85	1.38	0.63
Locations 2, Large Hole, Receive 3 NO COLUMNS	7.25	7.48	6.42	6.22	5.48	3.09	1.47	0.71

DISCUSSION

Reverberation Times

The reverberation times appear similar for scenarios with both the "labyrinth" open and closed for the scenarios tested to date. However, the reverberation times when the columns are removed are noticeably higher.

Echograms

The comparative echograms for corresponding source and receive positions with and without the hole to the labyrinth do not appear to show significant differences for the scenarios tested to date. Analysis of each individual octave band rather than the sum of all octave bands may yield more conclusive differences. There is noticeably smoother echo decay traces with the columns than without, a likely result of the additional diffusion provided by the surface and location of the columns of reflections from the smooth cylindrical wall behind.

Auralization

The comparative audio files for corresponding source and receive positions with and without the hole to the "labyrinth" appear to indicate that for some positions there is no noticeable difference in auralization when the "labyrinth" was open or closed. However, it is also evident that at certain send and receive locations, the model with the hole to the "labyrinth" open produced more listenable files; i.e. there are less early loud reflections which could be considered to disrupt the listening experience. The longer reverberation time and altered echogram resulting from removal of the columns as described above is also audible within the auralization files in some instances. There are also some notable differences for some locations with the small hole compared to the large hole, most likely due to the way in which early reflections are altered creating some interesting effects.

SUMMARY

The modeling undertaken, as detailed in our report, considers many varying scenarios of source and receive positions for the thymele's interior space with, and without, the "labyrinth" exposed. The reverberation time values predicted do not indicate much variation. However, the auralized files appear to suggest that the intentional exposing and/or concealing of the "labyrinth" hole could have been used to alter the reflection characteristics of the space to suit differing uses or to create different acoustical environments/effects as desired by the users of the space. Specifically, the labyrinth at some positions appeared to "absorb" some reflections, possibly directed into the labyrinth from the shape of the ceiling, resulting in a more pleasant, a more soothing, and a more controlled listening experience than when the labyrinth was closed off, i.e. when it reflected sound energy directly back up into the thymele's cella. The strength of some early reflections (up to around 100 ms relative to the direct sound) can have a large impact on the way a space "sounds" to a listener or worshipper.

Illustrations

Figure 1. Map of Greece, the sanctuary of Asklepios at Epidauros indicated. (© Theran Press.)

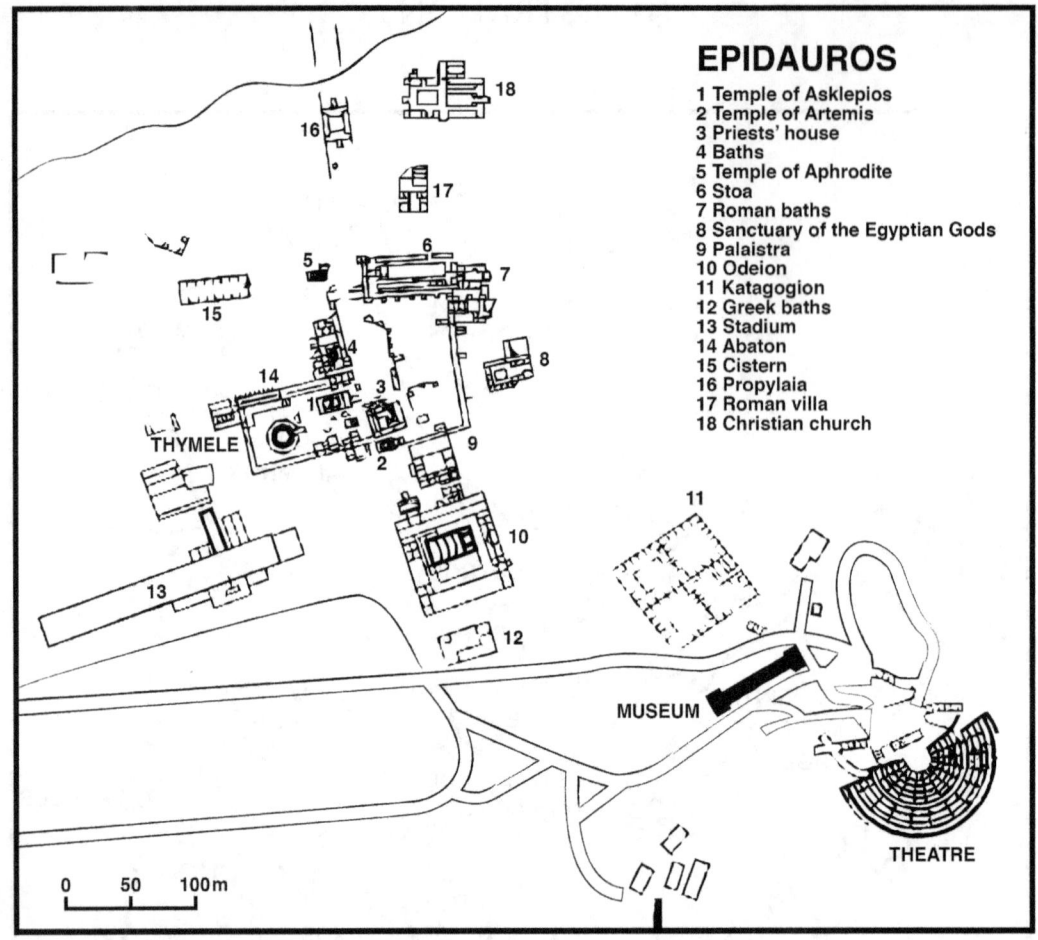

Figure 2. Plan of the Asklepieion at Epidauros, including theater, museum, and modern parking and paths. (© Theran Press.)

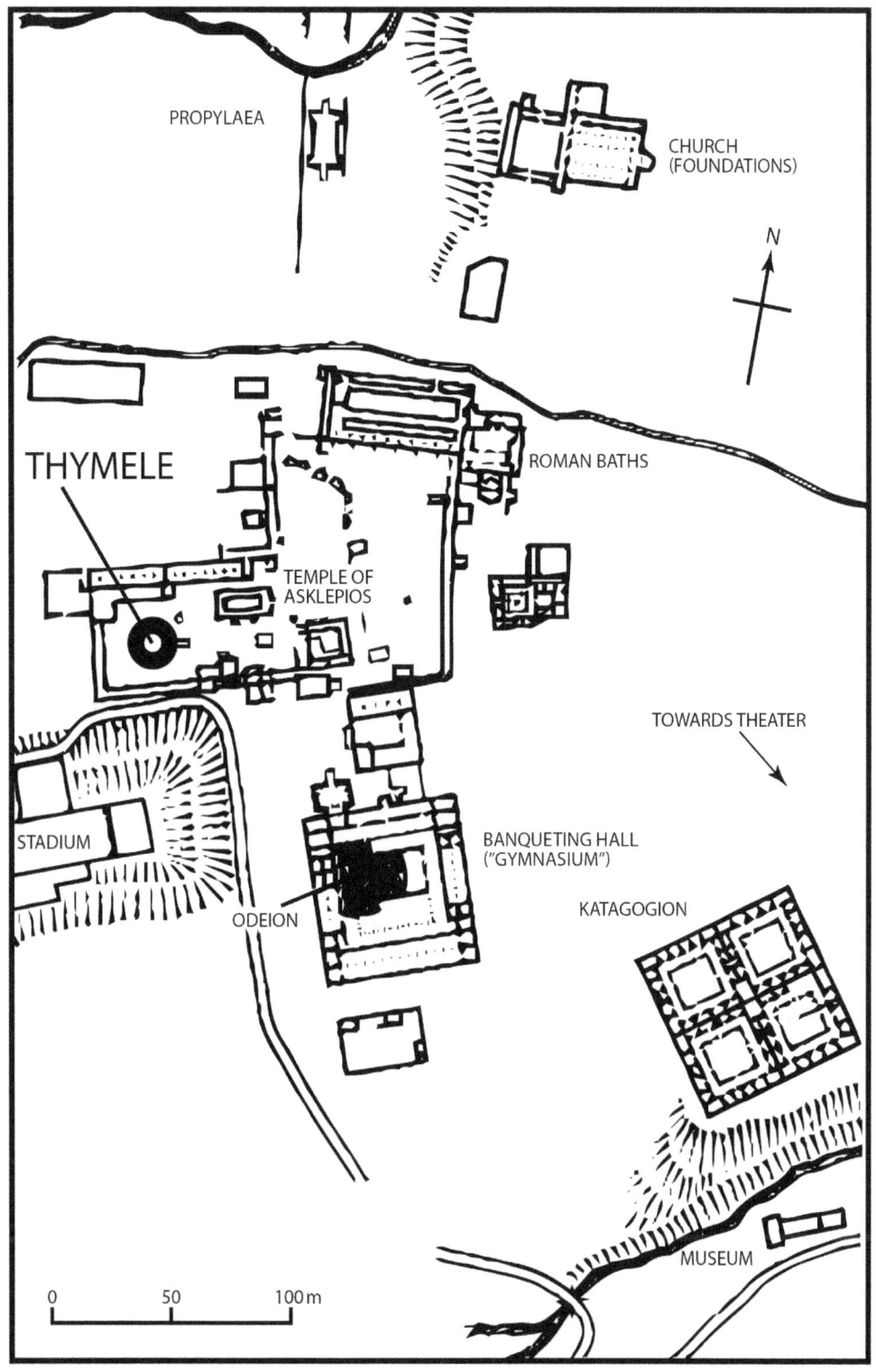

Figure 3. Plan of the central area of the Asklepieion at Epidauros, the thymele indicated. (© Theran Press.)

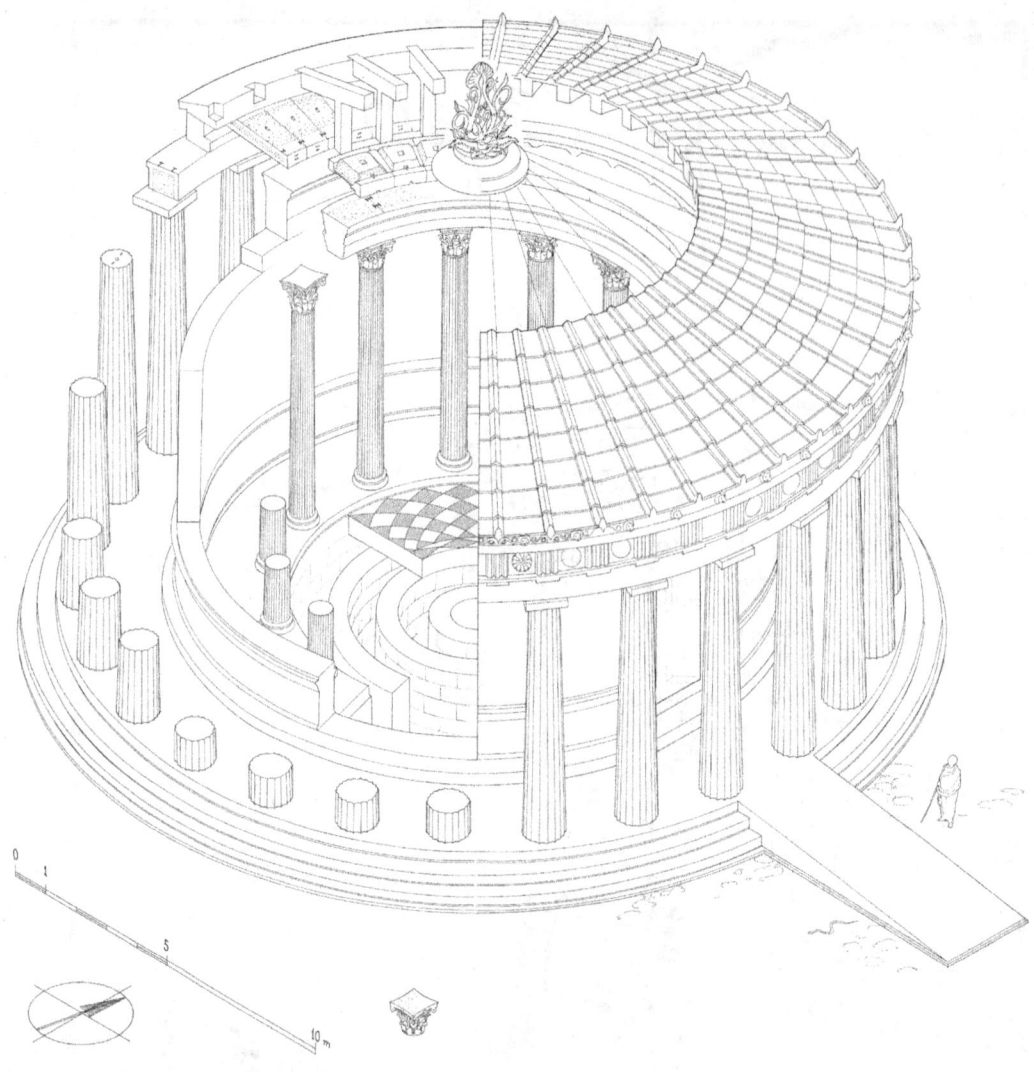

Figure 4. Cutaway plan of the thymele at Epidauros, from the southeast.
(© C. Kanellopoulos.)

Figure 5. Restored cutaway elevation of the façade and foundations of the thymele at Epidauros, from the south. Full color digital renderings are available at https://www.theranpress.org/the-thymele-at-epidauros. (© J. Goodinson; J. Svolos, scientific advisor.)

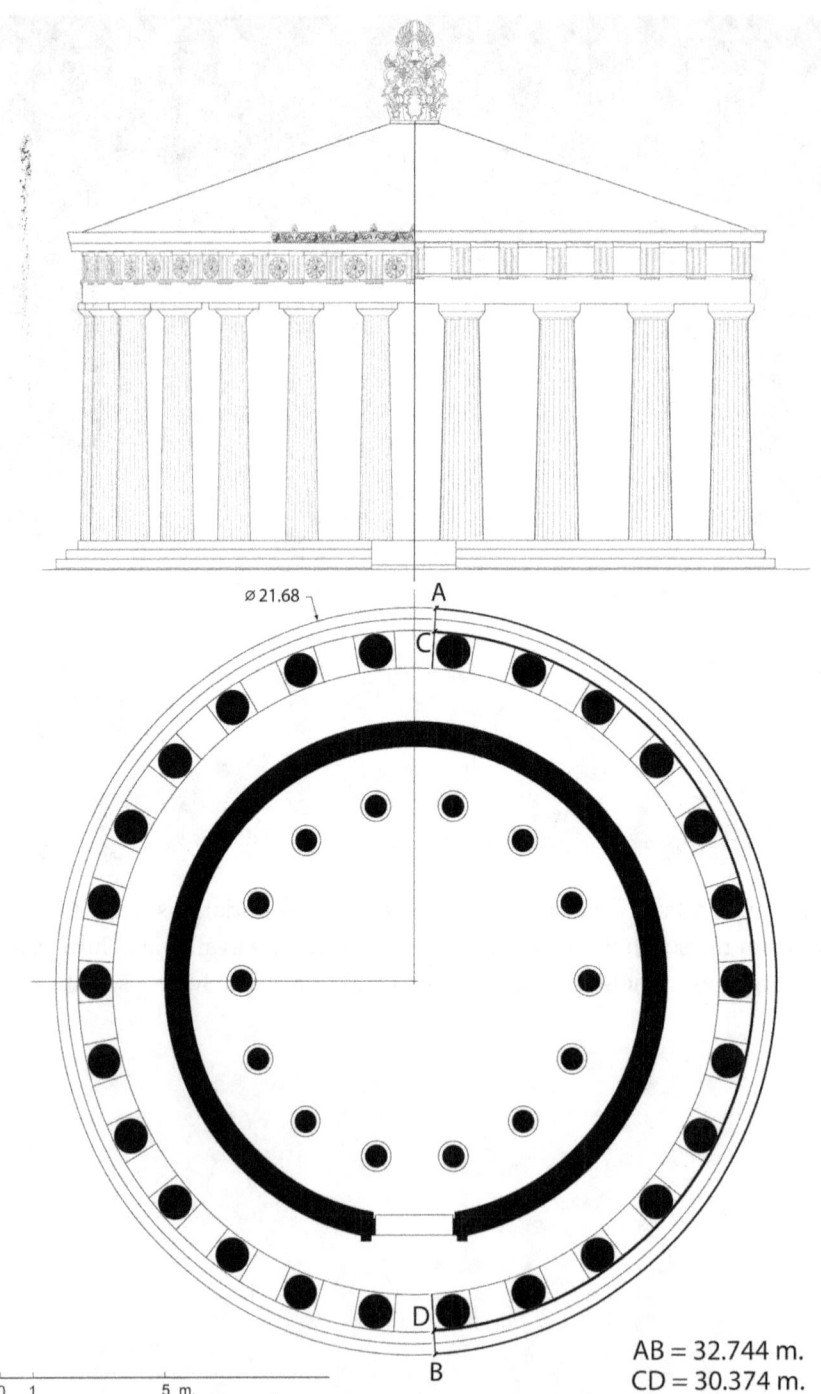

Figure 6. Top: The Parthenon's façade elevation (right) superimposed on the krepis and elevation of the thymele (left), with scaled stylobate width. Bottom: Ground plan of the thymele with section AB of the circumference marked on the first step of the krepis and with section CD marked on stylobate level (© C. Kanellopoulos.)

Figure 7. Restored elevation of the thymele and temple of Asklepios at Epidauros, from the southeast, over the "altar court." Full color digital renderings are available at https://www.theranpress.org/the-thymele-at-epidauros. (© J. Goodinson; J. Svolos, scientific advisor.)

Figure 8. Restored elevation of the thymele and temple of Asklepios at Epidauros, from the east along the axis of the "altar court." Full color digital renderings are available at https://www.theranpress.org/the-thymele-at-epidauros. (© J. Goodinson; J. Svolos, scientific advisor.)

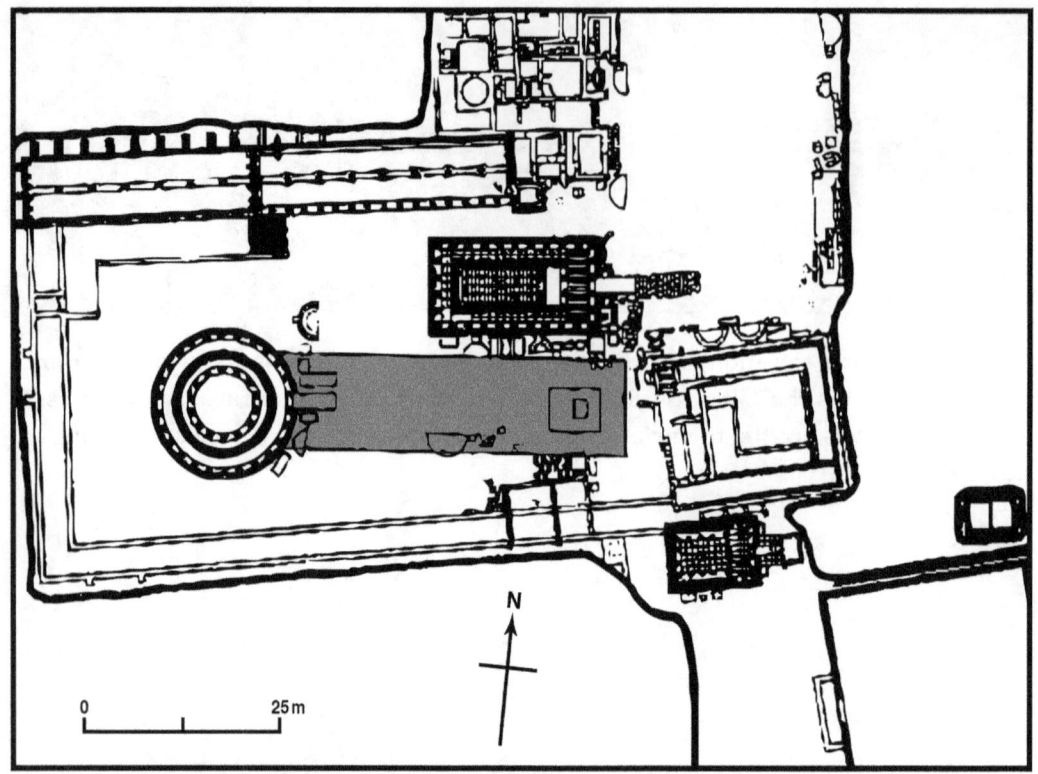

Figure 9. Plan of the central area of the Asklepieion at Epidauros in the third century BCE. The thymele and its "altar court" (© P. Schultz, after P. Kavvadias.)

Figure 10. A Corinthian capital from the thymele at Epidauros. (© Bryn Mawr College Library Lantern Slide Collection.)

Figure 11. Detail of a Corinthian capital from the thymele at Epidauros.
(© Greek Ministry of Culture; photograph, P. Schultz.)

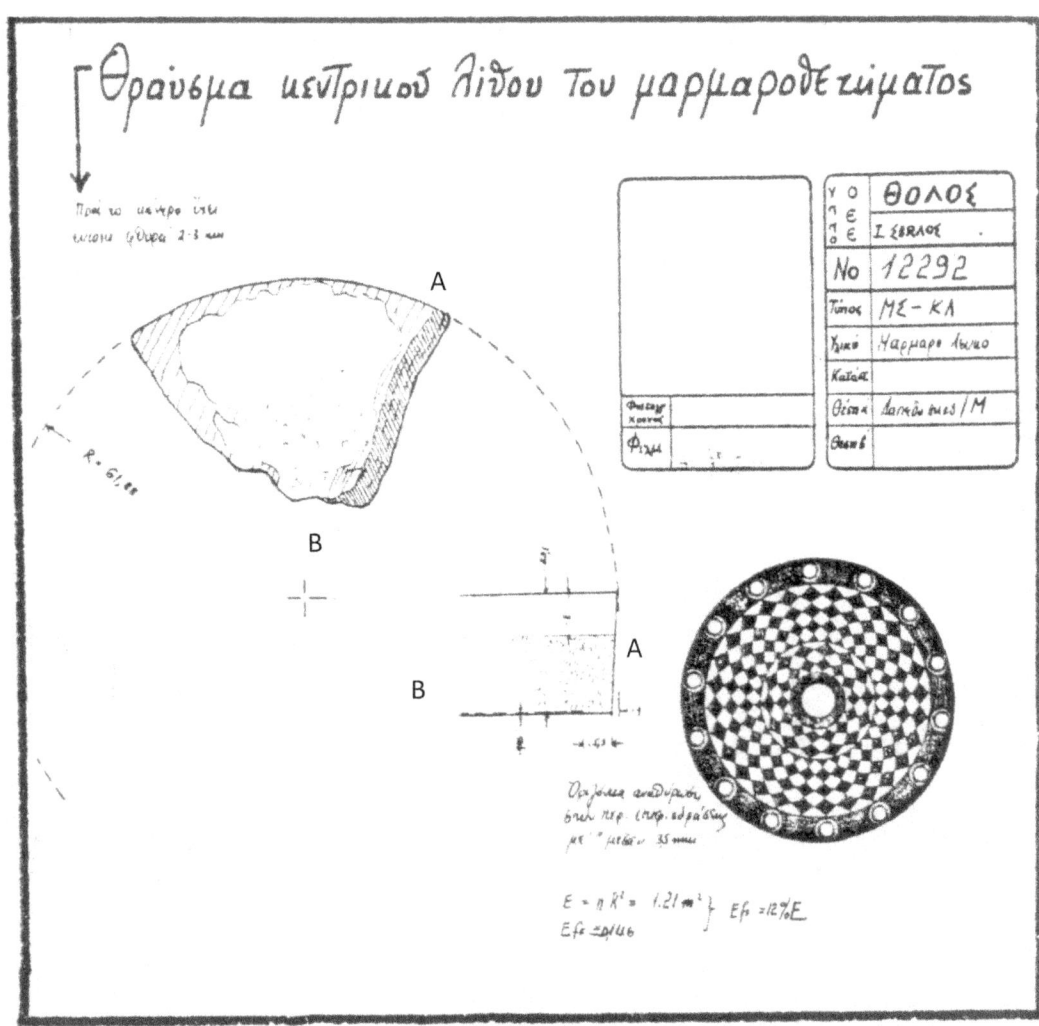

Figure 12. Drawing of the central capstone of the thymele's floor, inv. no. 12292. Point A marks the most well-preserved edge of the capstone's outer circumference; the restored diameter of the stone (ca. 1.236 m) was taken from this point. Point B marks the most well-preserved interior edge of the capstone's central hole; the restored diameter of the hole (ca. 0.38 m) was taken from this point. (© J. Svolos.)

Figure 13. Excavation photograph of the thymele at Epidauros showing the building's hollow foundation, and the size, scale, and position of the "labyrinth" corridors. ("Fundamente der Tholos zur Zeit der Ausgrabungen mit W.Dörpfeld." © D-DAI-ATH-Epidauros 7.)

Figure 14. Detail of the thymele's harlequin floor. Full color digital renderings are available at https://www.theranpress.org/the-thymele-at-epidauros. (© J. Goodinson; J. Svolos, scientific advisor.)

Figure 15. Oblique, detailed view of the thymele's central elements and restored bronze grille. Full color digital renderings are available at https://www.theranpress.org/the-thymele-at-epidauros. (© J. Goodinson; J. Svolos, scientific advisor.)

Figure 16. Phiale. The Painter of London D12. Attic. Ca. 450-440 BCE. (Museum of Fine Arts, Boston. Edwin E. Jack Fund. Photograph © Museum of Fine Arts, Boston.)

Figure 17. Digital reconstruction of the interior of the thymele with dancers and musician, as seen from the interior door lintel, door open. Full color digital renderings are available at https://www.theranpress.org/the-thymele-at-epidauros. (© J. Goodinson; J. Svolos, scientific advisor.)

Figure 18. Digital reconstruction of the interior of the thymele with dancers and musician, as seen from the interior door lintel, door shut and lamps lit. Full color digital renderings are available at https://www.theranpress.org/the-thymele-at-epidauros. (© J. Goodinson; J. Svolos, scientific advisor.)

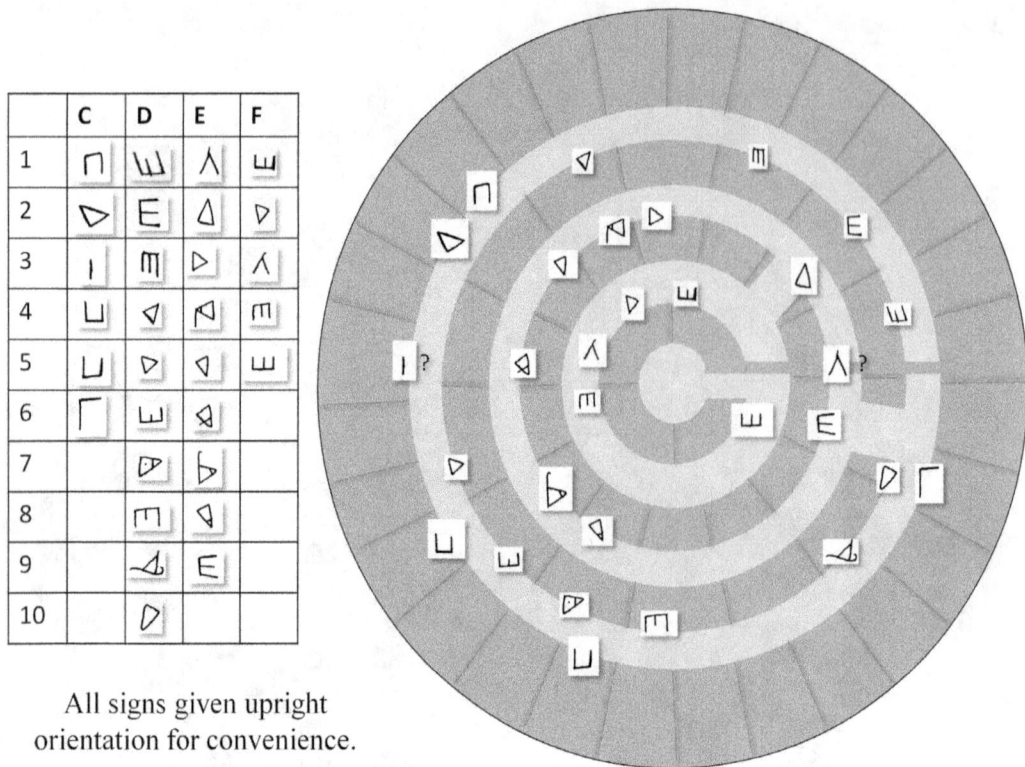

All signs given upright orientation for convenience.

Figure 19. Right: Distribution of signs within the labyrinth, following figures in Svolos 1988 (with minor corrections to his composite sign-charts by reference to his actual plans of the rings). Left: Composite chart to establish alphanumeric equivalents for each sign (for ease of reference in the main text). (© J. Franklin.)

Figure 20. Drawing of the marks in the substructure of the thymele. (© J. Svolos.)

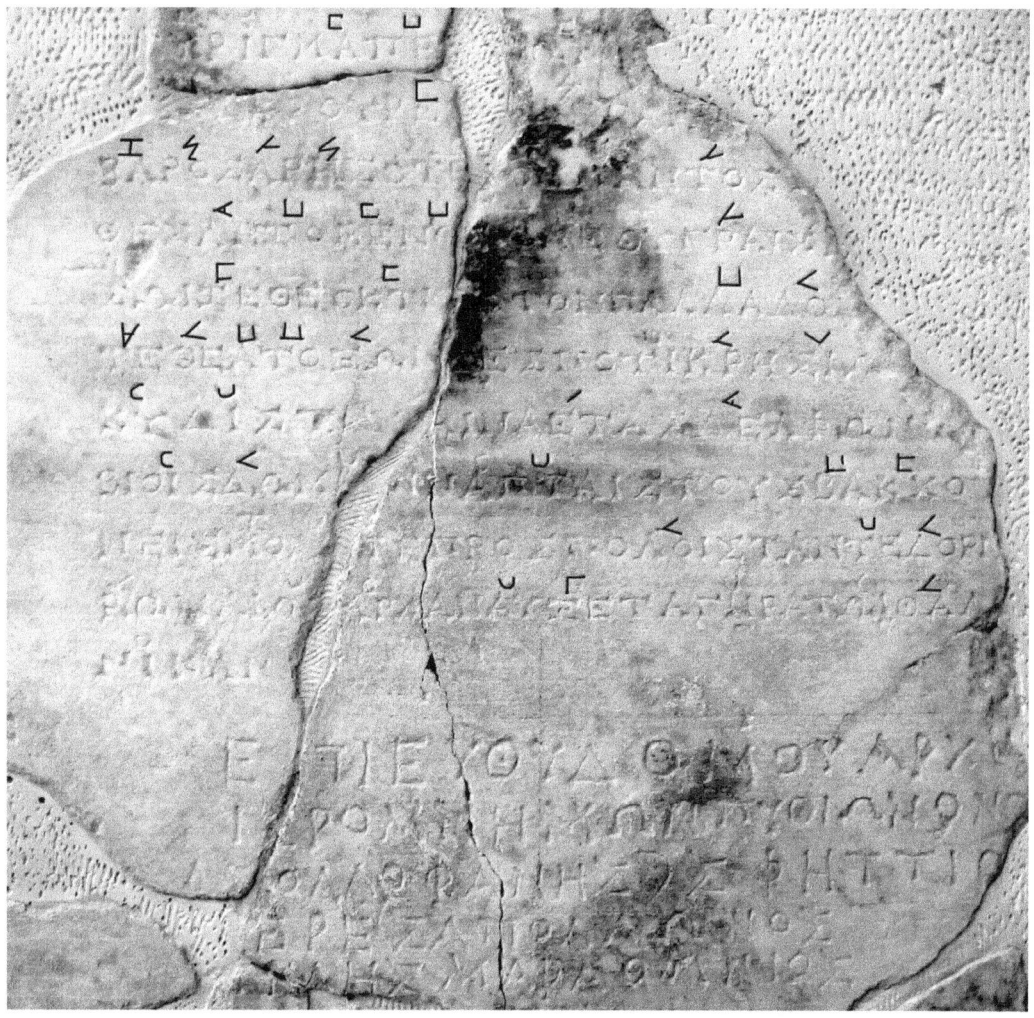

Figure 21. Photograph of an inscription recording the text and musical notations of a paean by Limenios, ca. 128 BCE, inscribed on the Athenian treasury at Delphi. Musical notations are highlighted. (Delphi Museum, Inv. Nos. 489, 1461, 1591, 209, 212, 226, 225, 224, 215, 214; © Greek Ministry of Culture.)

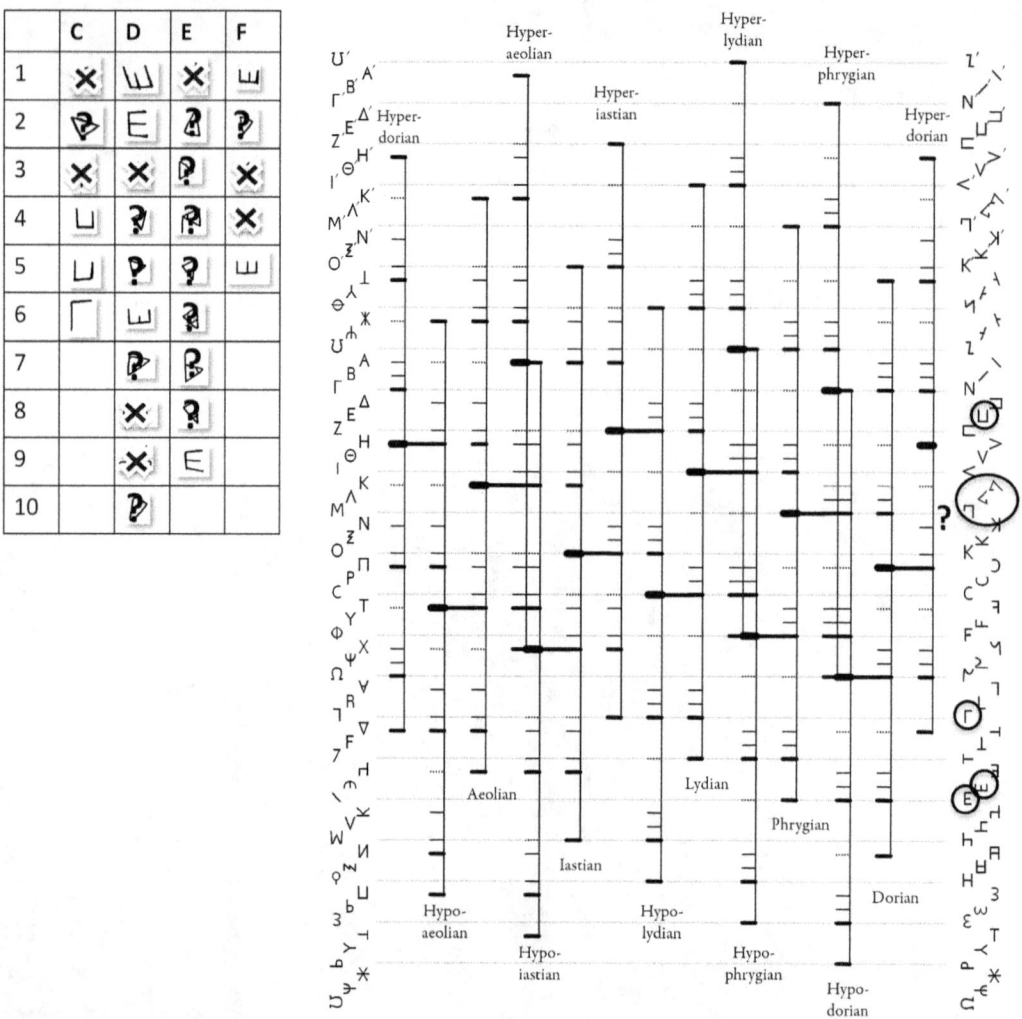

Figure 22. Labyrinth signs compared with instrumental notation symbols. Those which are unmarked in left-hand chart find matches in the notation, as indicated by circles on the right-hand chart (taken from Hagel 2000). Those with "X" have no matches. Those with "?" could match if one permits alternative rotations. (© J. Franklin.)

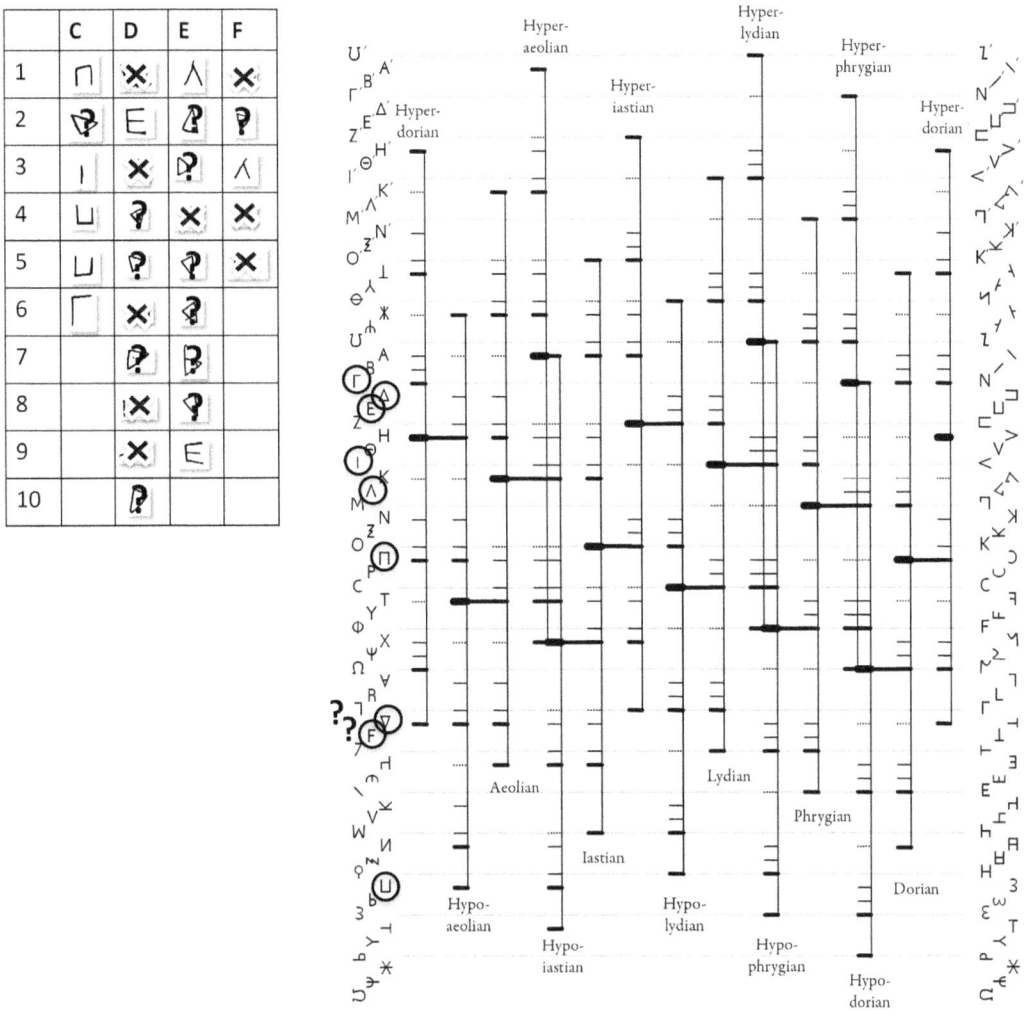

Figure 23. Labyrinth signs compared with vocal notation symbols, following conventions of Figure 22. (© J. Franklin.)

Bibliography

Unless otherwise noted, all journal abbreviations follow those given by the *American Journal of Archaeology* at http://www.ajaonline.org/submissions/abbreviations. Ancient literary and epigraphic sources have been abbreviated according to *The Oxford Classical Dictionary*.

Alcock, S. 1991. "Tomb Cult and the Post-Classical Polis." *AJA* 95: 447-67.

Aleshire, S.B. 1989. *The Athenian Asklepieion: The People, Their Dedications, and the Inventories.* Amsterdam: J.C. Gieben.

Aly, W. 1914. "Lexikalische Streifzüge." *Glotta* 5: 57-79.

Anderson, W.D. 1994. *Music and Musicians in Ancient Greece.* Ithaca and London: Cornell University Press.

Antonaccio, C. M. 1995. *An Archaeology of Ancestors: Tomb Cult and Hero Cult in Early Greece.* Lanham, MD: Rowman and Littlefield.

Ashby, C. 1999. *Classical Greek Theatre: New Views on an Old Subject.* Iowa City: University of Iowa Press.

Askitopoulou, H. et al. 2002. "Surgical Cures Under Sleep Induction in the Asclepieion of Epidauros." *International Congress Series (The History of Anesthesia)* 1242: 11-17.

Austin, C., and G. Bastianini, eds. 2002. *Posidippi Pellaei quae supersunt omnia.* Milan: LED.

Backman, E.L. 1952. *Religious Dances in the Christian Church and in Popular Medicine.* London: George Allen & Unwin.

Barker, A. 1984–1989. *Greek Musical Writings.* Cambridge: Cambridge University Press.

—. 2004. "Transforming the Nightingale: Aspects of Athenian Musical Discourse in the Late Fifth Century." In *Music and the Muses: The Culture of 'Mousike' in the Classical Athenian City*, edited by P. Murray and P. Wilson, 185-204. Oxford: Oxford University Press.

—. 2007. *The Science of Harmonics in Classical Greece*. Cambridge: Cambridge University Press.

—. 2009. "Shifting Conceptions of 'Schools' of Harmonic Theory, 400 BC-200 AD." In *La musa dimenticata: aspetti dell'esperienza musicale greca in età ellenistica*, edited by M.C. Martinelli, 165-90. Pisa: Edizioni della Normale.

Barron, M. 1993. *Auditorium Acoustics and Architectural Design*. London: E&FN Spon.

Bassi, K. 1989. "The Poetics of Exclusion in Callimachus' *Hymn to Apollo*." *TAPA* 119: 219–31.

Battezzato, L. 2009. "Metre and Music." In *The Cambridge Companion to Greek Lyric*, edited by F. Budelmann, 130-46. Cambridge: Cambridge University Press.

Baunack, J.F. 1890. *Aus Epidauros. Eine Epigraphische Studie*. Leipzig: Otto Dürr.

Beekes, R. 1969. *The Development of the Proto-Indo-European Laryngeals in Greek*. The Hague and Paris: De Gruyter.

—. 2010. *Etymological Dictionary of Greek*. Leiden: Brill.

Bélis, A. 1992. *Corpus des inscriptions de Delphes*. Vol. 3: *Les hymnes à Apollon*. Paris: École Française d'Athènes.

Bennett, J. 2010. *Vibrant Matter: A Political Ecology of Things*. Durham, NC: Duke University Press.

Bérard, C. 1970. *Eretria. Fouilles et recherches III: L'Héroon à la Porte d'Ouest*. Berne: Editions Francke.

Berges, D., V. Patsiada, and J. Nollé. 1996. *Rundaltäre aus Kos und Rhodos*. Berlin: Mann.

Berrey, M. forthcoming. *Hellenistic Science at Court.* Berlin: De Gruyter.

Biddle, M. 1962. "Acoustic Pots: A Proposed Study." *Medieval Archaeology* 6: 304.

Blake, E.C., and I. Cross. 2015. "The Acoustic and Auditory Contexts of Human Behavior." *Current Anthropolgy* 56.1: 81-103.

Blesser, B., and L.-R. Salter. 2007. *Spaces Speak, Are You Listening? Experiencing Aural Architecture.* Cambridge, MA: MIT Press.

Bohn, R. 1896. *Altertümer von Pergamon. IV. Die Theater-Terrasse.* Berlin: W. Spemann.

Bommelaer, J.-F., and D. Laroche. 1991. *Guide de Delphes. Le site.* École française d'Athènes. Sites et monuments VII. Paris: De Boccard.

Bona, G., ed. 1988. *Pindaro, I peani; testo, traduzione, scoli e commento.* Cuneo: Saste.

Bourguet, É. 1914. *Les ruines de Delphes.* Paris: Fontemoing.

Branigan, K. 1993. *Dancing with Death: Life and Death in Southern Crete c. 3000−2000 BC.* Amsterdam: A.M. Hakkert.

Bremer, J.M. 1981. "Greek Hymns." In *Faith, Hope, and Worship: Aspects of Religious Mentality in the Ancient World*, edited by H. Versnel, 193-215. Leiden: Brill.

Budelmann, F., ed. 2009. *The Cambridge Companion to Greek Lyric.* Cambridge: Cambridge University Press.

Bundrick, S.D. 2005. *Music and Image in Classical Athens.* Cambridge: Cambridge University Press.

Burford, A. 1966. "Notes on the Epidaurian Building Inscriptions." *ABSA* 61: 254–334.

—. 1969. *The Greek Temple Builders at Epidauros: A Social and Economic Study of Building in the Asklepian Sanctuary, During the Fourth and Early Third Centuries B.C.* Liverpool: Liverpool University Press.

Burkert, W. 1972. *Lore and Science in Ancient Pythagoreanism.* Cambridge, MA: Harvard University Press.

—. 1985. *Greek Religion.* Translated by J. Raffan. Cambridge, MA: Harvard University Press.

—. 1994. "Orpheus, Dionysos und die Euneiden in Athen: das Zeugnis von Euripides' Hypsipyle." In *Orchestra. Drama, Mythos, Bühne,* edited by A. Bierl and P. v. Möllendorff, 44–49. Stuttgart: Teubner.

Butler, S., and A. Purves, eds. 2014. *Synaeathesia and the Ancient Senses.* London and New York: Routledge.

Calame, C. 1992. *The Poetics of Eros in Ancient Greece.* Translated by J. Lloyd. Princeton: Princeton University Press.

—. 1997 (rev. ed. 2001). *Choruses of Young Women in Ancient Greece: Their Morphology, Religious Role, and Social Functions.* Translated by D. Collins and J. Orion. Lanham, MD: Rowman & Littlefield.

Calder, W.M. 1912. "Inscriptions d'Iconium." *RPh* 36: 48-77.

Cameron, A. 1995. *Callimachus and His Critics.* Princeton: Princeton University Press.

Canac, F. 1967. *L'Acoustique des théâtres antiques, ses enseignements.* Paris: Éditions du Centre national de la recherche scientifique.

Caton, R. 1899. *Two Lectures on the Temples and Ritual of Asklepios at Epidaurus and Athens, Delivered at the Royal Institution of Great Britain.* Hertford: S. Austin and Sons.

Ceccarelli, P. 2013. "Circular Choruses and the Dithyramb in the Classical and Hellenistic Period. A Problem of Definition." In *Dithyramb in Context,* edited by B. Kowalzig and P. Wilson, 153-170. Cambridge and London: Cambridge University Press.

Chaniotis, A. 2009. "A Few Things Hellenistic Audiences Appreciated in Musical Performances." In *La musa dimenticata: aspetti dell'esperienza musicale greca in età ellenistica,* edited by M.C. Martinelli, 75-97. Pisa: Edizioni della Normale.

—. 2011. "The Ithyphallic Hymn for Demetrios Poliorketes and Hellenistic Religious Mentality." In *More than Men, Less than Gods: Studies on Royal Cult and Imperial Worship*. Proceedings of the International Colloquium Organized by the Belgian School at Athens (November 1-2, 2007), edited by P.P. Iossif, A.S. Chankowski, and C.C. Lorber, 157-95. Leuven: Peeters.

Chantraine, P. 2009 (1968-80). *Dictionnaire étymologique de la langue grecque: histoire des mots*. Rev. ed. Paris: Klincksieck.

Charbonneaux, J. 1925. "Tholos et prytanée." *BCH* 49: 158–78.

Cheshire, K.A. 2008. "Kicking ΦΘΟΝΟΣ: Apollo and His Chorus in Callimachus' Hymn 2." *CP* 103: 354-73.

Chion, M. 2000. "Audio-Vision and Sound." In *Sound*, edited by P. Kruth and H. Stobart, 201-21. Cambridge: Cambridge University Press.

Collingwood, R.G. 1946. *The Idea of History*. Oxford: Oxford University Press.

Comotti, G. 1989. *Music in Greek and Roman Culture*. Baltimore and London: Johns Hopkins University Press.

Cooper. F., and S. Morris. 1990. "Dining in Round Buildings." In *Sympotica: A Symposium on the Symposion*, edited by O. Murray, 66-85. Oxford: Oxford University Press.

Cooper, F.A., ed. 1995. *The Temple of Apollo Bassitas. Vol. 1: The Architecture*. Princeton: American School of Classical Studies at Athens.

Cremer, L. 1975. "The Different Distributions of the Audience." *Applied Acoustics* 8.3: 173–91.

Cross, I., and A. Watson. 2006. "Acoustics and the Human Experience of Socially-organized Sound." In *Archaeoacoustics*, edited by C. Scarre and G. Lawson, 107–16. Cambridge: McDonald Institute for Archaeological Research.

Csapo, E. 2004. "The Politics of the New Music." In *Music and the Muses: The Culture of 'Mousike' in the Classical Athenian City*, edited by P. Murray and P. Wilson, 207-48. Oxford: Oxford University Press.

Csapo, E., and P. Wilson. 2009. "Timotheus the New Musician." In *The Cambridge Companion to Greek Lyric*, edited by F. Budelmann, 277-93. Cambridge: Cambridge University Press.

D'Angour, A. 1997. "How the Dithyramb Got Its Shape." *CQ* 47.2: 331-51.

—. 2011. *The Greeks and the New. Novelty in Ancient Greek Imagination and Experience.* Cambridge and New York: Cambridge University Press.

Dakaris, S. 1993. *Dodona*. Athens: Zaravinos.

Danner, P. 1989. *Griechische Akrotere der archaischen und klassichen Zeit (RdA* Supplement 5), Rome.

Darvill, T., Marshall, P., Parker Pearson, M., and Wainwright, G. 2012. "Stonehenge Remodelled." *Antiquity* 86.334: 1021-1040.

Davison, J.A. 1958. "Notes on the Panathenaea." *JHS* 78: 23–42.

Day, J.W. 2000. "Epigram and Reader: Generic Force as (Re-)Activation of Ritual." In *Matrices of Genre: Authors, Canons, and Society*, edited by M. Depew and D. Obbink, 37-57. Cambridge MA: Harvard University Press.

—. 2010. *Archaic Greek Epigram and Dedication: Representation and Reperformance.* Cambridge and New York: Cambridge University Press.

Declercq, N.F., and C.S.A. Dekeyser. 2007. "Acoustic Diffraction Effects at the Hellenistic Amphitheater of Epidaurus: Seat Rows Responsible for the Marvelous Acoustics." *Journal of the Acoustical Society of America* 121.4: 2011–22.

D'Errico, F., and G. Lawson. 2006. "The Sound Paradox: How to Assess the Acoustic Significance of Archaeological Evidence?" In *Archaeoacoustics*, edited by C. Scarre and G. Lawson, 41–58. Cambridge: McDonald Institute for Archaeological Research.

Defrasse, A., and H. Lechat. 1895. *Epidaure: restauration & description des principaux monuments du sanctuaire d'Asclépios*. Paris: Librairie-imprimeries réunies.

Denniston, J.D. 1939. *Euripides. Electra.* Oxford: Clarendon Press.

Depew, M. 2000. "Enacted and Represented Dedications: Genre and Greek Hymn." In *Matrices of Genre: Authors, Canons, and Society*, edited by M. Depew and D. Obbink, 59-79. Cambridge MA: Harvard University Press.

Devereaux, P. *RCA Landscape and Perception Project.* http://www.landscape-perception.com/

Diels, H. 1952 (6th ed.). *Die fragmente der Vorsokratiker.* Rev. by W. Kranz. Berlin: Weidmann.

Dillon, J., and J. Hershbell, eds. and trans. 1991. *Iamblichus, On the Pythagorean Way of Life: Text, Translation, and Notes*. Atlanta: Scholars Press.

Dillon, M. 1997. *Pilgrims and Pilgrimage in Ancient Greece*. London and New York: Routledge.

Dinsmoor, W.B., and W.J. Anderson. 1950. *The Architecture of Ancient Greece: An Account of its Historic Development* (third ed.). London and New York: Batsford.

Dodds, E.R. 1951. *The Greeks and the Irrational*. Berkeley: University of California Press.

Dörpfeld, W. 1902. "Thymele und Skene." *Hermes* 37: 249-57.

Downey, C. 2003. "The Architecture of the Greek Federal Leagues, 4th—2nd C. B.C.E," Ph.D. dissertation, University of Minnesota.

Edelstein, L., and E.J. Edelstein. 1945 (repr. 1998). *Asclepius: Collection and Interpretation of the Testimonies*. 2 vols. Baltimore: Johns Hopkins University Press.

van den Eijnde, F. 2000. "The Theatre Cavea in Early Greece: A Study of the History and Form of the Greek Cavea, 2000-330 B.C." Ph.D. dissertation, University of Amsterdam.

Ekroth, G. 2002. *The Sacrificial Rituals of Greek Hero-Cults in the Archaic to the Early Hellenistic Periods.* Liège: Centre Interantional d'Étude de la Religion Grecque Antique.

Elderkin, G.W. 1911. "Tholos and Abaton at Epidaurus." *AJA* 15.2: 161-67.

Eneix, L.C., 2016. *Listening for Ancient Gods.* New York: CSIPP.

Eneix, L.C., and E.B.W. Zubrow, eds. 2014. *Archaeoacoustics. The Archaeology of Sound.* Publication of the Proceedings from the 2014 Conference in Malta. New York: CSIPP.

Fairbanks, A. 1900. *A Study of the Greek Pæan, With Appendixes Containing the Hymns Found at Delphi, and the Other Extant Fragments of Pæans.* New York: Macmillan.

Falkener, E. 1854. *Description of Some Important Theatres & Other Remains in Crete; from a ms. History of Candia by Onorio Belli in 1586. Supplement to the Museum of Classical Antiquities.* London: Trübner.

Faraone, C.A. 2006. "Magic, Medicine, and Eros in the Prologue to Theocritus' Id. 11." In *Brill's Companion to Greek and Latin Pastoral,* edited by M. Fantuzzi and T. Papanghelis, 75-90. Leiden: Brill.

Fazenda, B.M. 2013. "The Acoustics of Stonehenge." *Acoustics Bulletin* 38.1: 32-37.

Fazenda, B.M., and I. Drumm. 2013. "Recreating the Sound of Stonehenge." *Acta Acustica united with Acustica* 99.1: 110-117.

Fehr, B. 1971-1972. "Zur Geschichte des Apollonheiligtums von Didyma, II: Tholos." *Marburger Winckelmannsprogramm*: 29-34.

Fermer, A. 2012. "Tholos of Epidauros. Draft Room Acoustic Report 17587/RAR1."

Feyel, C. 1998. "La structure d'un groupe socio-economique: les artisans dans les grands sanctuaires grecs du IVe siecle." *TOPOI* 8: 561-579.

Fischer, E., ed. 1974. *Die Ekloge des Phrynichos*. Berlin: de Gruyter.

Fitton, J.W. 1973. "Greek Dance." *CQ* 23: 254-74.

Ford, A. 2006. "The Genre of Genres: Paeans and *Paian* in Early Greek Poetry." *Poetica* 38: 277-96.

—. 2011. *Aristotle as Poet: The Song for Hermias and Its Contexts*. Oxford: Oxford University Press.

Franklin, J.C. 2005. "Hearing Greek Microtones." In *Ancient Greek Music in Performance*, edited by S. Hagel and C. Harrauer, 9–50. Vienna: Verlag der Österreichischen Akademie der Wissenschaften.

—. 2006a. "Lyre Gods of the Bronze Age Musical Koine." *JANER* 6.2: 39–70.

—. 2006b. "The Wisdom of the Lyre: Soundings in Greece, Cyprus and the Ancient Near East." In *Musikarchäologie im Kontext: Archäologische Befunde, historische Zusammenhänge, soziokulturelle Beziehungen. Serie Studien zur Musikarchäologie 5*, edited by E. Hickmann, A. A. Both, and R. Eichmann, 379–98. Rahden: Verlag Marie Leidorf.

—. 2012. "The Lesbian Singers: Towards a Reconstruction of Hellanicus' 'Karneian Victors'." In *Poesia, musica e agoni nella Grecia antica* (Proceedings of the 2010 MOISA Conference, Lecce), edited by D. Castaldo, and A. Manieri, 720–764. Galatina: Congedo.

—. 2013. "Song-Benders of Circular Choruses": Dithyramb and the 'Demise of Music'." In *Song Culture and Social Change: The Contexts of Dithyramb*, edited by P. Wilson, and B. Kowalzig, 213–36. Oxford: Oxford University Press.

—. 2016. *Kinyras: The Divine Lyre*. Washington D.C.: Center for Hellenic Studies/Harvard University Press.

Fraser, P.M., and E. Matthews. 1987–2010. *A Lexicon of Greek Personal Names*. Oxford and New York: Oxford University Press.

Frei, J. 1900. *De certaminibus thymelicis*. Basil: Ex officina E. Birkhaeuser.

Frisk, H. 1943. "Zur griechischen Wortkunde." *Eranos* 41: 46-54.

—. 1960-72. *Griechisches etymologisches Wörterbuch*. Heidelberg: Carl Winter.

Furley, W.D. 1995. "Praise and Persuasion in Greek Hymns." *JHS* 115: 29-46.

Furley, W.D., and J.M. Bremer. 2001. *Greek Hymns: Selected Cult Songs from the Archaic to the Hellenistic Period*. 2 vols. Tübingen: Mohr Siebeck.

Garber, J.J. 2008. *Harmony in Healing: The Theoretical Basis of Ancient and Medieval Medicine*. New Brunswick: Transaction.

Garfinkel, A.P., and S.J. Waller. 2012. "Sounds and Symbolism from the Netherworld: Acoustic Archaeology at the Animal Master's Portal." *PCASQ* 46.4:37-60.

Gell, A. 1998. *Art and Agency: An Anthropological Theory*. Oxford: Oxford University Press.

Giangrande, G. 1963. "Konjekturen zur Anthologia Palatina." *RhM* 106: 255-63.

Gibson, S. 2005. *Aristoxenus of Tarentum and the Birth of Musicology*. New York: Routledge.

Gilula, D. 2000. "Stratonicus, the Witty Harpist." In *Athenaeus and his World*, edited by D. Braund and J. Wilkins, 423–33. Exeter: University of Exeter Press.

Godman, R. 2006. "The Enigma of Vitruvian Resonating Vases and the Relevance of the Concept for Today." *Working Papers in Art and Design* 4. http://sitem.herts.ac.uk/artdes_research/papers/wpades/vol4/rgfull.html

Godwin, J. 1987. *Harmonies of Heaven and Earth: The Spiritual Dimension of Music from Antiquity to the Avant-Garde*. London: Inner Traditions.

Goette, H.R. 2000. *Ὁ ἀξιόλογος δῆμος Σούνιον: Landeskundliche Studien in Südost-Attika*. Rahden: Marie Leidorf.

Gogos, S. 2011. *Das Theater von Epidauros. Mit einem Beitrag zur Akustik des Theaters von Georgios Kampourakis*. Vienna: Phoibos.

Goodyear, W.H. 1912. *Greek Refinements: Studies in Temperamental Architecture.* New Haven: Yale University Press.

Gow, A.S.F. 1912. "On the Meaning of the Word ΘΥΜΕΛΗ." *JHS* 32: 213–38.

Gow, A.S.F., and D.L. Page. 1968. *The Greek Anthology. II. The Garland of Philip and Some Contemporary Epigrams.* Cambridge: Cambridge University Press.

Grandjean, Y., and F. Salviat. 2000. *Guide de Thasos.* 2nd ed. Paris: de Boccard.

Gros, P., A. Corso, and E. Romano. 1997. *Vitruvio. De architectura.* Torino: Giulio Einaudi.

Gruben, G. 2001. *Griechische Tempel und Heiligtümer.* Munich: Hirmer.

Gumbrecht, H.U. 2004. *The Production of Presence: What Meaning Cannot Convey.* Stanford: Stanford University Press.

Gurd, S.A. 2016. *Dissonance: Auditory Aesthetics in Ancient Greece.* New York: Fordham University Press.

Gutzwiller, K.J. 1995. "Cleopatra's Ring." *GRBS* 36: 383-98.

Hackstein, O. 2002. *Die Sprachform der homerischen Epen. Faktoren morphologischer Variabilität in literarischen Frühformen. Tradition, Sprachwandel, Sprachliche Anachronismen.* Wiesbaden: Reichert Verlag.

Hagel, S. 2000. *Modulation in altgriechischer Musik: Antike Melodien im Licht antiker Musiktheorie.* Frankfurt am Main: P. Lang.

—. 2002. "Musik zwischen Apollon und Dionysos—der delphische Paian des Athenaios." In *Archäologie früher Klangerzeugung und Tonordnungen*, edited by E. Hickmann, R. Eichmann, and A. Kilmer, 403–11. Rahden: Verlag Marie Leidorf.

—. 2005. "Twenty-four in Auloi. Aristotle, Met. 1093b, the Harmony of the Spheres, and the Formation of the Perfect System." In *Ancient Greek Music in Performance*, edited by S. Hagel and C. Harrauer, 51–92. Vienna: Verlag der Österreichischen Akademie der Wissenschaften.

—. 2009. *Ancient Greek Music: A New Technical History*. Cambridge: Cambridge University Press.

—. 2010. *Ancient Greek Music: A Technical History*. Cambridge: Cambridge University Press.

Hamilakis, Y. 2002. "The Past as Oral History: Towards an Archaeology of the Senses." In *Thinking Through the Body: Archaeologies of Corporeality*, edited by Y. Hamilakis, M. Pluciennik, and S. Tarlow, 121-36. New York: Kluwer Academic/Plenum.

—. 2013. *Archaeology and the Senses. Human Experience, Memory, and Affect*. Cambridge and New York: Cambridge University Press.

—. 2017. "Sensorial Assemblages: Affect, Memory, and Temporality in Assemblage Thinking." *CAJ* 27.1: 169-182.

Harrison, J. E. 1921 (repr. 1962). *Epilegomena to the Study of Greek Religion and Themis*. Cambridge: Cambridge University Press. Repr. New York: University Books.

Harrison, K. 1967–1968. "Vitruvius and Acoustic Jars in England during the Middle Ages." *Transactions of the Ancient Monuments Society* 15: 49–58.

Hartigan, K.V. 2009. *Performance and Cure: Drama and Healing in Ancient Greece and Contemporary America*. London: Duckworth.

Hedreen, G. 2010. "The Trojan War, Theoxenia, and Aegina in Pindar's Paean 6 and the Aphaia Sculptures." In *Aegina: Contexts for Choral Lyric Poetry*, edited by D. Fearn, 323-69. Oxford: Oxford University Press.

—. 2013. "The Semantics of Processional Dithyramb: Pindar's Second Dithyramb and Archaic Athenian Vase Painting." In *Dithyramb in Context*, edited by B. Kowalzig and P. Wilson, 171-97. Cambridge and London: Cambridge University Press.

Helmholtz, H.L.F. 1895. *On the Sensations of Tone as a Physiological Basis for the Theory of Music*. London: Longmans, Green, & Co.

Herrlich, S. 1898. *Epidaurus, eine antike Heilstätte*. Berling: R. Gaertners.

Hills, G.M. 1882. "Earthenware Pots (Built into Churches) Which Have Been Called Acoustic Vases." *Transactions of the Royal Institute of British Architects* Session 1881–82: 81–96.

Hinge, G. 2006. *Die Sprache Alkmans: Textgeschichte und Sprachgeschichte.* Wiesbaden: Reichert Verlag.

—. 2009. "Cultic persona and the Transmission of the Partheneions." In *Aspects of Ancient Greek Cult: Context, Ritual, Iconography*, edited by J.T. Jensen, G. Hinge, P. Schultz, and B. Wickkiser, 215-36. Aarhus: Aarhus University Press.

Hodder, I., and S. Hutson. 2003. *Reading the Past.* Cambridge: Cambridge University Press.

Holland, L. 1948. Review of Robert 1939, *AJA* 52: 307-10.

Hollinshead, M.B. 1999. "'Adyton,' 'Opisthodomos,' and the Inner Room of the Greek Temple." *Hesperia* 68.2: 189-218.

—. 2012. "Monumental Steps and the Shaping of Ceremony." In *Architecture of the Sacred: Space, Ritual, and Experience from Classical Greece to Byzantium*, edited by B.D. Wescoat and R.G. Ousterhout, 27-65. Cambridge: Cambridge University Press.

—. 2015. *Shaping Ceremony: Monumental Steps and Greek Architecture.* Madison, WI: University of Wisconsin Press.

Holmes, B. 2010. *The Symptom and the Subject: The Emergence of the Physical Body in Ancient Greece.* Princeton: Princeton University Press.

Hölscher, T. 2002. "Rituelle Räume und politische Denkmäler im Heiligtum von Olympia." In *Olympia 1875-2000: 125 Jahre deutsche Ausgrabungen*, edited by H. Kyrieleis, 331-45. Mainz: Philipp von Zabern.

Holwerda, J.H. 1904. "Die Tholos in Epidauros." *RhM* 59: 532-41.

Huffman, C.A. 2005. *Archytas of Tarentum: Pythagorean, Philosopher and Mathematician King.* Cambridge: Cambridge University Press.

Huffman, C.A., ed. 2012. *Aristoxenus of Tarentum: Discussion.* Rutgers University Studies in Classical Humanities vol. XVII. New Brunswick: Transaction Publishers.

—. 2014. *A History of Pythagoreanism.* Cambridge: Cambridge University Press.

Huguenot, C. 2003. "La réutilisation des édifices funéraires helladiques à l'époque hellénistique." *NumAntCl* 32: 81-140.

Hurwit, J. 2004. *The Acropolis in the Age of Pericles.* Cambridge and London: Cambridge University Press.

Jacoby, F., ed. 1926. *Die Fragmente der griechischen Historiker.* Berlin: Weidmann.

Jeffery, L.H. 1990. *The Local Scripts of Archaic Greece: A Study of the Origin of the Greek Alphabet and its Development from the Eighth to the Fifth Centuries B.C.* (rev. ed.). Oxford and New York: Clarendon Press.

Johansen, H. F., and E.W. Whittle. 1980. *Aeschylus. The Suppliants.* Copenhagen: Gyldendal.

Jones, M.W. 2003. *Principles of Roman Architecture.* New Haven: Yale University Press.

—. 2013. *Origins of Classical Architecture. Temples, Orders, and Gifts to the Gods in Ancient Greece.* New Haven: Yale University Press.

Jouanna, J. 2009. "Does Galen Have a Medical Programme for Intellectuals and the Faculties of the Intellect?" In *Galen and the World of Knowledge*, edited by C. Gill, T. Whitmarsh, and J. Wilkins, 190-205. Cambridge: Cambridge University Press.

Jucker, I. 1963. "Frauenfest in Korinth." *Antike Kunst* 6: 47-61.

Kaiser, S.I., ed. 2010. *Die Fragmente des Aristoxenos aus Tarent.* Hildesheim: Olms.

Kaltsas, N. 1997. *Olympia.* Athens: Epikoinonia.

Kanellopoulos, C., and E. Zavvou. 2014. "The Agora of Gytheion." *ABSA* 109: 357-378.

Käppel, L. 1989. "Das Theater von Epidauros: Die mathematische Grundidee des Gesamtentwurfs und ihr möglicher Sinn." *JdI* 104: 83-106.

—. 1992. *Paian: Studien zur Geschichte einer Gattung*. Berlin: de Gruyter.

Karanika, A. 2005. "Ecstasis in Healing: Practices in Southern Italy and Greece from Antiquity to the Present." In *Performing Ecstasies: Music, Dance, and Ritual in the Mediterranean*. Edited by L. del Giudice and N. van Deusen, 25-36. Ottawa: Institute of Medieval Music.

Kassel, R., and C. Austin, eds. 1983-. *Poetae comici Graeci*. Berlin: de Gruyter.

Kavvadias, P. 1900. *To Hieron tou Asklēpiou en Epidaurō kai hē Therapeia tōn Asthenōn*. Athens: Archaeologikē Hetaireia.

Kearns, E. 1989. *The Heroes of Attica*. London: University of London, Institute of Classical Studies.

Kennedy, J.B. 2011. *The Musical Structure of Plato's Dialogues*. Durham: Acumen.

Kerényi, K. 1959. *Asklepios: Archetypal Image of the Physician's Existence*. Translated by R. Manheim. New York: Pantheon.

—. 1976. *Dionysos: Archetypal Image of the Indestructible Life*. Translated by R. Manheim. Princeton: Princeton University Press.

Kolar, M. A., and J.W. Rick, P.R. Cook, and J.S. Abel. 2012. "Ancient Pututus Contextualized: Integrative Archaeoacoustics at Chavín de Huántar, Perú." In *Flower World: Music Archaeology of the Americas*, Vol. 1. Edited by M. Stöckli and Arnd Adje Both, 23-54. Berlin: Ekho Verlag.

Kolar, M.A. 2013a. "Archaeological Psychoacoustics at Chavín de Huántar, Perú." Ph.D. dissertation, Stanford University.

—. 2013b. "New Evidence for Ritual Sound Environment Use and Design at Chavín de Huántar, Perú." Lecture presented at the 78th Annual Meeting of the Society for American Archaeology, 5 April 2013, Honolulu. Symposium: "Ritual Innovation, Material Culture, and Environment in Chavín de Huántar, Perú."

—. 2014. "Pututus, Resonance, and Beats. Acoustic Wave Interference Effects at Ancient Chavín de Huántar, Perú." Lecture presented at the 168th Annual Meeting of the Acoustical Society of America, Indianapolis, 30 October 2014. Session 4pAAa: "Architectural Acoustics and Speech Communication: Acoustic Trick-or-Treat. Eerie Noises, Spooky Speech, and Creative Masking."

Kolb, F. 1981. *Agora und Theater, Volks- und Festversammlung*. Deutsches Archäologisches Institut, Archäologische Forschungen Bd. 9. Berlin: Mann.

Kolde, A. 2003. *Politique et religion chez Isyllos d'Epidaure*. Basel: Schwabe.

Kotsidu, H. 1991. *Die musischen Agone der Panathenäen in archaischer und klassischer Zeit: eine historisch-archäologische Untersuchung*. München: Tuduv.

Kourinou, E. 2000. *Σπάρτη. Συμβολή στη μνημειακή τοπογραφία της*. Athens: Horos.

Kovacs, D. 1998. *Euripides. Suppliant Women, Electra, Heracles*. Cambridge, MA and London: Harvard University Press.

Kowalzig, B. 2007. *Singing for the Gods: Performances of Myth and Ritual in Archaic and Classical Greece*. Oxford: Oxford University Press.

Kowalzig, B., and P. Wilson, eds. 2013. *Dithyramb in Context*. Oxford: Oxford University Press.

Krause, B. 1972. "Zum Asklepios-Kultbild des Thrasymedes in Epidauros." *AA*: 240-57.

Kritzas, C.B. 1998. "Nouvelle inscription provenant de l'Asclépiéion de Lébéna (Crète)." *ASAtene* 70-1 (1992-93): 275-90.

—. 2006. "Choroi. The Dancing Floors of Greek Sanctuaries." Paper read at the 107th Annual Meeting of the Archaeological Institute of America, Montreal, January 6, 2006.

Kurke, L. 2005. "Choral Lyric as 'Ritualization': Poetic Sacrifices and Poetic Ego in Pindar's Sixth Paian." *CA* 24.1: 81-130.

Laferrière, C. 2016. "The Vari Cave as a Vibrant Soundscape." Paper read at the Sound and Auditory Culture in Greco-Roman Antiquity conference, University of Missouri, April 1-2, 2016.

—. 2017. "The Complex Sensations of Divine Music in Archaic and Classical Greek Art." Ph.D. Dissertation, Yale University.

Laidlaw, A. 1985. *The First Style in Pompeii. Painting and Architecture.* Rome: G. Bretschneider.

Lambrinoudakis, V.K. 2014. "Theurgic Medicine." In *Hygieia: Health, Illness and Treatment from Homer to Galen*, edited by N.C. Stampolidis and Y. Tassoulas, 17-31. Athens: Museum of Cycladic Art.

Lambrinoudakis, V.K., and S.E. Katakis. 2017. "The University of Athens New Excavation Project in the City and the Asklepieion of Epidauros." Paper read at the National and Kapodistrian University of Athens, Eleventh Archaeological Symposium, Fieldwork and Research XI: The Work of the Department of Archaeology and History of Art, April 6, 2017.

Landels, J.G. 1967. "Assisted Resonance in Ancient Theatres." *GaR* 14: 80-94.

—. 1999. *Music in Ancient Greece and Rome.* London: Routledge.

Langdon, M., and L.V. Watrous. 1977. "The Farm of Timesios: Rock-cut Inscriptions in South Attica." *Hesperia* 46: 162-77.

Lapatin, K. 2001. *Chryselephantine Statuary in the Ancient Mediterranean World.* Oxford: Oxford University Press.

Larson, J. 2007. *Ancient Greek Cults. A Guide.* London and New York: Routledge.

Lattimore, S. 1997. "Art and Architecture." In *The Greek World in the Fourth Century*, edited by L. Tritle, 249-82. London: Routledge.

Lawler, L.B. 1947. "The Dance in Ancient Greece." *CJ* 42: 343-49.

Lawrence, A.W. 1957. *Greek Architecture.* New York and London: Penguin.

Lawson, G. 2006. "Large Scale—Small Scale: Medieval Stone Buildings, Early Medieval Timber Halls and the Problem of the Lyre." In *Archaeoacoustics,* edited by C. Scarre and G. Lawson, 85-94. Cambridge: McDonald Institute for Archaeological Research.

Lawson, G., C. Scarre, I. Cross, and C. Hills. 1988. "Mounds, Megaliths, Music and Mind: Some Thoughts on the Acoustical Properties and Purposes of Archaeological Spaces." *Archaeological Review from Cambridge* 15.1: 111–34.

Lee, K.H. 1997. *Euripides. Ion.* Warminster: Aris & Phillips.

Lempidaki, E. 2003. "Μικρά Ιερά του Ασκληπιείου Επιδαύρου." Ph.D. dissertation, University of Athens.

van Lennep, D.J. 1822. *Hieronymi de Bosch observationum et notarum in Antologiam Graecam volumen alterum.* Utrecht: J. Altheer.

LeVen, P.A. 2014. *The Many-Headed Muse: Tradition and Innovation in Late Classical Greek Lyric Poetry.* Cambridge and New York: Cambridge University Press.

Leventi I. 2003. *Hygieia in Classical Greek Art*. Archaiognosia Supplementary Volume 2. Athens: University of Athens Press.

Lewcock, R., R. Pirn, and J. Meyer. 2007–2011. "Acoustics, §I: Room Acoustics." In *Grove Music Online*, edited by S. Sadie, s.v. London and New York: Macmillan/Grove's Dictionaries of Music.

Liddell, H.G. and R. Scott. 1996. *A Greek-English Lexicon. With a Revised Supplement.* Oxford: Clarendon Press.

LiDonnici, L.R. 1995. *The Epidaurian Miracle Inscriptions: Text, Translation, and Commentary.* Atlanta: Scholars Press.

Lind, T.T. 2009. "Music and Cult in Ancient Greece." In *Aspects of Ancient Greek Cult: Context, Ritual, Iconography*, edited by J.T. Jensen, G. Hinge, P. Schultz, and B. Wickkiser, 195-214. Aarhus: Aarhus University Press.

Lonsdale, S. H. 1995. *Dance and Ritual Play in Greek Religion*. Baltimore: Johns Hopkins University Press.

Ma, J. 2013. *Statues and Cities. Honorific Portraits and Civic Identity in the Hellenistic World*. Oxford: Oxford University Press.

Maas, P. 1933. *Epidaurische Hymnen*. Halle: M. Niemeyer.

Maas, M., and J.M. Snyder. 1989. *Stringed Instruments of Ancient Greece*. New Haven: Yale University Press.

Machemer, G.A. 1993. "Medicine, Music, and Magic: The Healing Grace of Pindar's *Fourth Nemean*." *HSCP* 95: 113-41.

Marchetti, P., and Y. Rizakis. 1995. "Recherches sur les mythes et la topographie d'Argos. IV. L'Agora revisitée." *BCH* 119: 437-72.

Marriott, H.P.F. 1895. *Facts About Pompei: Its Masons' Marks, Town Walls, Houses, and Portraits*. London: Hazell, Watson & Viney.

Marsá, V. 2008. *Himnos Délficos Dedicados a Apolo: Análisis Histórico y Musical*. Castelló de la Plana: Universitat Jaume I.

Martin, R. 1965. *Manuel d'Architecture Grecque*. Paris: Éditions A. et J. Picard.

Martinelli, M.C., ed. 2009. *La musa dimenticata: aspetti dell'esperienza musicale greca in età ellenistica*. Pisa: Edizioni della Normale.

Mathiesen, T.J. 1999. *Apollo's Lyre: Greek music and music theory in antiquity and the Middle Ages*. Lincoln, NE: University of Nebraska Press.

Mayrhofer, M. 1986-2001. *Etymologisches Wörterbuch des Altindoarischen*. Heidelberg: Winter Verlag.

McCredie, J. R. 1968. "Samothrace: Preliminary Report on the Campaigns of 1965-1967." *Hesperia* 37: 200-34.

McKenny Hughes, T. 1915. "Acoustic Vases in Churches Traced Back to the Theatres and Oracles of Greece." *Cambridge Antiquarian Society Communications* 19: 63–90.

Meier-Brügger, M. 1989. "Griech. θῡμός und seine Sippe." *MusHelv* 46: 243-46.

Melfi, M. 2007. *I santuari di Asclepio in Grecia.* Rome: Erma di Bretschneider.

Miller, M.C. 1997. *Athens and Persia in the Fifth Century B.C.: A Study in Cultural Receptivity.* Cambridge: Cambridge University Press.

Mills, S. 2014. *Auditory Archaeology. Understanding Sound and Hearing in the Past.* London and New York: Routledge.

Mitchell-Boyask, R. 2008. *Plague and the Athenian Imagination: Drama, History, and the Cult of Asclepius.* Cambridge: Cambridge University Press.

Mitsos, M.T. 1967. "Ἐπιγραφικὰ ἐξ Ἀσκληπιείου Ἐπιδαύρου." *AE*: 1-28.

Morris, I. 2000. *Archaeology as Cultural History: Words and Things in Iron Age Greece.* London: Wiley-Blackwell.

Muller-Dufeu, M. 2002. *La Sculpture Grecque: Sources Littéraires et Épigraphiques.* Paris: École superieure des beaux arts.

Musti, D. 2000. "Musica greca tra aristocrazia e democrazia." In *Synaulia: Cultura Musicale in Grecia e Contatti Mediterranei,* edited by A. Cassio, D. Musti, and L. Rossi, 7-55. Naples: AION.

Mylonopoulos, J. 2011. "Divine Images Behind Bars: The Semantics of Barriers in Greek Temples." In *Current Approaches to Religion in Ancient Greece,* edited by M. Haysom and J. Wallensten, 269-91. Stockholm: Svenska institutet i Athen.

Nielsen. I. 2002. *Cultic Theatres and Ritual Drama.* Aarhus: Aarhus University Press.

Nilsson, M.P. 1968. *The Minoan-Mycenaean Religion and its Survival in Greek Religion,* 2nd Ed. Lund: Gleerup.

Niniou-Kindeli, V., and N. Chatzidakis. 2016. "The Roman Theatre at Aptera: a Preliminary Report." In *Roman Crete: New Perspectives*, edited by J.E. Francis and Anna Kouremenos, 127-154. Oxford. Philadelphia: Oxbow Books.

Nisbett, A. 1965. *The Technique of the Sound Studio*. New York: Hastings House.

Ohnesorg, A. 1991. "Altäre auf Paros." In *L'Espace Sacrificiel dans les Civilisations Méditerranéennes de l'Antiquité: Actes du Colloque Tenu à la Maison de l'Orient, Lyon, 4-7 Juin 1988*, edited by R. Etienne and M.-T. Le Dinahet, 121-26. Lyon: Bibliothèque Salomon-Reinach, Université Lumière-Lyon 2.

—. 2005. *Ionische Altäre. Formen und Varianten einer Architekturgattung aus Insel- und Ostionien*. Berlin: Mann.

Otto, W. 1995. *Dionysos: Myth and Cult*. Bloomington: Indiana University Press.

Page, D.L. 1962. *Poetae Melici Graeci*. Oxford: Clarendon Press.

Pakkanen, J. 2008. "The Erechtheion and the Length of the 'Doric-Pheidonic' Foot." *Talanta. Proceedings of the Dutch Archaeological and Historical Society* 28–29: 97–122.

—. 2013. *Classical Greek Architectural Design: A Quantitative Approach*. Helsinki: Foundation of the Finnish Institute at Athens.

—. 2014. "Observations on the Reconstruction of the Late Classical Temple of Athena Alea." In *Tegea II, Investigations in the Sanctuary of Athena Alea 1990-94 and 2004*, edited by E. Østby, 353-370. Papers and Monographs from the Norwegian Institute at Athens 4. Athens: The Norwegian Institute at Athens.

Paton, J.M., et.al. 1927. *The Erechtheum*. Cambridge, MA: American School of Classical Studies at Athens.

Peek, W. 1969. *Inschriften aus dem Asklepieion von Epidauros*. Berlin: Akademie-Verl.

Petrakos, V.C. 1968. Ὁ Ὠρωπὸς καὶ τὸ ἱερὸν τοῦ Ἀμφιαράου. Athens: Archaiologike Etaireia.

Petsalis-Diomidis, A. 2005. "The Body in Space: Visual Dynamics in Graeco-Roman Pilgrimage in Classical Greece." In *Pilgrimage in Graeco-Roman and Early Christian Antiquity: Seeing the Gods*, edited by J. Elsner and I. Rutherford, 183-218. Oxford: Oxford University Press.

—. 2010. *'Truly Beyond Wonders': Aelius Aristides and the Cult of Asklepios.* Oxford: Oxford University Press.

Pigeaud, J.-M. 1978. "Du rythme dans le corps: Quelques notes sur l'interprétation du pouls par le médecin Hérophile." *Bulletin de l'Association Guillaume Budé* 3: 258-67.

Platt, V. 2011. *Facing the Gods: Epiphany and Representation in Graeco-Roman Art, Literature, and Religion.* Cambridge: Cambridge University Press.

—. 2016. "Sight and the Gods: On the Desire to See Naked Nymphs." In *Sight and the Ancient Senses*, edited by M. Squire, 161-79. London and New York: Routledge.

Plommer, H. 1983. "Scythopolis, Caesarea, and Vitruvius: Sounding-Vessels in Ancient Theatres." *Levant* 15: 132-40.

Pöhlmann, E., and M.L. West, eds. 2001. *Documents of Ancient Greek Music: The Extant Melodies and Fragments Edited and Transcribed with Commentary.* Oxford: Clarendon Press.

Polacco, L. 1998. *Kyklos: la Fenomenologia del Cerchio nel Pensiero e nell' Arte dei Greci.* Venice: Istituto Veneto di Scienze, Lettere ed Arti.

Polacco, L., et al. 1990. *Il Teatro Antico di Siracusa: pars Altera.* Padua: Programma.

—. 1990. *The Art of Ancient Greece: Sources and Documents*, 2nd Ed. Cambridge and London: Cambridge University Press.

Poule, B. 2000. "Les vases acoustiques du theâtre de Mummius Achaicus." *RA* 2000.1: 37–50.

Powell, J.U., ed. 1925. *Collectanea Alexandrina.* Oxford: Clarendon Press.

Power, T. 2007. "Ion of Chios and the Politics of *Polychordia*." In *The World of Ion of Chios*, edited by V. Jennings, and A. Katsaros, 179–205. Leiden and Boston: Brill.

—. 2010. *The Culture of Kitharoidia*. Cambridge, MA: Harvard University Press.

—. 2012. "Aristoxenus and the 'Neoclassicists'." In *Aristoxenus of Tarentum: Discussion*, Rutgers University Studies in Classical Humanities vol. XVII, edited by C.A. Huffman, 129-54. New Brunswick: Transaction Publishers.

Prauscello, L. 2009. "Wandering Poetry, Travelling Music: Timotheus' Muse and Some Case-Studies of Shifting Cultural Identities." In *Wandering Poets in Ancient Greek Culture: Travel, Locality and Panhellenism*, edited by R. Hunter, and I. Rutherford, 168–94. Cambridge: Cambridge University Press.

Prignitz, S. 2014. *Bauurkunden und Bauprogramm von Epidauros (400-350): Asklepiostempel, Tholos, Kultbild, Brunnenhaus*. Munich: C.H. Beck.

Provenza, A. 2006. "Medicina e musica in Platone: il Timeo e il progetto paideutico della Repubblica." *Seminari romani di cultura greca* 9.1: 105-28.

—. 2007. "La musicoterapia nell'antica Grecia." Ph.D. dissertation, l'Università degli Studi di Palermo.

—. 2009. "Phobos, incantamento e catarsi. Alcune riflessioni su ascolto dell'aulos e tragedia." *RivFil* 137.3–4: 280–301.

—. 2010. "Tra incantamento e phobos. Alcuni esempi sugli effetti dell'aulos nei dialoghi di Platone e nella catarsi tragica." In *La musica nell'Impero Romano. Testimonianze teoriche e scoperte archeologiche*, edited by E. Rocconi, 141–52. Pavia: Pavia University Press.

—. 2012. "Aristoxenus and Music Therapy: Fr. 26 Wehrli within the Tradition on Music and Catharsis." In *Aristoxenus of Tarentum: Discussion*, Rutgers University Studies in Classical Humanities vol. XVII, edited by C.A. Huffman, 91-128. New Brunswick: Transaction Publishers.

—. 2014. "Soothing Lyres and *epodai*: Music Therapy and the Cases of Orpheus, Empedocles, and David." In *Music in Antiquity: The Near East and the Mediterranean*, edited by J. Goodnick Westenholz, Y. Maurey, and E. Seroussi, 298-339. Berlin and Boston: de Gruyter.

Purser, J. 2014. "The Significance of Music in the Gàidhealtachd in the Pre- and Early-Historic Period." *ScS* 37: 207-221.

Purves, A. Forthcoming. *Touch and the Ancient Senses*. London and New York: Routledge.

Rainer, B.L. 1975. "Philodamus' Paean to Dionysus: A Literary Expression of Delphic Propaganda." Ph.D. dissertation, University of Illinois at Urbana.

Ramsay, W. 1941. *The Social Basis of Roman Power in Asia Minor*. Aberdeen: Aberdeen University Press.

Rehm, R. 2002. *The Play of Space: Spatial Transformation in Greek Tragedy*. Princeton: Princeton University Press.

—. 2006. "Going in Circles: Speculations on the Introduction of the Circular Orchestra in Greek Theatres." Abstract for a paper delivered at the 107th Annual Meeting of the Archaeological Institute of America, Montreal. http://www.archaeological.org/webinfo.php?page=10248&searchtype=abstract&ytable=2006&sessionid=4D&paperid=774.

Rekowska, M. 2012. "Architectural Decoration of the House of Leukaktios: Preliminary Remarks." In *Ptolemais in Cyrenaica, Studies in Memory of Tomasz Mikocki*, edited by J. Zelazowski, 157-182. Warsaw: Institute of Archaeology, University of Warsaw.

Renberg, G.H. 2017. *Where Dreams May Come. Incubation Sanctuaries in the Greco-Roman World*. Leiden: Brill.

Reznikoff, I. 2002. "Prehistoric Paintings, Sound and Rocks." In *Archäologie früher Klangerzeugung und Tonordnungen*, edited by E. Hickmann, R. Eichmann, and A. Kilmer, 39–56. Rahden: Verlag Marie Leidorf.

—. 2006. "The Evidence of the Use of Sound Resonance from Palaeolithic to Medieval Times." In *Archaeoacoustics*, edited by C. Scarre, and G. Lawson, 77–84. Cambridge and Oakville, CT: McDonald Institute for Archaeological Research/David Brown.

Richards-Madzoulinou, E. 1981. "Η φυτική διακοσμήση των κλασικων χρόνων." *AAA* 14: 208-29.

Richter, L. 1999. "Struktur und Rezeption antiker Planetenskalen." *Die Musikforschung* 52: 289–306.

—. 2000. *Momente der Musikgeschichte: Antike und Byzanz*. Anif and Salzburg: Mueller-Speiser.

Ridgway, B.S. 1997. *Fourth Century Styles in Greek Sculpture*. Madison: University of Wisconsin Press.

Riethmüller, J.W. 1996. "Die Tholos und das Ei. Zur Deutung der Thymele von Epidauros." *Nikephoros* 9: 71-109.

—. 2005. *Asklepios: Heiligtümer und Kulte*. 2 vols. Heidelberg: Archäologie und Geschichte.

Rix, H. 2001. *Lexikon der indogermanischen Verben*. 2nd ed. Wiesbaden: Reichert Verlag.

Robert, C. 1897. "Zur Theaterfrage." *Hermes* 32: 421-53.

Robert, F. 1939. *Thymélè: recherches sur la signification et la destination des monuments circulaires dans l'architecture religieuse de la Grèce*. Paris: E. de Boccard.

Rocconi, E. 2006. "Theatres and Theatre Design in the Greco-Roman World: Theoretical and Empirical Approaches." In *Archaeoacoustics*, edited by C. Scarre and G. Lawson, 71–76. Cambridge and Oakville, CT: McDonald Institute for Archaeological Research/David Brown.

Rolley, C. 1999. *La sculpture grecque. 2: La période classique*. Paris: A. and J. Picard.

Rosen, R.M. 2002. "Cratinus' Pytine and the Construction of the Comic Self." In *The Rivals of Aristophanes: Studies in Athenian Old Comedy*, edited by F.D. Harvey and J. Wilkins, 23-39. London: Duckworth.

—. 2013. "Galen, Plato, and the Physiology of Eros." In *Eros in Ancient Greece*, edited by C. Sanders et al., 111-128. Oxford: Oxford University Press.

Roussel, P. 1911. "L'Hestia à l'Omphalos." *RA* 1911: 86-91.

Roux, G. 1961. *L'architecture de l'Argolide aux IVe et IIIe siècles avant JC*. Paris: E. de Boccard.

—. 1976. *Delphes. Son oracle et ses dieux.* Paris: Belles Lettres.

—. 1988. "La tholos d'Athena Pronaia dans son sanctuaire de Delphes." *CRAI* 132.2: 290-309.

Rowland, I.D., and T.N. Howe. 1999. *Vitruvius: Ten Books on Architecture.* New York: Cambridge University Press.

Rudolph, K., ed. Forthcoming. *Taste and the Ancient Senses.* London and New York: Routledge.

Rutherford, I. 1995. "Apollo in Ivy: The Tragic Paean." *Arion* 3.1: 112-35.

—. 2001. *Pindar's Paeans: A Reading of the Fragments with a Survey of the Genre.* Oxford: Oxford University Press.

Rynearson, N. 2009. "A Callimachean Case of Lovesickness: Magic, Disease, and Desire in Aetia frr. 67-75 Pf." *AJP* 130: 341-65.

Saliou, C. 2009. *Vitruve: De l'architecture. Livre v.* Paris: Les belles lettres.

Sanders, E., C. Thumiger, C. Carey, and N.J. Lowe, eds. 2013. *Eros in Ancient Greece.* Oxford: Oxford University Press.

Sandin, P. 2005. *Aeschylus' Supplices: Introduction and Commentary on Vv. 1-523.* Lund: Symmachus.

Scahill, D. 2012. "The South Stoa at Corinth: Design, Construction and Function of the Greek Phase." Ph.D. dissertation, University of Bath.

Scarre, C. 2006. "Sound, Place, and Space: Towards an Archaeology of Acoustics." In *Archaeoacoustics*, edited by C. Scarre and G. Lawson, 1–10. Cambridge: McDonald Institute for Archaeological Research.

Scarre, C., and G. Lawson, eds. 2006 *Archaeoacoustics*. Cambridge and Oakville, CT: McDonald Institute for Archaeological Research/ David Brown.

Schafer, R. 1977. *The Soundscape. Our Sonic Environment and the Tuning of the World*. New York: Knopf.

Schofield, M. 2014. "Archytas." In *A History of Pythagoreanism*, edited by C. Huffman, 69-87. New York and Cambridge: Cambridge University Press.

Schrijver, P. 1991. *The Reflexes of the Proto-Indo-European Laryngeals in Latin*. Amsterdam and Atlanta, GA.: Rodopi.

Schröder, S. 1999. *Geschichte und Theorie der Gattung Paian: eine kritische Untersuchung mit einem Ausblick auf Behandlung und Auffassung der lyrischen Gattungen bei den alexandrinischen Philologen*. Stuttgart: Teubner.

Schultz, P. 2001. "The Akroteria of the Temple of Athena Nike." *Hesperia* 70.1: 1-47.

—. 2007a. "Leochares' Argead Portraits in the Philippeion." In *Early Hellenistic Portraiture. Image, Style, Context*, edited by P. Schultz and R. von den Hoff, 205-33. Cambridge and New York: Cambridge University Press.

—. 2007b. "Style and Agency in an Age of Transition." In *Debating the Athenian Cultural Revolution: Athenian Art, Literature, Language, Philosophy and Politics, 430-380 B.C.*, edited by R. Osborne, 144-87. Cambridge and New York: Cambridge University Press.

Schultz, P., and B.L. Wickkiser. 2010. "Communicating with the Gods in Ancient Greece: The Design and Functions of the 'Thymele' at Epidauros." *The International Journal of Technology, Knowledge and Society* 6.6: 143–64.

Schwyzer, E. 1939. *Griechische Grammatik. Erster Band: Allgemeiner Teil. Lautlehre, Wortbildung, Flexion.* München: C.H. Beck.

Scott, M. 2010. *Delphi and Olympia: The Spatial Politics of Panhellenism in the Archaic and Classical Periods.* New York and London: Cambridge University Press.

Scranton, R. 1969. "Greek Building." In *The Muses at Work. Arts, Crafts, and Professions in Ancient Greece and Rome,* edited by C. Roebuck, 2-34. Cambridge, Mass. and London: MIT Press.

Seaford, R. 2006. *Dionysos.* New York and London: Routledge.

Sear, F. 2006. *Roman Theatres: An Architectural Study.* Oxford: Oxford University Press.

Segal, A. 1995. *Theatres in Roman Palestine and Provincia Arabia.* Leiden: Brill.

Seiler, F. 1986. *Die griechische Tholos: Untersuchungen zur Entwicklung, Typologie und Funktion kunstmäßiger Rundbauten.* Mainz am Rhein: P. von Zabern.

Shankland, R.S. 1973. "Acoustics of Greek Theatres." *Physics Today* 26: 30–35.

Sider, D. 1997. *The Epigrams of Philodemos.* New York and Oxford: Oxford University Press.

Small, C. 1998. *Musicking: The Meanings of Performing and Listening.* Hanover and London: Wesleyan University Press.

Smith, A.C. .1993. "Athenianizing Associations in the Sculpture of the Temple of Asklepios at Epidauros." *AJA* 97: 300.

Snyder, J.M. 1984. "The Harmonia of Bow and Lyre in Heraclitus Fr. 51 (DK)." *Phronesis* 29.1: 91-5.

Squire, M., ed. 2016. *Sight and the Ancient Senses.* London and New York: Routledge.

von Staden, H. 1989. *Herophilus: The Art of Medicine in Early Alexandria: Edition, Translation and Essays.* Cambridge: Cambridge University Press.

Stafford, E. 2000. *Worshipping Virtues: Personification and the Divine in Ancient Greece.* London: Duckworth.

Stewart, A. 1982. "Dionysos at Delphi: The Pediments of the Sixth Temple of Apollo and Religious Reform in the Age of Alexander." *Studies in the History of Art* 10: 205-227.

Sullivan, L. 1896. "The Tall Office Building Artistically Considered." *Lippincott's Magazine* 57 (March 1896): 403-09.

Svolos, J. 1988a. "The History of the Tholos from the 4th Century B.C. to the Present." In *The Propylon of the "Gymnasium" and the Tholos in the Asklepieion at Epidauros: Preservation and Partial Restoration Proposals,* V. Lambrinoudakis et al., 225-33. Translated by J. Binder, et al. Athens: Ministry of Culture.

—. 1988b. "The Graphic Restoration of the Crepidoma of the Tholos." In *The Propylon of the "Gymnasium" and the Tholos in the Asklepieion at Epidauros: Preservation and Partial Restoration Proposals,* V. Lambrinoudakis et al., 243-88. Translated by J. Binder, et al. Athens: Ministry of Culture.

Swift, L.A. 2010. *The Hidden Chorus: Echoes of Genre in Tragic Lyric.* Oxford: Oxford University Press.

Tate, J. 1955. "The Backwards-Looking Greeks: B. A. Van Groningen; In the Grip of the Past. Essay on an Aspect of Greek Thought." *The Classical Review* 5 (01): 64-66.

Thiersch, H. 1909. "Antike Bauten für Musik." *Zeitschrift für Geschichte der Architektur* 2: 67-95.

Thomas, R. 1992. *Literacy and Orality in Ancient Greece.* New York and Cambridge: Cambridge University Press.

von Thüngen, S. 1994. *Die frei stehende griechische Exedra.* Mainz: P. von Zabern.

Till, R. 2010. "Songs of the Stones: The Acoustics of Stonehenge." In *The Sounds of Stonehenge.* CHOMBEC Working Papers No. 1, edited by Stephen Canfield, 17-44. Oxford: Archaeopress.

Tomlinson, R.A. 1969. "Two Buildings in Sanctuaries of Asklepios." *JHS* 89: 106-17.

—. 1983. *Epidauros*. Austin: University of Texas Press.

—. 1988. Review of Seiler 1986. *CR* 38: 350-52.

Toner, J, ed. 2014. *A Cultural History of the Senses in Antiquity*. London and New York: Bloomsbury.

Townsend, R. 2003. "The Philippeion and Fourth Century Athenian Architecture." In *The Macedonians in Athens 322-229 B.C.*, edited by O. Palagia and S.V. Tracy, 93-101. Oxford: Oxbow.

Truitt, P. 1969. "Attic White Ground Pyxis and Phiale, ca. 450 B.C." *Boston Museum Bulletin* 67: 72-92.

Ure, A.D. 1955. "Threshing Floor or Vineyard." *CQ* 5: 225-30.

de Vaan, M. 2008. *Etymological Dictionary of Latin and the other Italic Languages*. Leiden and Boston: Brill.

Vanderpool, E. 1982. "ΕΠΙ ΠΡΟΥΧΟΝΤΙ ΚΟΛΩΝΩΙ. The Sacred Threshing Floor at Eleusis." In *Studies in Athenian Architecture, Sculpture and Topography: Presented to Homer A. Thompson*, 172-74. Princeton: Princeton University Press.

Veronese, F. 2006. *Lo spazio e la dimensione del sacro. Santuari greci e territorio nella Sicilia arcaica*. Padova: Esedra.

Voigt, E.-M. 1971. *Sappho et Alcaeus. Fragmenta*. Amsterdam: Athenaeum.

Wagman, R. 1995. *Inni di Epidauro*. Pisa: Giardini.

—. 2012. "From Song to Monument: Sacred Poetry and Religious Revival in Roman Epidaurus." In *Hymnes de la Grèce antique: approches littéraires et historiques*. Actes du colloque international de Lyon, 19-21 juin 2008, Collection de la Maison de l'Orient (CMO) 50, Série littéraire et philosophique 17, 219-231. Lyon: Maison de l'Orient et de la Méditerranée.

Wallace, R.W. 1995. "Speech, Song and Text, Public and Private: Evolutions in Communications Media and Fora in Fourth-Century Athens." In *Die athenische Demokratie im 4. Jahrhundert v. Chr.: Vollendung oder Verfall einer Verfassungsform?*, edited by W. Eder, 199-224. Stuttgart: Steiner.

Waller, S. 2006. "Intentionality of Rock-art Placement Deduced from Acoustical Measurements and Echo Myths." In *Archaeoacoustics*, edited by C. Scarre and G. Lawson, Cambridge and Oakville, CT: McDonald Institute for Archaeological Research/David Brown.

Watson, A., and D. Keating. 1999. "Architecture and Sound: An Acoustic Analysis of Megalithic Monuments in Prehistoric Britain." *Antiquity* 73: 325-36.

Wehrli, F. 1945. *Die Schule des Aristoteles: Texte und Kommentare.* vol. 2. Basel: B. Schwabe.

—. 1967. *Die Schule des Aristoteles. Texte und Kommentare.* Basel: B. Schwabe.

Wescoat, B.D. 2012. "Coming and Going in the Sanctuary of the Great Gods, Samothrace." In *Architecture of the Sacred: Space, Ritual, and Experience from Classical Greece to Byzantium*, edited by B.D. Wescoat and R.G. Ousterhout, 66-113. Cambridge and New York: Cambridge University Press.

West, M.L. 1992. *Ancient Greek Music.* Oxford: Oxford University Press.

—. 2000. "Music Therapy in Antiquity." In *Music as Medicine: The History of Music Therapy since Antiquity*, edited by P. Horden, 51-68. Aldershot: Ashgate.

Whitely, J. 2001. *The Archaeology of Ancient Greece.* Cambridge: Cambridge University Press.

Wickkiser, B.L. 2008. *Asklepios, Medicine, and the Politics of Healing in Fifth-Century Greece: Between Craft and Cult.* Baltimore: Johns Hopkins University Press.

von Wilamowitz-Moellendorff, U. 1886. *Isyllos von Epidauros.* Berlin: Weidmann.

Wiles, D. 1997. *Tragedy in Athens*. Cambridge: Cambridge University Press.

Wilson, P. 1999. "The Aulos in Athens." In *Performance Culture and Athenian Democracy*, edited by S. D. Goldhill and R. Osborne, 58–95. Cambridge and New York: Cambridge University Press.

—. 2007. "Pronomos and Potamon: Two Pipers and Two Epigrams." *JHS* 127: 141–49.

Winnington-Ingram, R.P. 1976. "The Delphic Temple in Greek Tragedy." In *Miscellanea Tragica: In Honorem J.C. Kamerbeek*, edited by J.M. Bremer, S.L. Radt, and C.J. Ruijgh, 483-500. Amsterdam: Hakkert.

Woerther, F. 2008. "Music and the Education of the Soul in Plato and Aristotle: Homeopathy and the Formation of Character." *CQ* 58: 89–103.

Wright, J.P., and P. Potter, eds. 2000. *Psyche and Soma: Physicians and Metaphysicians on the Mind-Body Problem from Antiquity to Enlightenment*. Oxford: Clarendon Press.

Wyatt, W.F., and C.N. Edmonson. 1984. "The Ceiling of the Hephaisteion." *AJA* 88.2: 135–67.

Yalouris, N. 1992. *Die Skulpturen des Asklepiostempels in Epidauros, AntP* 21. Munich: Hermer.

Young, J.H. 1956. "Studies in South Attica: Country Estates at Sounion." *Hesperia* 25: 122-46.

Zhmud, L. 2014. "Sixth-, Fifth- and Fourth-Century Pythagoreans." In *A History of Pythagoreanism*, edited by C.A. Huffman, 88-111. Cambridge: Cambridge University Press.

Zimonyi, A. 2014. "The Context of Medical Competitions in Ephesus." *Acta Antiqua Academiae Scientiarum Hungaricae* 54.4: 355-70.

Ziolkowski, J.E. 1999. "The Bow and the Lyre: Harmonizing Duos in Plato's Symposium." *CJ* 95.1: 19-35.

INDEX

Abaton, 23
acoustics, 28-29, 75-78, 121-144,
       167-169, and 172-177
    ancient theories of, 76, 80-81, 83
    and architecture, 79, 89, 106, 121, 136
    modeling, 120, 144, 172-77
Achilles, 110, 115
Aelius Aristides, 94, 98, 111
Aeschylus, 49, 51, 62
Agamemnon, 53, 115
akroterion, floral, 35
Alexander of Macedon (the Great), 59
Alexandria, 37, 92, 125
Alkmaeon, 76, 102
altar
    of Apollo, 22, 97, 103, 106
    of Apollo at Didyma, 69
    of Asklepios, 22-23, 38-39, 90, 106, 111
    of Demeter at Arkouda on Thasos, 68
    of Dionysos, 46
    of Hestia, 98
altar court, 38-39, 69, 103, 105
Amesbury, 167
Amphiaraos, 68
Antioch, 50
Aphrodite, 55
Apollo (see also, Phoebus), 21-22, 30, 49,
    52, 55, 69, 72, 81, 86-88, 90-97, 101-
    103, 106, 109, 112, 114-17, 119, 147-48,
    164, 166
Apollo Pythios, 103, 106
Apollo, sanctuaries at
    Bassai, 147, 148, 156
    Delos, 90
    Delphi, 49, 52, 72, 87-88, 90, 93-94,
        96, 106, 148
    Didyma, 69
    Epidauros (see: Epidauros, sanctuary
        of Apollo)
    Erythrae, 95, 97, 99, 105

archaeoacoustics, 28-29, 73-83, 121-135,
    157-63
architecture
    Alexandrian, 37
    aural, 79, 106
    circular, 21-22
    sacred, 26, 35
architectural orders
    Doric, 35-37
    Ionic, 36-37
    Corinthian, 36-37, 39-40, 45, 104
Archytas, 73-74, 83
Argos
    Heraion at, 38
    stone from, 28, 40-41, 150
Ariphron, 94-95, 117
Aristonoos, 49, 55, 94, 96
Aristophanes, 107
Aristotle, 80, 83, 92
    De audibilibus, 129
    Problems, 129
Aristoxenos, 80-81, 83, 108-110, 125,
    130-131, 161-162, 170
Arsinoe II, 35
Asklepiades, 108
Asklepieion, 21-22, 25, 34, 38-39, 89, 94,
    107, 114, 133, 145-46, 150
Asklepios, 21-30, 33-34, 37-39, 55, 70,
    81, 84, 87-96, 98-99, 101, 103-115,
    117-19, 144, 151-52
Asklepios, sanctuaries at
    Athens (Acropolis), 107
    Epidauros, 26, 28, 30, 33-34, 84, 89,
        91-92, 103, 112
    Erythrae, 94-95
    Lebena, 70
    Lissos, 37
    Pergamon, 94, 98
Asklepios, tomb of, 23-24, 26
assembly marks (see also, masons' marks),
    146-48

Athena Alea at Tegea, 37
Athena Pronaia at Delphi (see also: Delphi, sanctuary of Athena Pronaia), 35
Athenaios, 100, 159
Athenian craftsmen, 36, 38
Athens
    Acropolis, 38, 107, 114
    City Dionysia, 87
    Erechtheion, 35, 40
    Hephaisteion, 146
    Parthenon, 36, 45
    Sacred Way, 88
    Theater of Dionysos, 68, 130
audience, 31, 66, 71, 74, 77, 86, 99, 104-107, 112, 116, 126, 128-129, 132, 134, 138, 157, 168
αὐλός / aulos / auloi, 47, 69, 102, 109, 119-20, 132, 156

Bacchus (see also, Dionysus), 95
Bacchylides, 94, 102
βῆμα (see also, speaking platform), 47, 143
βωμός (see also, altar), 46-47, 51, 53, 98
bronze, 25, 41, 71, 73, 75, 79-80, 82, 85, 93, 113, 119, 122-23, 125-126, 129, 135, 137, 143, 159, 164, 167

Calydon, 73
capstone, 41, 75, 139-141, 143, 174
cavea, 136, 157
cella, 24, 26, 40, 42, 66, 75-77, 102-104, 120, 135-36, 138-39, 141-43, 151, 158, 174, 177
Chavín de Huántar, Peru, 77, 167
Cheiron, 81, 115
choral song, 104, 137
choros / choroi, 67, 70-72
chorus, 46-49, 53-54, 93, 97, 103-104, 138, 165
Chryselephantine, 21
chthonic, 23, 142

circle / circularity, 26, 29, 40, 42-43, 66-74, 85, 97-98, 104, 109, 116, 119, 136, 139, 160, 165-67
cithara / citharoedi, 47, 81, 84-85, 101, 115
citharode(s): 76, 83, 93, 130, 132-35, 137
competition, musical, 27, 59, 88-89, 170
concert hall (see also, odeion) 31, 118, 133-34
contractor(s), 34, 78-79, 146-55, 162
Corinth, stone from, 150-51
costume, sacred, 69
Crete, 37, 68, 70, 108, 126
cult
    healing, 99, 107, 110-11, 119, 169-70
    mystery, 24, 42
    statue, 21
cyma recta frieze, 37
Cyprus / Cypriot, 138
Cyrenaean, 37

Damokritos, 154
dance, 29-30, 45, 49, 55-56, 65-66, 68-72, 74-75, 93, 97-99, 103-104, 107, 109, 111, 115, 132, 139
dancing floor, 67, 70-71
dedication (see also, votive), 38-39, 48, 50, 55, 103, 106
Delos, sanctuary of Apollo, 90
Delphi
    sanctuary of Athena Pronaia, 35, 98
    sanctuary of Apollo Pythios, 106
    Athenian Treasury, 49, 88, 101
    halos, 68, 72, 90
    Sacred Way, 68, 88, 90
    Stoa of the Athenians, 90
    Temple of Apollo, 52, 72, 87
Demeter, 68, 118
Demetrios Poliorketes, 98, 101
Demokritos, 122
Didyma, 69
Dionysos (see also, Bacchus), 46, 56, 68, 71, 95, 97, 113, 129-30, 138
Dionysos Melpomenos, 138

disease, 115
dithyramb, 71, 102, 133
door / doorways, 37, 42
drama, 107-108, 127, 130, 135

echea (see also, resonating vessels), 79-80, 82-83, 122
emotional imbalance, 110, 114-15
emotions, 86, 110-11
Ennodia, 50
ἐναγιστήριον (see also, offering pit), 24
Ephesus, 133
Epidauros
    excavations at, 21-23, 118
    healing therapy at (see: cult, healing; space, healing; music, and healing)
    musical performance at, 26-27, 29, 84, 86, 88-92, 106, 111
    paeans from, 27, 91-92, 94-96, 103-105
    sanctuary of Apollo (see also, Apollo, sanctuaries at), 30, 84, 91-92, 103, 112, 164
    sanctuary of Asklepios (see also, Asklepios, sanctuaries at), 26, 28, 30, 33-34, 84, 89, 91-92, 94, 103, 111-12, 164
    theater (see: theater, at Epidauros)
    thymele at (see: thymele)
epiphany, 98-99, 103, 105, 137
Episthenes, 152
Erechtheion, 35, 40
Eros, 66, 84-85, 110, 112-14, 116-17
Erythrae, 94-95, 97, 99, 105
Eryximachos, 116
Ἑστία (see also, Hestia), 53, 98
ἐσχάρα / eschara, 51, 53, 98
Euclid, 83
Eukles, 154
Eunikos, 79, 149-152
Eupolis, 55
Euripides, 45, 49, 52-54, 87, 107, 160
exedrae, 38-39, 72, 90, 103-104

ἠχεῖα (see also, resonators and resonance), 122-23, 128, 130-31, 134-35, 138

θῦμα / θύω (see also, sacrifice), 46-48, 57, 60-63, 65
θυμέλη (see also, thymele), 45-65, 76, 131, 137

"form and function", 26-29, 31, 66-83
foundations (see also, labyrinth), 23, 25, 29, 41-42, 66, 75, 77-82, 142, 145, 149

Galen, 108, 110-11
games, Pythian, 88, 93
γένος, 110, 123
geometry, sacred (see also, Pythagoras), 35, 40, 73, 144
gilding, 35
Glaukos, 153
Gorgias, 107
grille, 41-42, 75, 140, 143

halos (see also, threshing floor), 67-68, 71-72, 90
harlequin floor mosaic, 39-40
harmonia, 73-74, 105, 118, 156
healing inscriptions (see also, iamata), 105, 112
hearth, 23-24, 26, 46, 49-50, 52-54, 56, 59, 63
hekatompedos, 36
Herakleitos, 116
hero shrine (see also, heröon), 25
Herodotus, 71, 111
heröon / heroa (see also, hero shrine), 24-25
Herophilos, 108, 110
Hesiod, 107
Hestia (see also, Ἑστία), 49-50, 96-98
hexastyle, 36
Hippasus of Metapontum, 122

Hipponax, 62
holokautesis (see also, ritual burning), 23-25
Homer
    Iliad, 109-10, 115
    Odyssey, 116
Homeric Hymn to Apollo, 93, 102
Homeric Hymn to Hestia, 49
Hygieia, 94-95, 100, 116-17
hymn(s) (see also, paean[s]), 49-50, 86-88, 93-97, 100, 102, 116, 159
    inscribed, 88-89
    to Aphrodite, 55
    to Apollo, 95
    to Asklepios, 81, 95
    to Hestia, 49-50, 95
    to Hygieia, 94
    to Pan, 95
Hyperboreans, 93

iamata (see also, healing inscriptions), 112
Iamblichos, 109-10
Ikonion, 50-51
incubation, 23-24, 97, 110-12, 142
innovation (see also, novelty), 29, 36-37, 40, 43-44, 78, 83-84, 97, 101-102, 161, 169-70
inscriptions, funerary, 51
Istron, 70
Isyllos, 89, 96, 101

Julius Pollux, 47-48

katabasis, 142
keys, musical
    Dorian, 160-61
    Hypodorian, 160-61
    Hypophrygian, 161
    Lydian, 159-61
    Phrygian, 161
Kinesias, 83

κιθάρα / kithara, 118, 132
Kinyras, 138
Knossos, 71
Kronos, 49

labyrinth (see also, foundation[s]), 27, 42, 75-76, 79, 102, 104, 120, 135-36, 138-39, 141-63, 173-74, 176-77
Lakonia, 154
"landscapes of power", 39
Lasus of Hermione, 122, 161
λαμπρότης, 129, 144
Lebena, sanctuary of Asklepios at, 70
letter-forms, 154, 162
libation, 24-25, 81, 113-14, 163
Limenios, 82, 106
Lucian, 54-56, 71
Lucius Mummius, 122, 124
Lykourgos, 130
lyre, 66, 74, 81, 84-86, 93, 97, 102-103, 109-10, 112-16, 119-20, 122-23, 129, 132, 137-38, 161, 165, 168
Lysikrates, 151-52, 155

Makedonikos, 96
marble, 35, 41, 75, 79, 85, 140, 173
masons' marks (see also, assembly marks), 78-79, 119, 121, 145-47, 149, 155, 158-59, 163
medicine, 86-87, 104-105, 107-12, 114-16
    ancient Greek, 108
    and Asklepios, 107-109, 169
    and music, 74, 107, 109-10, 115
Megalopolis, 34
Melanippides, 83
Menander, 113
meter, 22, 50, 83, 101-102
metopes, 34, 113
models (see also, paradeigma / paradeigmata), 43
Mnemosyne, 50

music
    and healing, 26, 30, 74, 86-87, 107-12, 115, 119
    competitions, 27, 88-89
    performance, 26-27, 29, 31, 46, 56, 59, 74-76, 83-90, 92-93, 106, 108, 118-19, 130, 134, 140, 170
    sacred, 26, 30, 69-70, 77, 87, 90, 170
musical notation, 81-82, 101, 119, 135, 145, 147, 149, 156-58, 163
musical therapy
    to treat the body, 55, 87, 108, 119
    to treat the soul, including the mind and/or emotions, 65, 86, 110-11
musician(s), 31, 76-77, 81, 83, 88, 91, 104, 108, 139, 143, 158-59, 165, 170
Mycenae, Mycenaean, 25, 53, 63, 137
mysticism, 98-99, 103-105, 119, 137

Nemea, 25, 34, 74, 90
Nero, 134
"New Music", 83, 132-33
notation (see: musical notation)
novelty (see also, innovation), 29, 38, 43-44, 78, 113, 163

octastyle, 36
odeion (see also, concert hall), 27, 89, 118, 132-34
Odeion
    of Herodes Atticus, 133
    of Pericles, 118, 132-33
offering pit (see also, ἐναγιστήριον), 24
Olympia, 25, 34, 68, 90, 98
Omphalos, 50
Onorio Belli, 126
ὀρχήστρα / orchestra, 27, 45-46, 59, 67, 70-71, 73, 76, 78, 128, 136-38
Oropos, sanctuary of Amphiaraos at, 68
Ovid, 115

paean(s) (see also, hymn[s]), 27, 30, 55, 84, 87-89, 91-110, 112, 115, 117, 119, 120
    composed by:
        Ariphron, 94-95, 117
        Aristonoos, 49, 55, 94, 96
        Athenaios, 100, 159
        Bacchylides, 94, 102
        Isyllos, 96, 101
        Limenios, 82, 106
        Makedonikos, 96
        Philodamos, 94-95, 97, 100
        Pindar, 91, 93-94, 102, 163
        Sophocles, 94
        Thaletas, 108
Paieon, 86, 91, 92, 96, 100-101, 109
Panathenaia, 132, 134
Pangrates, 148
paradeigma / paradeigmata (see also, models), 40
paradigms
    architectural, 40, 43, 125
    musical, 125, 161
    verbal, 61
Parthenon, 36, 45
Pausanias, 28, 38, 59, 71, 84, 112-13, 118
Pausias, 66, 84-85, 112-13, 116-17
Pentelic marble, 41
Perachora, 34
"Perfect System", 123, 131-32
performance (see: music, performance; music, sacred)
performance space, 26-27, 30, 47, 66-68, 70-73, 75-76, 87, 90, 103, 106, 118, 120, 130-30
performers, 58, 70, 86, 88, 97-100, 102, 104-105, 129
Pergamon, 50, 94, 98, 148
Pericles, 21, 118, 132-33
Persia, 58
personification
    of Eros, 116
    of Gout, 54-55
    of Methe / Drunkenness, 113, 116
Petra, 37

Pherekrates, 58
phiale, 69, 84, 113-14, 166
Philip of Macedon, 96, 98, 101
Philodamos, 94-95, 97, 100
Philolaos, 73
Phoebus (see also, Apollo), 52
Phorminx, 97, 102
Phrynis of Lesbos, 132
Phylios, 152
Pindar, 91, 93-94, 102, 138, 163
platform (stage), 46-47, 58, 71-72, 76, 143
Plato, 47, 74, 88-89, 92, 110, 116
Plutarch, 58
Polykleitos, 21, 28, 38, 78
Polykleitos the Younger, 21, 28, 78, 82, 161, 170
Polyphemos, 115
Pompeii, 37, 146
Porphyry, 110
Posidippos, 114
Pratinas, 55, 108
Praxiteles, 113
Pronomos of Thebes, 156-57
proportions, architectural, 22, 35-37
propylaea on Samothrace, 37
prosodion, 106
prosopography, Epidaurian, 144-56
Pythagoras (see also, geometry, sacred), 74, 76, 102
    and music, 109-10
    and musical theory, 111, 122

resonance effects, 121-123
resonating vessels (see also, echea), 79-80, 82, 84, 93, 119-20, 135, 138, 144
resonators (see also, vessels, resonant), 120, 123-32, 134-35, 138, 157, 159, 161-63
rhythm, 31, 88, 99, 101, 108, 164
ritual burning (see also, holokautesis), 24
rituals, 31, 42, 68, 91, 104, 110, 112, 119, 170
rosettes, 34-35, 40, 113

sacrifice (see also, altar; libation; θῦμα / θύω), 23, 25-26, 46, 48, 53, 57, 60-63, 65, 68, 75, 91, 99, 166
Samothrace, Sanctuary of the Great Gods at, 37, 68-69, 73
σκηνή / scene building, 46-48, 56, 137
snakes, sacred, 23-24
song, 25, 29-30, 45, 55, 58, 65-66, 68-71, 75, 78, 88, 91, 93, 97-99, 104, 107, 115-16, 130, 132, 137, 168
Sophocles, 94, 107
soul, 65-66, 73-74, 86, 88, 109-11, 114
sound, 31, 45, 76-77, 79-80, 84-85, 87-88, 95, 102-103, 105-106, 109, 112, 120-22, 125, 127-33, 136-44, 158, 165-68, 172-74, 177
soundscape, 77, 121, 167-68
space
    circular, 26-27, 30, 43, 66-73, 90, 125, 136, 143-44
    healing, 86-87, 107, 112
    ritual, 23, 26, 38, 51-52, 55-56, 60, 65, 68, 72-73, 75, 90. 104-105, 112
    sacred, 53, 66, 68, 72, 90, 104, 144
Sparta, 25, 71, 96, 108, 118
speaking platform (see also, βῆμα), 47
stage, 46-47, 55-56, 59, 80, 85, 103, 127-28, 134-35, 138, 149, 152-53, 156, 160, 169
Stepterion, 72, 90
stoa, 37-38, 68, 72, 90, 111-12, 114, 164-66
Stonehenge, 28, 77, 167

temenos, 26, 38, 89, 112, 164-65
Tempe, valley of, 72
temple / temples, 21-23, 25, 33-34, 36-39, 45, 49-50, 52-55, 63, 69, 72, 75, 87-91, 103, 106, 111, 113, 122, 124, 147-48, 151-53, 164
temple of
    Asklepios at Lissos, 37
    Apollo at Bassai, 147
    Apollo at Delphi, 49, 106
    Apollo at Didyma, 69

Athena Alea at Tegea, 37
Luna, 122, 124
terrace, 23, 38, 72
Thaletas, 108
Thasos
    sanctuary of Demeter at Arkouda, 68
    sanctuary of Zeus Agoraios, 69
theater (see also, theatron), 46-48, 55-60, 67-68, 70-73, 82-89, 107-108, 122-128, 130-138
    acoustical design of, 27, 76, 78, 82, 85, 127-28, 134-36, 138
    at Aezani, 125
    at Athens, 68, 107, 130
    at Avaricum Biturigum, 125-26
    at Corinth, 83, 122, 127
    at Epidauros, 21, 28, 78, 88-9, 111, 127-28, 136
    at Gioiosa Ionica, 125
    at Hippo Regius, 125
    at Nemus Aricinum, 125
    at Nora, 125
    of Pompey (Rome), 127, 133
    at Saguntum, 125
    at Syracuse, 76, 138
    at Scythopolis, 125-26
    at Thorikos, 73
theatron (see also, theater), 68, 71-73
Themis, 50
Theodotos, 21
Theokritos, 115
tholos, 21-22, 25, 27-28, 35, 37, 45, 68, 98, 119, 164-65
Thorikos, 73
Thrasymedes, 21
threshing floor (see also, halos), 67, 71-72
thymele (see also, θυμέλη)
    architect of, 42-43, 77-78, 82, 135, 161
    construction of, 21-23, 28, 33-34, 38, 42-43, 45, 83, 90, 133, 141, 143-44, 169-70
    design, 22, 25-28, 35, 38-41, 43-45, 74-76, 78, 84, 87, 93, 113, 136, 144, 163, 167
    etymology of, 45-64
    interface between foundations and cella, 40-43, 75-78
    interior, 36, 39, 42, 66, 75, 84, 132, 174, 177
    exterior, 38, 40, 105, 113, 142
    function(s) of, 25-26, 29, 44-46, 55, 66-67, 78, 85, 87, 90, 107, 119-20, 138-39, 142, 163
Timotheos, 81, 83, 101-102, 118, 130
tomb, 23-26, 37
Torrin, 168
θυμέλη (see also, thymele), 45-65, 76, 131, 137
tripod, 93, 141
Troy / Trojan, 53
Tyche, 50

ὑπατή, 124

Vari, 70, 86
vessels, resonant (see also, resonators), 25, 79-80, 82-85, 93, 108, 119-20, 122-25, 127, 129-31, 135, 138-39, 144, 158
Vitruvius, 79-80, 82, 84, 118-20, 122-30, 134, 138-39, 156-57, 162
votive (see also, dedication), 50, 90, 99, 112, 164, 166

χρόαι, 124

Zeus, 49, 68-69

www.ingramcontent.com/pod-product-compliance
Lightning Source LLC
Chambersburg PA
CBHW060419300426
44111CB00018B/2908